European Papers in American History
SERIES EDITOR : DAVID K. ADAMS

1. REFLECTIONS ON AMERICAN EXCEPTIONALISM
Edited by David K. Adams and Cornelis A. van Minnen

2. FROM THEODORE ROOSEVELT TO FDR: INTERNATIONALISM AND ISOLATIONISM IN AMERICAN FOREIGN POLICY
Edited by Daniela Rossini

3. TOWARDS A NEW AMERICAN NATION? REDEFINITIONS AND RECONSTRUCTION
Edited by Anna Maria Martellone

TOWARDS A NEW AMERICAN NATION ?
REDEFINITIONS AND RECONSTRUCTION

Towards a New American Nation?
Redefinitions and Reconstruction

Edited by Anna Maria Martellone

SERIES EDITOR : DAVID K. ADAMS

EP
AH

RYBURN PUBLISHING
KEELE UNIVERSITY PRESS

First published in 1995
by Ryburn Publishing
an imprint of Keele University Press
Keele University, Staffordshire, England

Composed by
Keele University Press
and printed by Hartnolls
in Bodmin, England

ISBN 1 85331 160 X

Contents

Notes on Contributors

Raffaella Baritono received a Ph.D. in 'Storia delle Americhe' from the University of Genoa in 1992. Her interests include the rise of the administrative state with particular regard to the analysis of Progressive social scientists. Her doctoral dissertation was awarded the 1992 'Premio Opera Prima Roberto Ruffilli' and she is author of *Oltre la politica: La crisi politica e istituzionale negli Stati Uniti tra Otto e Novecento* (1993).

Thomas Bender is Professor of Humanities and History at New York University. His books include *Toward an Urban Vision* (1982); *Community and Social Change in America* (1982); *New York Intellect: A History of Intellectual Life in New York City, from 1750 to the Beginning of Our Own Times* (1987) and *Intellect and Public Life: Essay on the Social History of Academic Intellectuals* (1993). He has been a Getty Scholar, a Rockefeller Humanities Fellow, and a Guggenheim Fellow. He received the Frederick Jackson Turner Award of the Organization of American Historians in 1975.

Stephan G. Bierling is Assistant Professor at the Geschwister-Scholl-Institute for Political Science of the University of Munich and executive director of the Interdisciplinary Center for American Studies. In 1993 he was Visiting Professor at Austin College, Texas. His fields of research include the domestic and foreign policies of the United States and the interdependence of politics and economics. Among his publications are *The National Security Advisor of the US President: Anatomy and Background of a Career 1947–1989* (1990) and *Partners or Opponents? The Presidency and Congress in US Foreign Policymaking 1974–1988* (1992).

John Bodnar is Professor in the Department of History, Indiana University, Bloomington. His research interests include political struggle over cultural meaning in modern America; class, ethnic and racial conflicts, and the creation and uses of social memory. He is the author of *The Transplanted: A History of Immigrants in Urban America* (1985); *Remaking America: Public Memory, Commemoration, and Patriotism in the Twentieth Century* (1992).

Emory Elliott is Professor of English, University of California, Riverside. He taught at Princeton University (1972–1989) where he was Chair of the English Department (1986–9). He has held fellowships from the Woodrow Wilson Foundation, the Guggenheim Foundation, the ACLS, the NEH, and the University of California Center for Research in the Humanities. Among his publications are *Power and the Pulpit in Puritan New England* (1975); *Revolutionary Writers: Literature and Authority in the New Republic, 1725–1810* (1986); '*New England Puritan literature*' in *The Cambridge History of American Literature* (1994). He has also edited *The Columbia Literary History of the United States* (1988), which received an American Book Award.

Sergio Fabbrini is Professor of Political Science at the University of Naples. His research interests include welfare policies, the making of economic and social policies in Western democracies, and the comparative approach to US politics. He has been a Visiting Fellow at Cambridge University, Visiting Scholar at the University of California, Riverside, and Fulbright Visiting Scholar at Harvard University. He is in charge of the European Consortium for Political Research Standing Group on American Politics. Among his numerous publications are *Neoconservatorismo e politica americana: Attori e processi politici in una società in trasformazione* (1988); *Politica e mutamenti sociali: Alternative al confronto sullo stato sociale* (1988); *La politica dei cittadini: Argomentazioni sulla democrazia che cambia* (1991); *Il presidenzialismo negli Stati Uniti* (1993).

Ferdinando Fasce teaches American History at the University of Bologna and is a Researcher at the University of Genoa. His main interests are in twentieth-century American politics, society and culture. He is a member of the executive committee of the Associazione Italiana di studi Nord-Americani, and a member of the organizational committee for the 1995 Organization of American Historians Conference. He has been Howard B. Taft Special Lecturer at the University of Cincinnati and Visiting Scholar at Ohio University (1990). Among his publications are *Dal mestiere alla catena* (1983); *Una famiglia a stelle e strisce: Grande Guerra e cultura di impresa in America* (1993), which received the OAH award for the best book on American History written in a foreign language, and *Tra due sponde: Lavoro, affari e cultura fra Italia e Stati Uniti nell'età della grande immigrazione* (1994).

Eric Foner is DeWitt Clinton Professor of History at Columbia University from which he received his Ph.D. He has been Pitt Professor of History and American Institutions at Cambridge University and Fulbright Professor of American History at Moscow State University. Among his books are *Free Soil, Free Labor, Free Men: The Ideology of the Republican*

Party before the Civil War (1970); *Tom Paine and Revolutionary America* (1976); *Reconstruction* (1988); and *A House Divided* (1990).

Daria Frezza is a Researcher at the History Department of the University of Siena. Her current interests include the history of nineteenth-century culture, and the history of psychoanalysis in the United States. She has done research and published on Italy and the US during the Fascist period. Among her works are *F. D. Roosevelt: Il presidente e l'opinione pubblica* (1982) and an essay on 'Information or propaganda', in *L'estetica della politica* (M. Vaudagna, ed., 1989). She is working on a book on crowd psychology and the concept of leadership in American democratic culture.

Saverio Giovacchini graduated *magna cum laude* from the University of Florence in 1990. He has recently participated in a research project on cinematic narrative strategies of historical knowledge and is currently finishing a Ph.D. at New York University. He contributed with an essay entitled 'Fritz Lang and the "Moguls"' to *Lo straniero interno* (M. Pozzi, ed., 1993) and his 1992 essay 'Did private Nolan get his glory?' was finalist for the Peltzer Prize of the Organization of American Historians.

David M. Kennedy is Professor of History and American Studies at Stanford University. He is the author of numerous publications including *Birth Control in America: The Career of Margaret Sanger* (1970); *Over Here: The First World War and American Society* (1980); *The American Pageant* (co-author, 1991); *The American Spirit* (co-author, 1991). He has received honors and awards such as the Bancroft Prize and a Guggenheim fellowship. He is currently working on a volume covering the years 1933–43 in the *Oxford History of the United States*.

Alessandra Lorini received a Ph.D. from Columbia University in 1991 and is now a Researcher in the Department of History of the University of Florence, and teaches American History at the University of Pisa. Her main interests are in American cultural history in the nineteenth and twentieth centuries. She is author of *Ingegneria umana e scienze sociali negli USA, 1890–1920* (1980) and of numerous articles. She is editor of and contributor to a special issue of *Storia Nordamericana* entitled *African-Americans and the Urban Experience: A Collection of Essays by European Scholars* (1990). Her forthcoming book is entitled *Breaking through the Color Line: Public Rituals and Race Ideology in New York City (1827–1917)*.

Stefano Luconi is a doctoral candidate in American Studies at the University of Rome where he is completing his dissertation on the voting behavior of Pennsylvania's Italian-Americans during the New Deal realignment. On that topic he has contributed a number of articles to

Studi Emigrazione, *Passato e Presente*, *The Pennsylvania Magazine of History and Biography*, the *Journal of American Studies* and *Italian Americana*.

Anna Maria Martellone is Professor of American History at the University of Florence. She has extensively researched on issues related to immigration in the United States and is the author of *Una Little Italy nell'Atene d'America: La comunità italiana di Boston, 1880–1920* (1973), has published numerous essays and edited *La 'questione' dell' immigrazione negli Stati Uniti* (1980). She has been the general editor of the journal *Storia Nordamericana*, member of the executive committee of the Comitato Italiano per la Storia Nordamericana and of the Associazione Italiana di Studi Nord-Americani. She is also on the scientific committee of the journal *Altreitalie*.

Foreword

This volume contains 13 of the 19 papers originally presented at the international conference 'Toward a New American Nation? Redefinitions and Reconstruction' held in Florence, Italy, between 24 and 26 March, 1994. The two languages of the conference were Italian and English, and papers were delivered by scholars from Italy, Germany and the United States.

The conference was promoted by the Istituto di Studi Americani in Florence and co-sponsored by the University of Florence. It was first conceived of early in 1992, well before the American presidential election that was to result in the victory of Bill Clinton and in the establishment of a Democratic majority in both branches of Congress. The title of the conference itself, with its question mark, indicates that the attitude behind its planning was one of expectancy but also of doubt: expectancy of a much needed turnabout in American politics but also doubts as to the real extent of the change that could be achieved. The United States had been in economic recession since July 1990, and the number of the poor and homeless was increasing. Many came from the ranks of a newly impoverished and jobless middle class. In 1990, a quarter of the Massachusetts unemployed held a college degree. Was it the end of the 'American dream'?

While the political circumstances (the end of the presidency of Bush and of the Reagan era and the probable outcome of the presidential election), conferred on the proposed conference an aura of timeliness, it was not our intention to restrict the enquiry to politics. In fact, the main stimulus for the project came not from political concerns but from an interest in the current state and future prospects of the American multicultural 'nation'. This interest was grounded in the recent extensive discussions by American scholars on the necessity of 'reconstructing' the unity of American history, both in the historiographical narrative and in the self-awareness of Americans, without forfeiting the enrichment of diversity.

It is well known that since the Sixties many elements of diversification and even of fragmentation had asserted their presence in, and relevance to, the texture of the American identity. Suffice it to think of the unprecedented importance attributed to class, race, ethnicity and gender in American society; this new awareness had led to the parallel opening of new fields of study based on an understanding of the American past far more articulate, complex and conflictual than the one presented by the old 'consensus history'. Innovative contents and methodologies had been introduced into scholarly work in the various disciplines, from history and sociology to economics and literary studies; new issues had been discussed with unaccustomed fervor in academic milieus and publicized in enraged debates on a variety of topics ranging from the literary canon to political correctness, from affirmative action to the rewriting of a national identity through the interpretation of constitutional rights and the process of constitutional politics, from the making of collective memory to the changing meaning of citizenship. Searching for a unifying context of so many diversified approaches and discussions unavoidably led many American scholars and opinion makers to ask the all-embracing question of what it means to be an American today and to probing the processes of constructing and perceiving national identity as a dialectics of unity and diversity, of inclusion and exclusion.

To say that this is the re-proposing in new terms of the old and confident motto 'E pluribus unum' and of that ancient conundrum 'What is then an American?' may be an undue simplification of new and urgent questions of national identity that today concern not only the United States but also many European countries faced with ethnic insurgencies and internal divisions. When a standard bearer of American liberalism like Arthur Schlesinger Jr. voices alarm over the dangers of a 'new tribalism' tearing asunder the American nation, the fact that he addresses his remarks primarily to the American situation does not prevent the European reader from speculating on the possible import of Schlesinger's rebuke for those European nations with long standing ethnic disputes or others with more recent, although predictable, racial and ethnic explosions or regional conflicts. To Italians, for instance, questions of what is a nation and of the meanings of national unity, along with the conjoined issues of federalism versus centralization, of solidarity versus market economy and individualism, have acquired relevance because of political and economic developments that have deeply shaken accepted assumptions concerning the very existence of an Italian national community.

Once we had defined the theme of the conference, we next turned in 1993 to selecting the subjects to be treated in three days of discussions that, of necessity, could touch on only a few aspects of the multi-layered text of contemporary America. Citizenship, solidarity, concepts of inclusion/exclusion, dialectics of culture seemed of paramount importance. In addition, we decided to devote the opening day of the conference to a detailed consideration of two aspects. One was the extent to which the economic crisis then besetting the United States endangered the practical realization of inclusiveness and equity in the granting of social rights. The other was whether the recent Democratic victory marked the beginning of a new political cycle in American history, of an enduring realignment that would be the starting point of a long process of 'reconstructing' social unity and national identity.

By the time the conference convened in March 1994, the Clinton administration had been in office for a little over a year, and the economic recession was on its way out, although the two occurrences were not necessarily related. In opening the conference, I commented on the positive outlook of the American economy: the gross internal product had increased 7.5 per cent with respect to the third quarter of 1993 and the forecast for 1994 was hopeful. If the economy improved, perhaps a more equitable distribution of resources and a willingness on the part of the Administration to launch health care and welfare programs would assuage ethnic conflicts and prevent disorders like the 1992 Los Angeles riots. In politics, it was too early to say whether there had been a lasting realignment of the electorate and whether the new Administration could undertake long ranging social legislation with any certainty of mustering congressional support.

The three-day conference dealt in succession with three main themes, one for each day: crisis of economic growth and in political systems; the frontiers of community and related processes of inclusion/exclusion; fragmentation and the making of national identity, plus a panel discussion on identity politics and the cultural market place.

One year and one midterm election later, the papers presented at the conference have lost none of their analytical value and a few of them have turned out to be quite accurate predictions of what was yet to happen. Hence the idea of making them available in print and their submission to Keele University Press for inclusion in its series of *European Papers in American History*. I am grateful to the General Editor of the series, Professor David Adams, for his willingness to accept and recommend the proposal of publication and to Keele University Press for carrying out the project with speed and accuracy.

I would like to thank all conference speakers, chairpersons and participants and to gratefully mention the cultural institutions which lent their sponsorship and financial support: the University of Florence, the Scientific Committee of the Istituto di Studi Americani, the Department of History, the Consiglio Nazionale delle Ricerche, the Ministry for the University and Scientific Research. The conference would not have been possible without the financial assistance of USIS, in the person of the then Cultural Attaché of the United States in Rome, Mr. Warren Obluck, who generously helped us in many ways including bringing our American speakers to Florence. To Mr. Obluck and to his Assistant, Mr. Daniele Fiorentino, go our thanks, which are also extended to the Consul General, to the Consul for Cultural Affairs and the personnel of the Cultural Office of the Consulate of the United States in Florence.

Many people helped in organizing the conference. I would like to give special recognition to Elisabetta Vezzosi whose always generous help was invaluable, and to thank Corso Boccia and Raffaella Baritono for giving valid support and attending to many necessary and painstaking details while the conference was in progress. Members of my Department, Alessandra Lorini and Massimo Rubboli, helped in more ways than I could mention, both on the cultural and the practical level. Stefano Luconi has been most attentive, duly fastidious and greatly helpful in preparing the texts for publication.

Anna Maria Martellone
President, Istituto di Studi Nordamericani, Florence

1

The Legacy of the Reagan Years

David M. Kennedy

We live in an urgent age. We take for granted fast food, simultaneous translation, instant replays, and instantaneous electronic communication. In this environment, it is hardly surprising that we also clamor for instant history.

By training and temperament historians are inclined to believe that we can only see clearly in the long slanting light of time distant. To offer some reflections on the implications of an era that is scarcely five years old is to commit what members of the scholarly guild will regard as a criminal assault on the sacred principle of 'historical perspective'. The tone is therefore more ruminative than definitive, more speculative than conclusive. At this stage in our appraisal of the 1980s, it will be an achievement just to get some of the questions right, never mind the answers. There is a profound truth in Gertrude Stein's alleged last words: when on her death bed she asked her companion Alice B. Toklas, 'What is the answer?' Toklas replied: 'But Gertrude, what is the question?' To which Stein legendarily responded: 'Ah – that is the answer.'

Specifically, I would like to pursue two questions about the Reagan presidency. What effect did it have on economic and social policy? What effect did it have on American political culture? These questions will be approached by drawing some comparisons with more safely settled historical subjects, especially the presidency of Franklin Roosevelt, but there will also be allusions to Jimmy Carter, Dwight Eisenhower, Lyndon Johnson, and even Andrew Jackson, directed toward the conclusion that Ronald Reagan will prove to have been the most consequential President since Franklin Roosevelt – for better or worse.

President Reagan had his own ideas about the judgments of history. 'What I'd really like to do', he told his biographer Lou Cannon in 1981, 'is to go down in history as the president who made Americans believe in themselves again.'[1] That remark suggests Reagan's instinctive preoccupation with feeling and sentiment, with perception and image, a preoccupation that became a hallmark of his presidency and prompted many critics to accuse him of caring more for psychology than substance. But Reagan's remark to Cannon also reveals one of his many similarities with his immediate predecessor, Jimmy Carter. It is premised on the assumption that Americans did in fact disbelieve in themselves before his election in 1980 – a consideration on which Jimmy Carter dwelt at length in his notorious 'malaise' speech in July of 1979.

The list of continuities from Carter to Reagan is quite impressive, and, given the political polemics of the early 1980s, somewhat surprising: Carter in 1976, like Reagan in 1980, originally ran as a 'beyond-the-Beltway' anti-big-government outsider. It was Carter, as early as 1977, who called the US tax code nothing less than 'a disgrace to the human race'. It was on Carter's watch, in 1979, that the Federal Reserve Board's tight-money policies began to screw down the lid on inflation. It was Carter who pioneered economic de-regulation by relaxing federal controls over the airline industry. It was Carter who first called in 1980 for 5 per cent real growth in the defense budget. It was Carter who demonstrated the continuing indispensability of the South to putting together a winning presidential electoral coalition. And, to look ahead a little, there is the consummate irony that Reagan, like Carter, eventually saw his presidency crippled and his reputation clouded by entanglement with Iran.

All these points of comparison between Carter and Reagan suggest the existence in the 1970s and 1980s of a set of objective realities in the economic realm, in the political landscape, and in the international arena to which both presidents made more or less common response. History may in the end conclude, therefore, that only distinctions of personality, style, and political skill, rather than deep divisions over the substance of policy, separated the two men who presided over what may come to be called the Carter–Reagan era – or the era of adjustment to the end of the national and international regime that had endured for three decades following World War II, a period for which we have as yet only imperfect and awkward terminology like the 'post-Vietnam era', or the 'post-post-war era'. Reagan's partisans, of course, resist the assimilation of their man to Carter, and insist on the reality of the 'Reagan Revolution'. But other observers have already concluded that the 'Reagan Revolution' was more apparent than real, and that Reagan will ultimately be regarded as a kind of latter-day Dwight Eisenhower – a custodial president, who despite his rhetoric of drastic change was in fact content not to disturb the essential character of American life.

In the realm of domestic policy, the comparison with Eisenhower – who is conventionally regarded as having legitimated the New Deal by not dismantling it when he supposedly had the chance – is instructive, because it raises the question of what it was, exactly, over which Eisenhower and Reagan exercised protective custody. Reflection on that question suggests that Franklin Roosevelt's New Deal perhaps defined the outer-most limits of legitimacy in American political culture for collectivist, government-interventionist policies, while Lyndon Johnson's Great Society programs, in contrast, dangerously breached those limits.

In this regard consider George Will's observation about Reagan's victory in 1980 – that it took sixteen years to count the ballots from the election of 1964, and it turned out that Barry Goldwater won. That analysis is surely mistaken. Goldwater ran before the Great Society had taken shape; he campaigned explicitly against the New Deal heritage. He commanded, as a consequence, the barest of audiences. Reagan, in contrast, ran not against the New Deal, but against the perceived legacy of the Great Society, and won handsomely. For a large majority of voters, Reagan not once but twice, in 1980 and 1984, made a convincing case that the 1960s' brand of liberalism had by the late 1970s over-reached itself, had subordinated the public interest, however difficult that was to define, to the treacherously easy-to-define interests of a host of discrete groups. Rather ingeniously, Reagan therefore exploited the sentiment that Theodore White once described as the popular conviction that the job of the president is to protect citizens from other citizens' congressmen. The depth and durability of that preference for political paralysis in American political culture, for a stasis sustained by the literal working of checks and balances, is reflected in 1994 polls showing that a heavy majority of the American public prefers to have different parties in control of the congress and the presidency.

Reagan told a New York audience in 1982 that:

> Like FDR, may I say that I'm not trying to destroy what is best in our system of humane, free government, I'm doing everything I can to save it, to slow down the destructive rate of growth in taxes and spending, to prune nonessential programs so that enough resources will be left to meet the requirements of the truly needy ...[2]

Evidence like this has prompted several observers to note, as the political scientist Hugh Heclo puts it, that 'much as FDR and the New Deal had the effect of conserving capitalism, so Reaganism will eventually be seen to have helped conserve a predominantly status-quo, middle-class welfare state'.[3] Or, as a Democratic congressman told Lou Cannon in 1981, 'Some of our programs are out of hand. We can't cut them. Reagan can and it will save us, and him'.[4] Here, in fact, may be the essential explanation for the pliability of the Democratic congress in the face of Reagan's legislative program.

Of course Reagan's appropriation of the Roosevelt mantle galls liberals. But they might consider that Roosevelt, damned in his day by conservatives as a traitor to his class and the scourge of capitalism, is now widely regarded as his enemies' best friend, if only they had seen clearly what he was up to. By taming the raw, unbridled, unstable, laissez-faire business world of his day he arguably saved the free enterprise system from extinction at the hands of more radical foes. So it is not implausible that Reagan may one day be judged as having performed a similar salvage operation on the welfare state. If the American political system was due for a Thermidor after half a century of liberal ascendancy, perhaps liberals should be thankful that it was presided over by someone like Reagan, rather than, say, by the likes of George Wallace or John Connally.

The comparison with FDR can be taken still further. Ironically enough, both Roosevelt and Reagan ran on pledges to balance the federal budget. One of the first, though often forgotten, measures of the famed 100 Days in 1933 was the Economy Act, designed to reduce federal expenditures by about 15 per cent. More notoriously, Roosevelt never did find a policy short of war to cure the Great Depression. Through two full New Deal administrations, down to 1940, the unemployment rate averaged 17 per cent per year, and the budget remained unbalanced. As for Reagan, his budget deficits, and those of his successor, George Bush, were monumental in scale, dwarfing those of the New Deal, or even those of World War II, and mocking his 1980 pledges to bring the federal budget into balance. Although the Reagan–Bush economic policies did, after the painful recession of 1981–2, produce a sustained economic recovery, its dimension were hardly spectacular, certainly far short of the alluring promises of the supply-side prophets in 1980.

Yet both Roosevelt and Reagan displayed traits of political genius in turning their economic policy failings into enduring political triumphs. Had FDR swiftly banished the Depression in 1933, there might never have been a New Deal as we know it. Roosevelt shrewdly used the continuing economic crisis of the 1930s to drive an epochal legislative program through Congress, culminating in major institutional reform, like the Social Security and the National Labor Relations Acts in 1935.

So, too, did Reagan use the gargantuan deficits resulting from what George Bush, no less, called his 'voodoo' economic policies to secure and ensure the longevity of his dearest political objectives. Only the archives will yield the truth of Senator Daniel Patrick Moynihan's charge that the deficits were deliberately created, with malice aforethought, in order to block any further social spending. But whatever the origins and the intention behind the mountains of debt piled up in the Reagan and Bush years – more than three trillion dollars, a sum greater than that accumulated by all their predecessors combined, including those who had fought protracted global wars – that debt constitutes a formidable barrier to even the thought of new domestic programs, a barrier that is President Clinton's greatest challenge as he contemplates health care and welfare reform.

Reagan's deficits thus ensure that, in a sense, he institutionalized and perpetuated the achievement of his highest political priority – shrinking the growth of the welfare state – to a degree that few presidents have managed to accomplish. Whatever the final judgement on the wisdom of such an accomplishment, in terms of sheer political consequentiality it is no small achievement. Reagan built and bequeathed to the future a fiscal edifice with no easy exits in which Americans will dwell at least until the end of the century, and probably beyond. In this sense he wrote a definite 'finish' to the Great Society chapter in American history.

From policy to politics

Of all the promises of Reaganism, none excited more debate as the 1980s opened than the possibility that he might be the architect of a new and lasting Republican majority. That prospect had traumatized Democrats and tantalized Republican strategists at least since 1969, when Kevin Phillips published *The Emerging Republican Majority*.

Phillips drew on the concept of 'party systems' to make his case. In this view, familiar to political scientists and historians, American political history has evolved through five identifiable stages, or party systems. These are periods with distinct political identities marked by electoral behavior, salient issues, and, most importantly, the composition and relationship of the major political parties. These systems, first appearing in the early republic at the end of the eighteenth century, have succeeded one another at remarkably regular intervals of approximately three-and-one-half decades – with the prominent, and problematic, exception of the fifth, or the New Deal party system, which has apparently persisted with a unique stubbornness well beyond the usual life-cycle of other such systems.

In his 1969 book, Phillips reasoned that the fifth party system, born in the mid-1930s, was approaching the end of its life-span. The famed New Deal coalition, so the argument ran, that dominant Democratic grouping composed of the Solid South, urban ethnic workers, and blacks, and committed to the expansion of the welfare state and the enfranchisement and advancement of minorities, including women, was showing signs of age and was about to unravel. Thus the fifth party system, Phillips urged, was ripe for replacement by a new Republican majority recruited from religious traditionalists, white southerners choking on the success of the civil rights movement, and suburbanites, many of them the sons and daughters of the old New Deal ethnics. All of these elements of the presumptive new Republican majority were thought to be sick of 'favoritism' for minorities and of the aura of cultural licentiousness that blossomed in the 1960s. Significantly, economic issues figured far less prominently in Phillips's calculus than did cultural concerns, none more conspicuously than affirmative action.

In Phillips's analysis, the election of 1972 should have been the precipitating event that forced the realignment of American politics. This expectation lay behind Richard Nixon's 'southern strategy', which shrewdly focussed on a culturally conservative region that was being convulsed by the upheavals of the 1960s. But Watergate, Phillips later reflected, thwarted the full crystallization of this realignment. The aberration of born-again southerner Jimmy Carter's candidacy in 1976 further suppressed it. Thus by 1980, in this view, the American body politic was tumescently overripe for the kind of massive restructuring that the party systems analysis predicted.

Ronald Reagan and his circle shared this appraisal, especially as it concerned cultural issues and the South. Some Republicans, sensitive to the charge that they were exploiting racial tensions, denied that the southern strategy even existed. Yet Reagan unapologetically declared to a southern audience in 1973 that: 'there is a southern strategy and this country is better off for it'. In a 1976 television address he explicitly attacked affirmative action programs as 'federal distortion of the principle of equal rights', because such programs gave 'special treatment' to some groups and inflicted 'reverse discrimination' on others, including Americans of Czech, Polish, and Italian ancestry. A year later, in 1977, he identified the 'social issues' as 'law and order, abortion, busing, quota systems', and he emphasized their appeal to 'the blue-collar, ethnic, and religious groups who are traditionally associated with the Democratic Party'. 'The Democratic Party', he concluded, 'turned its back on the majority of social conservatives during the 1960s. The new Republican party of the late 1970s and 1980s', he urged, 'must welcome them, seek them out, enlist them ...'[5]

Following that strategy, along with exploiting frustrations over inflation and the Iran hostage crisis, got Reagan elected in 1980. In that election, for the first time, more white southerners identified themselves as Republicans than as Democrats. Demonstrating the enormous electoral appeal of the social issue themes that Reagan stressed, white 'born-again' Christians in 1984 voted Republican by a margin of four to one. And yet the permanent change in electoral patterns that the party systems analysis predicted did not occur. The House remained in Democratic hands all through the 1980s. The surprise Republican capture of the Senate in 1980 was reversed in 1986. A Democrat was elected President in 1992. In short, the long-awaited and repeatedly predicted realignment of American politics into a 'sixth party system' has not occurred. This unprecedented persistence of what is at least a recognizable version of the Democratic dominance characteristic of the fifth party system is a puzzle that challenges political analysts.

It may be that we have in fact entered a new, or sixth, party system without fully realizing it. Reagan may have so shifted the center of political gravity that both parties now orbit around his sun. The persistence of traditional two-party voting patterns, in other words, may cloak the fact that Democrats no less than Republicans have internally aligned themselves in a conservative, Reaganite direction – as the candidacy of Michael Dukakis in 1988 and the role of the centrist Democratic Leadership Council in Bill Clinton's rise to power suggest. Yet the failure of a more transparently obvious realignment to occur may have another, more ominous, implication. Kevin Phillips himself has suggested that the forces of cultural conservatism, corked up for so long in the 1970s, excited by Reagan in the 1980s, but still unable to impose their full agenda, may turn sour and volatile, even explosive. No longer containable in the vessels of either traditional party, they may contribute to what is sometimes called 'de-alignment', or the flow of voters out of formal party membership and into the roiling and inflammable pool of independents. The Perot phenomenon appears as a rather benign fulfillment of this prediction; the as-yet unmeasured strength of the Christian Coalition faction within the Republican party may prove to be a more troublesome confirmation of this unsettling prophecy.

The fact is that a yawning gap separated Reagan's promise and performance on a wide range of social issues. After twelve years of Reagan–Bush leadership, affirmative action programs were still in place, crime was still rampant, abortions were still legal, and school prayers were not. Does this represent the strength of the liberal opposition, or the weakness of Reagan's merely opportunistic attachment to social issues? The religious right might well wonder about the depth of Reagan's commitment to their agenda in the first place. Reagan himself informed an interviewer in 1982 that the social issues were on the 'periphery' of his agenda. A White House aide cited to Lou Cannon the line from the film *The Godfather* about holding your friends close and your enemies closer, and explained that 'we want to keep the moral majority types so close to us they can't move their arms'.[6]

If this is Reaganism's real relationship to the religious right, its adherents may eventually break out of the Republican embrace altogether and turn themselves into an impassioned, unyieldingly doctrinaire element in American politics. Alternatively, they may seize effective control of the Republican party, creating a cleavage between a secularized Democratic Party primarily concerned with economic issues, and an evangelical Republican party primarily concerned with social and cultural issues, a prospect strongly conjured by the Republican congressional campaign of 1994. To the extent either of these scenarios unfolds, Ronald Reagan may come to be regarded not as the leader of a conservative cultural revival, but as a grasping politician who short-sightedly, opportunistically, and cynically heated the cauldron of cultural politics without regard to the dangerously polarizing and potentially explosive results in the longer run.

Presidential personality and American political culture

Reagan defined his preferred role in the history books as the man who made Americans believe in themselves again, a remark reminiscent of a number of his predecessors, particularly Franklin D. Roosevelt.

Reagan knew that none of FDR's gifts to the American people was more precious than the gift of restoring their self-confidence in a menacing hour – a result that FDR accomplished, in large part, by managing to project, especially through the infant medium of radio, his own sense of self-confidence. Along with his even more colorful cousin, Theodore, Franklin Roosevelt demonstrated that the presidential personality can itself be a powerful instrument of governance. It is a mysterious element, to be sure, often even to those that wield it. But its power, especially in this electronic age, cannot be doubted. The legions of media advisers and spin-doctors surrounding President Clinton only confirm the point. As the late Tip O'Neill remarked in some perplexity about Ronald Reagan, 'There's just something about the guy that people like'.[7]

O'Neill's remark echoes the no less amazed comment of another political opponent about another popular president in an altogether different political era. 'The less informed – the unsophisticated classes of people', this observer mused, 'believed [the president] honest and patriotic; that he was the friend of the people, battling for them against corruption and extravagance and opposed by dishonest politicians. They loved him as their friend.' Yet another observer of that same president's inauguration exclaimed with comparable befuddlement: 'I never saw anything like it before. Persons have come 500 miles to see [the new president], and they really seem to think that the country is rescued from some dreadful danger.'[8] That observer was Daniel Webster. The year was 1829. The president about whom Webster was speaking was Andrew Jackson, the president who provides the most interesting comparison with Ronald Reagan. Like Jimmy Carter's 'malaise', the 'dreadful danger' about which Webster was so quizzical eluded precise definition. But it was a feeling abroad in 1820s America that was nurtured by developments with an eerily familiar appearance. Little more than a decade before Jackson's election in 1828, for example, the United States had lost the War of 1812, a defeat for American arms that would be repeated on only one other occasion in American history, a century and a half later, in Vietnam.

Other similarities between that time and this, and between Jackson and Reagan, abound. Born in backwoods South Carolina and moving to Tennessee, Jackson foreshadowed Reagan's own westerly migration in the twentieth century from Illinois to California. Indeed, Jackson personified the westward movement that was churning and scattering the American people in the early nineteenth century to a degree that is matched only by the explosive mobility of the post-World War II era. In a massive internal migration comparable to the huge population shifts of the 1940s, 1950s, and 1960s, the infant republic of Jackson's youth burst its colonial confines and poured its people over the Appalachian crest. In the process, old ties of kinship, community, and church were sundered. One profoundly significant result of this literally unsettling development was the proliferation of new religious sects and the upwelling of an enormous evangelical wave that historians call the 'Second Great Awakening'. The Awakening washed with special force over the rude, untutored, indeed anti-metropolitan, frontier communities that were Jackson's own home ground. It encouraged a return to biblical fundamentals and inspired countless campaigns for moral purification and reform. And it swiftly politicized its concerns and thrust them onto the agendas of the political parties, most notably and consequentially in the crusade for the abolition of African-American slavery. All of these developments are strikingly premonitory of the fluid, mobile, religiously preoccupied social conditions that nurtured Ronald Reagan's political career more than a century later.

Another feature of Jacksonian America that foreshadows the Reagan era was the pervasive feeling, on which Jackson largely built his career, that the purity of America's democratic experiment had been sullied by the cancerous growth of 'privilege'. Privilege was thought to be especially rampant in federal schemes to build up the country by constructing internal improvements and fostering industrial growth through subsidies and protective tariffs. Jackson's vice-president and successor, Martin Van Buren, until George Bush the only sitting vice-president to be elected to the presidency, complained that the government was beset by 'a little army of cunning contractors' trying to profit from these policies.[9]

Jackson's immediate predecessor, John Quincy Adams, had lost the public's confidence by doggedly persisting in proposing nationalistic enterprises, like roads, canals, and even a federal astronomical observatory, at the taxpayers' expense. Exasperated by popular resistance to his proposals, Adams at one point complained that his government was 'palsied by the will of our constituents', an oddly un-democratic observation that adumbrated Jimmy Carter's complaint in his 'malaise' speech that, in effect, he was trying to be a good leader but that the people were perversely refusing to follow.[10] Using Adams as a foil, as Reagan would later use Carter, Jackson swept onto this troubled political landscape trumpeting a summons to return to the values of the founding fathers. The revolutionary fathers, Jackson believed, taught that a powerful federal government, no matter how efficient an engine of economic growth it might be, no matter how artfully it was constructed or how compassionately it was administered, bred corruption, dependency, and, above all, 'artificial' inequalities.

In his veto of the bill to recharter the Bank of the United States in 1832 Jackson summed up this philosophy. 'Distinctions in society will always exist', he said.

> [B]ut when the laws undertake to add to these natural and just advantages artificial distinctions … and exclusive privileges … the humble members of society – the farmers, mechanics, and laborers – who have neither the

> time nor the means of securing like favors to themselves, have a right to complain of the injustices of their Government.[11]

A century and a half later, those words could have formed the manifesto of the 'Reagan Revolution', especially as it took aim at welfare and affirmative action programs.

Like Reagan, the first man to take the oath of office on the west façade of the Capitol, Jackson was a westerner, the first man from beyond the Appalachians to live in the White House. And like Reagan, accused by his critics of being an 'amiable dunce', he was jeered by many in the established eastern seaboard society of his day as a backwoods barbarian, unfit for the presidency. But as the crudely educated Jackson and the sometimes awesomely misinformed Reagan both demonstrated, presidents need not be philosophers to be effective. If a command of ideas were sufficient qualification for command over men, it would have been Aristotle, not his pupil Alexander, who wept at the Indus, and it would have been Machiavelli who was the Prince. Reagan's first budget director, David Stockman, might have had to learn the hard way, as he records in his memoir, *The Triumph of Politics*, that the world is ruled by 'passion and imperfection, not reason and doctrine', but the lesson is elementary political science.[12]

Ronald Reagan, like Andrew Jackson, incarnated some of the most elemental American passions and imperfections. Sometimes lumped together as defining a 'populist' political temperament, they include the glorification of the individual, suspicion of authority, hostility to privilege of any kind, a provincial and even isolationist nationalism, and a radical egalitarianism. These tenets may not describe the world actually shaped by either Jackson's or Reagan's policies, but they do powerfully account for both presidents' popular appeal.

Reagan's popularity was not built on his specific policies, nor even on his personality pure and simple. It grew rather from that cluster of populistic political values for which he ingeniously made himself a totem. Like Jackson, he brilliantly mined the American public's reverential regard for what are often, and somewhat thoughtlessly, taken to be the immutably sacred founding principles of the republic. No matter that those principles already showed signs of obsolescence in Jackson's day, and that their unmodified applicability a century and a half later defied common historical sense. Ronald Reagan laid no claim to a nuanced, textured understanding of the nation's past. In the old and famous formulation of the Greek poet Archilochus, he was not the fox who knew many things, but the hedgehog who knew one big thing – and knew its magnetic power over his constituents. His very simplicity, therefore, while it may be the despair of the professors, was among the supreme secrets of his popular success.

The axioms that compose 'Reaganism' stand squarely in a tradition that marches right off the pages of early American national history. Visiting the United States in the age of Jackson, the French commentator Alexis de Tocqueville coined the term 'individualism' to describe the unique social and political ethos he saw emerging in America. Jackson tapped the power of that ethos when he defined his principal goal as restoring 'to our institutions their primitive simplicity and purity', and preventing the government from becoming 'an engine of oppression to the people'.[13]

The vibrancy with which Reagan revived the antique beliefs of the American political tradition provided a stunning reminder of their enduring psychological power. Those beliefs seem especially susceptible to political mobilization in times of national anxiety and uncertainty of purpose. Franklin Roosevelt tapped the egalitarian, anti-authoritarian elements in those beliefs when he championed the common man and declared war on 'economic royalists'. Reagan similarly took up the cause of the common folk, but he reached back in time beyond Roosevelt to Andrew Jackson, when 'big government', not 'big business', loomed as the chief enemy of the people.

Like Jackson, Reagan made it his mission to redeem the Republic by harking back to the ancient, eighteenth-century wisdom of the founders. Jackson's and Reagan's revivals of Revolutionary-era sentiment, along with the religious revivals that surrounded and suffused Jacksonianism and Reaganism alike, suggest a perduring populistic fundamentalism in American culture that embraces both the political and religious realms. Reagan served as the paladin of that fundamentalist urge. It is only a slight exaggeration to say that he was a soul-brother to his nemesis the Ayatollah Khomeini; both men raged against modern history, seeking to recover a lost age of political purity, cultural consensus, and impregnable national security. Elected to guide his countrymen into an uncertain future, Ronald Reagan instead turned his face toward a safe but elusive past – a past when government was small, religion was vital, minorities quietly in their place, criminals un-Mirandized, and the Russians devoid of strategic parity.

Andrew Jackson sought to point the arrow of time backward to the Revolution, and contemporaries and historians alike have generally praised his effort as leaderly, even mythic. Perhaps the future will be comparably generous to Ronald Reagan, seeing him as the leader who in the hour of need played upon the mystic chords of national memory and revitalized the first principles of the republic. It is, however, at least as likely that scholars in the future will look back upon President Reagan less as a leader and more as a cheer-leader – a man who had no usable vision of a realizable future but who obsessively conjured an apparition of an irretrievable past. Did he educate his countrymen, they will ask, or only arouse them? Did he lift the American people to new levels of common commitment and purpose, or only take them down the worn path of least resistance, telling them what they most wanted to hear? Did he summon up timeless political values, or invoke primitive tribal myths no longer appropriate in the modern world?

President Reagan in a speech in 1986 quoted a famous observation of Clare Booth Luce to the effect that 'no matter how exalted or great a man may be, history will have time to give him no more than one sentence. George Washington – he founded our country. Abraham Lincoln – he freed the slaves and preserved the Union. Winston Churchill – he saved Europe'.[14] What will Ronald Reagan's single sentence be? That he perpetuated his political priorities to a degree that few presidents have achieved, thus checking the growth of the welfare state and preserving the best of the New Deal tradition? Or, that his deficits massively impaired the capacity of American society to deal with issues like poverty, the break-down of the family, health care, environmental quality, education, and the maintenance and modernizing of the nation's physical infrastructure? That he out-bluffed the Soviets by threatening to out-spend them, and thus ended the Cold War? Or, that he only belatedly understood the dynamics of Soviet decay, and nearly bankrupted his own country with a defense build-up targeted on an already dying foe? That he set the stage for a sixth party system of conservative dominance? Or, that his mischievous politicization of the social issues churned and agitated and divided and destabilized American politics for a generation to come?

These are questions of considerable gravity. Comparably weighty inquiries could be fairly directed to only a handful of American presidencies. Merely to recite these interrogatories is to be reminded of the extraordinary importance of the historical moment through which we passed in the 1980s, not only in America, but in the world at large. Whether the 1980s will be described economically as the dawn of the post-industrial age, in international terms as the end of the Cold War era, or politically as the end of the New Deal–post-World War II epoch, it was Ronald Reagan's destiny to preside over what was unarguably a pivotal decade. In that sense, whatever the answers to the specific questions posed, his consequentiality, and his fascination for future historians are assured.

Notes

1. L. Cannon, *Reagan* (Perigee, New York: 1982), p. 320.
2. Ibid., p. 416.
3. H. Heclo, 'Reaganism and the search for a public philosophy', in J. L. Palmer (ed.), *Perspectives on the Reagan Years* (The Urban Institute, Washington, DC: 1986), p. 60.
4. Cannon, *Reagan*, p. 410.
5. R. Reagan, *A Time for Choosing* (Regnery Gateway, Chicago: 1983), pp. 136, 169, 189.

6. Cannon, *Reagan*, p. 316.
7. Ibid., p. 407.
8. H. L. Watson, 'The Age of Jackson', *Wilson Quarterly* 9 (1985), p.102.
9. Ibid., p. 122.
10. Ibid., p. 118.
11. J. D. Richardson (ed.), *Messages and Papers of the Presidents* (Bureau of National Literature, Washington, DC: 1911), p. 1153.
12. D. A. Stockman, *The Triumph of Politics: Why the Reagan Revolution Failed* (Harper and Row, New York: 1986), p. 342.
13. Richardson (ed.), *Messages and Papers of the Presidents*, p. 1169.
14. Reagan's speech was given on 16 March 1986. The full text can be found in *Facts on File*, 21 March 1986, pp. 180–1.

2

From Reaganomics to Clintonomics: A Counterrevolution?

Stephan G. Bierling

William Jefferson Clinton rode into the White House on a wave of broad public dissatisfaction with the state of the American economy. However, Clinton was no passive beneficiary of circumstance but actively shaped the political agenda. He successfully convinced the voters that the slow recovery after the recession of 1990–1 revealed a fundamental economic decay. At practically every campaign stop the Democratic candidate replayed his favorite theme: the 1980s was a decade of decline caused by Reagan's and Bush's failed policies. He promised to focus on the economy 'like a laserbeam' and get America back on the right track. This more than anything else won him the election in 1992.

Since taking office, the desire to undo the legacy of his two immediate predecessors has been the driving force behind the economic initiatives put forward by the new President. In his policy outline *A Vision of Change for America* Clinton wrote: 'Twelve years of neglect have left America's economy suffering from stagnant growth and declining incomes.'[2] Accordingly, his Economic Plan, introduced on 16 July 1993, stated: 'The President's plan represents a fundamental break from the old, failed trickle-down policies of the past.'[3]

This harsh rejection of the economic policies of his predecessors constituted the very basis for Clinton's reform program. Such a political strategy is legitimate. However, it does not say anything about the justification of the accusations or the quality of his own proposals. To shed some light on that matter, this study analyses the following three questions: (1) Has the economic policy pursued by Reagan caused such damage to the United States as Clinton is suggesting? (2) How does President Clinton intend to overcome the alleged economic problems? and (3) What are the lessons to be learned from the last thirteen years of economic policy in America?

A fresh look at Reaganomics

When Ronald Reagan was elected President of the United States on 4 November 1980, he not only captured 51 per cent of the popular vote and 44 states, but also managed to defeat an elected incumbent for only the second time this century. The reason for his victory was that the voters held Carter responsible for economic difficulties: in 1980 inflation was running at almost 10 per cent, unemployment was up to 7.1 per cent and rising, Gross Domestic Product (GDP) was shrinking, the budget deficit was increasing.[4]

Reagan promised to cure these ills without asking anybody for painful sacrifices. Consequently, he rejected traditional Republican policies of 'austerity'. His 'all gain, no pain' economics emphasized incentives for people to work and save, stressed the need for deregulation to raise productivity, and proposed tax cuts for high-income individuals and business to stimulate growth.[5] The term attached to this spectrum of ideas was supply-side economics.[6] This agenda was flanked by Reagan's free trade philosophy and his support for the drastic steps of the Federal Reserve Board under Paul Volcker to restrain the supply of money along the doctrines of monetarism.

In practice Reagan was never either willing or able to pursue a policy based upon a single homogeneous economic theory.[7] To sell his tax cuts for the upper-rate brackets politically he extended them to the middle class; and to pursue his peace-through-strength policy he increased spending on defense. Both measures resembled more of ostracized Keynesianism than of propagated supply-side economics. Nevertheless, the President was able to convey the impression that he was following a coherent economic strategy. Friends and foes alike supported this view by dubbing the combination of these different instruments Reaganomics.

At the end of the decade not only the Democrats but also a majority of economic commentators denounced Reaganomics as failure.[8] Only a few voices came out in defense of the economic policies adhered to in the 1980s.[9] To get a realistic picture of the developments the central accusations must be checked.

Income and its distribution

The critics argue that Reaganomics led to a decrease in average wages. Beyond that, Republican economic policies are said to have deliberately redistributed the national income from have nots to haves.

As often with polemic accusations there is a grain of truth in their arguments, but they fail to give the whole picture. It is indisputable that the average real wage of Americans has fallen in the last decade. But wages are only one part of workers' compensation. The other part – non-money benefits like employer contribution to social security, retirement or health and life insurance – has risen. If they are figured in, real compensation per capita increased two-tenths of one per cent per year in the period 1973 to

1990.[10] Still, this is close to stagnation. The reason for this development is the slow growth of productivity.[11] This has to do with the fact that the composition of the workforce has changed dramatically in the past two decades. New workers entering the labor market were increasingly young, female, or members of minority groups. Since they tend to be less skilled, they do not earn as much as established workers, thereby lowering the overall hourly wage. At the same time, a higher percentage of American citizens working has meant more earners in many families. Therefore with 0.5 per cent annually, average family income has grown faster than individual compensation, and faster in the 1980s than in the 1970s.

However, not only did family income grow more slowly in the last twenty years than in the two decades after World War II, *inequality* has increased. One of the most widely used models of income distribution is the Gini ratio, which measures the difference between the actual situation and a state of perfect equality. If all incomes were distributed equally, the Gini ratio would be zero; if all income were received by one family, it would be one. Figure 1 shows the development of the Gini index since 1947.

After falling for twenty years, it has been rising again since the late 1960s. The claim that inequality is greater today than it was at the beginning of the Reagan era is therefore accurate. Yet, the catchiest explanation ('the rich got richer, the poor poorer') is not the correct one. A careful analysis reveals that the income of the upper quintiles has grown faster than that of the lower quintiles, thereby widening the gap between rich

Figure 1 Inequality of US family income, 1947–91

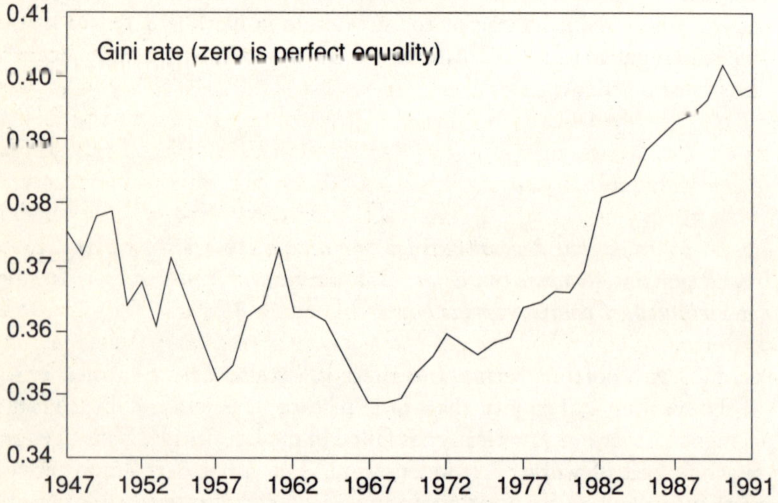

Source: US Bureau of the Census, Current Population Reports, series P-60, no. 142 (1984), p. 47; no. 180 (1992), p. B-11

and poor. Those better off in the early 1980s gained more in the following years. Therefore, to suggest that the rich became wealthier at the expense of the poor is an unscientific simplification for political purposes and not covered by the facts.[12] To make Republican tax policy responsible for the redistribution of income in this period is equally wrong. Of course, Reagan's 1981 tax cuts were regressive. But the 1986 Tax Reform Act and Bush's 1990 tax bill were progressive. The result: from 1981–91 there was as good as no change in the effective tax rates of almost all income groups.[13]

Additionally, to blame Reaganomics for the slow rise in average income and for the growing inequality misses the point. These are developments which originated in the early 1970s well before Reagan took office, and which are identifiable throughout the Western world. The growing inequalities have more to do with demographic trends, technological change[14] and the intensification of competition as a consequence of the internationalization of the marketplace than with specific government policies.[15] Obviously, government can influence these developments to some degree but not fundamentally shape or reverse them.

Deregulation

The Reagan administration is accused – driven by its ideological zest for reducing the government's role in the economy – of having ruined a variety of industries by its deregulation policies. The most frequently cited examples are the fiasco of the savings and loans associations and the huge losses of the airline industry in the early 1990s.

Again, Reaganomics is charged with – or given credit for, dependent on one's standpoint – something it was not mainly responsible for. The deregulation movement began in the mid-1970s and reached its peak under President Carter.[16] The AT&T telephone system was broken up in the Ford years, airlines were deregulated in 1978, railroads, trucks, and the savings and loans industry in 1980. In fact, despite his rhetorical support for deregulation, Reagan had little to do with the most prominent cases. But while under Carter there was also a substantial increase in the regulation of health, safety, the environment, and the uses of energy, under Reagan there was little activity either for new or against old government controls. Yet since most deregulations, when executed properly, worked out well, it is no wonder that Reagan took credit for them.

The Airline Deregulation Act of 1978 decontrolled air fares and routes – pricing structures and entry into and exit from markets – but did not touch federal responsibility for safety standards and inspections.[17] Within the next five years the number of airlines operating in the US doubled to over 400, but was halved again until 1988. These figures indicate that competition has increased dramatically in this industry. In the same period average air fares fell in real terms, with long-distance flights being reduced more than short-distance flights. Even with the further concentration of the industry – in 1993 three 'mega-carriers' controlled 70 per cent of the domestic market – competition remained high.

Additionally, the safety record for air travel improved in the 1980s. For instance, the annual average number of all accidents during the first thirteen years of deregulation was 50 per cent lower than in the same period before 1978. The death risk sank from one in 2.6 million flights prior to deregulation, to one in 10.2 million flights afterwards.[18] The point here is not whether these safety improvements are due to deregulation (e.g. through speeding up the buying and using of safer aircrafts or improving maintenance) or whether they only reflect a long-term trend. The point is that deregulation did not reduce safety.

Finally, the huge losses of almost all American airlines in the last three years result from bad management strategies (e.g. creating overcapacities on transatlantic flights, ordering too many airplanes) and the recession, and not from deregulation. In fact, deregulation has contributed to the fact that US carriers are 50 per cent more productive today than their still regulated European competitors.

While airline deregulation is one of the success stories of the 1980s, the crisis of the savings and loans associations is an example of the opposite. But contrary to the conventional wisdom the S&L debacle is no case in point against deregulation in general but more against politicians seeking to avoid confronting a problem by entrusting its solution to a magic formula. To prove this thesis, a closer look at the development of the S&L crisis is necessary.

The first savings and loans associations were founded in the nineteenth century to support members in buying or building homes.[19] The thrift industry had its golden days after World War II when the number of accounts tripled in a decade to 28 million. However, the whole system worked only under good weather conditions. Since S&Ls borrowed short-term from depositors and loaned long-term to home buyers, their fate depended on low and stable interest rates. When interest rates rose from the late 1960s on, the costs of deposits increased more quickly than the yield on loans. Moreover, government controls on interest rates that the S&Ls could offer to attract new savings remained in place for social reasons. Consequently, savers removed their money from thrifts in search of better yields. By 1980, the savings and loans industry was in shambles. In this situation, the political elite should have realized that the structure of the S&L system had been fundamentally flawed from the outset and should have tried to diminish the damage. Yet the S&Ls fulfilled a politically and socially wanted purpose and were popular with the voters; so Congress decided to cure the symptoms without dealing with the roots of the illness.

In 1980 a law was passed phasing out all interest rate controls and increasing the ceiling on insured accounts from $40,000 to $100,000. As the situation worsened two years later Congress, with the support of President Reagan, granted broad new lending powers to thrifts. To out-compete banks – and each other – the S&Ls now offered high interest rates on deposits and put those funds into high risk investments like real estate development, energy projects, and junk bonds.[20] When energy and real estate prices went sour in the second half of the 1980s hundreds of S&Ls became insolvent. The federal government had to bail out those thrifts whose insured deposits exceeded their assets. The entire tab for the taxpayer was calculated to be over $400 billion.

Reagan's policies can only partially be blamed for this financial fiasco. When he took office the S&L policy was already on the wrong track. The main cause for the disaster was that politicians of both parties and both branches of government did not have the will to abort a failed experiment and took refuge to a popular recipe without thinking through the consequences.

The budget deficit

Reaganomics is charged with having caused the biggest budget deficits in American history. Under Republican presidents, it is argued, the deficit has rarely been below $200 billion, while the overall federal debt quadrupled from $1 trillion to almost $4 trillion. This fiscal irresponsibility allegedly is a drain on the pool of national savings available for investment and threatens the future of the nation.

Before being able to analyze the causes and consequences of the fiscal crisis in America its real dimension has to be determined. Very often the deficit and the debt is measured in nominal dollars. Since these figures are not adjusted for inflation, they give a distorted view of what has happened in the 1980s. Even real dollars do not tell the entire story because they do not account for the growth of the economy. So, only the percentage share of the deficit at the Gross National Product (GNP) gives a realistic picture. Table 1 documents that the federal government has run a budget deficit of more than 2.5 per cent every year since 1975 with the exception of 1979.

Under Reagan, the deficit peaked in 1983 to decrease in tendency in later years. It started to climb again in the early Nineties. Two questions need to be answered: why is the United States running a deficit of such proportions for twenty years in a row and why did it worsen in Reagan's first term and under Bush?

The answer is that it is a combination of structural and cyclical causes. Since the mid-1970s real outlays for mandatory spending like social security and Medicaid rose substantially, while real receipts stagnated as a

Table 1 Federal Receipts and Outlays, 1975–90 (as percentage of GNP)

	Receipts	*Outlays*	*Surplus or Deficit* (–)
1975	18.3	21.8	–3.5
1976	17.6	21.9	–4.3
1977	18.4	21.2	–2.8
1978	18.4	21.1	–2.7
1979	18.9	20.6	–1.6
1980	19.4	22.1	–2.8
1981	20.1	22.7	–2.6
1982	19.7	23.8	–4.1
1983	18.1	24.3	–6.3
1984	18.1	23.1	–5.0
1985	18.6	23.9	–5.4
1986	18.4	23.7	–5.3
1987	19.3	22.7	–3.4
1988	19.0	22.3	–3.2
1989	19.3	22.3	–3.0
1990	19.1	23.2	–4.1

Source: *Budget of the United States Government, 1992*, VII, S. 17, table 1.3

consequence of slow economic growth after 1973. Until 1979 this trend was partially offset by the sharp decline in defense spending. When Carter and Reagan started the military buildup in the wake of Soviet intervention in Afghanistan, the defense budget not only lost its function as a major source of budgetary savings but was transformed into one of the fastest rising items of the budget.[21] Together with the increase in interest payments for the debt due to the tight monetary policy of the Fed, expenditures rose in 1983 to a post-World War II high of 24.3 per cent of GNP. Because of Reagan's reluctance to increase taxes, and the deepest recession since the 1940s in 1981–2, receipts fell to 18.1 per cent.[22] The budget deficit ballooned in 1983 to 6.3 per cent of GNP. Through rigid spending and higher taxes in his second term, and five years of substantial economic growth, the deficit fell to 3.2 per cent in 1988. Yet the structural deficit remained basically untouched. Under Bush, spending increased dramatically at the same time as a cyclical downturn began. Deficits went up again.

To sum up, no single source for the fiscal crisis of the United States can be identified. Reaganomics intensified the problem but did not cause it. Reagan's tax cuts, often singled out as the main reason of high deficits, merely prevented a sharp hike in taxes under existing law. Once again the roots for the negative developments rest more with long-term trends, like rapidly rising outlays for entitlement programs and the worsening of the general economic conditions since 1973, than with a specific policy.

A look over the national fence supports this view. Budget deficits have become commonplace in almost all of the Western democracies. Yet Republican presidents have to take a good deal of the blame. Reagan consciously accepted high deficits when he told his economic advisers in late 1981: 'I did not come here to balance the budget – not at the expense of my tax-cutting program and my defense program. If we can't do it in 1984 [balancing the budget], we'll have to do it later.'[23] By increasing borrowing Reagan and Bush chose the easiest political option – but only postponed hard choices.

The question remains whether the deficit and the accumulation of debt are really 'impoverishing the nation', as David Calleo has phrased it.[24] Conventional economic-policy wisdom explains the relationship between budget deficits and investment as follows: to finance its deficit the government competes with private-sector borrowers in the credit markets for a scarce pool of savings; more public borrowing forces business to pay higher interest rates if they want funds and thereby raises the cost for investment ('crowding out').

This logic, however, is increasingly challenged. Economists Robert Pindyck and Avinash Dixit have convincingly demonstrated in their recent book that investment decisions are most of all driven by perceptions of a stable, predictable business climate.[25] Additionally, there is no conclusive empirical evidence of a relationship between budget deficits and interest rates.[26] In a $6 trillion economy, deficits are not everything. This, of course, does not mean deficits have no negative effects on the economy, only that their immediate consequences have been exaggerated. If Americans really want to get serious about the fiscal crisis, they have to accept the fact that you cannot have a welfare state and refuse to pay for it.

America's standing in the world economy

A growing chorus of scholars and commentators denounces the Reagan years for speeding up the economic decline of the United States. America, they say, has lost its competitive edge; worse, it has become a second rank economic power. This decline is allegedly expressed in the huge trade deficits that America has run since 1983.

Indeed, it is undeniable that the American position as the dominant economic power on this globe has been eroding since World War II. But this is first of all a relative, not an absolute decline. And it is merely the natural consequence of the once destroyed economies in Europe and Asia rebuilding and trying to catch up with the United States. There is plenty of evidence that it is much easier for economic late-comers to have high growth rates than for the leader. However, this trend has come to a halt in the late 1970s. So, for example, the American share of the world product has remained remarkably stable at 23 per cent since 1975.[27] Figure 2 supports this statement.

Looking at the most important economic indicator – productivity, measured in GDP per capita – the US has kept its leadership position against its main economic rivals allowing only Japan to get closer. America has also not become industrially uncompetitive – on the contrary. A detailed study by the McKinsey Global Institute, comparing manufacturing productivity in nine different sectors for the US, Japan and Germany, comes to the conclusion that labor productivity reaches only 83 per cent and 79 per cent of America's in Japan and Germany respectively.[28] Figure 3 shows that only in metalworking and steel production is German productivity equal to America's. In five sectors – autos, auto parts, metalworking, steel, and consumer electronics – Japan has a significantly higher productivity than the US while lagging by large margins in beer and processed food. The study finds sectors exposed to international competition having a dramatically higher productivity than sectors with government protection. William Lewis of McKinsey concludes: 'Global competition breeds high productivity; protection breeds stagnation.'[29] Consequently, the best economic policy to strengthen further a nation's competitiveness is keeping markets open and enhancing free trade. This is exactly what Reagan supported in the 1980s.

Figure 2 GDP per capita, 1950–90 (Currencies converted at OECD purchasing power parities)

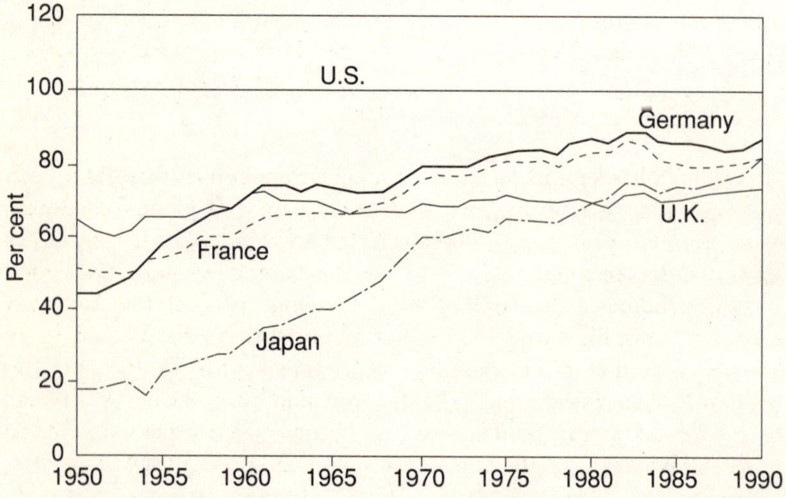

Source: McKinsey Global Institute, *Manufacturing Productivity* (McKinsey Global Institute, Washington, DC: 1993), exhibit 1–2

Figure 3 Labor Productivity (Value added at industry PPP per hour worked)

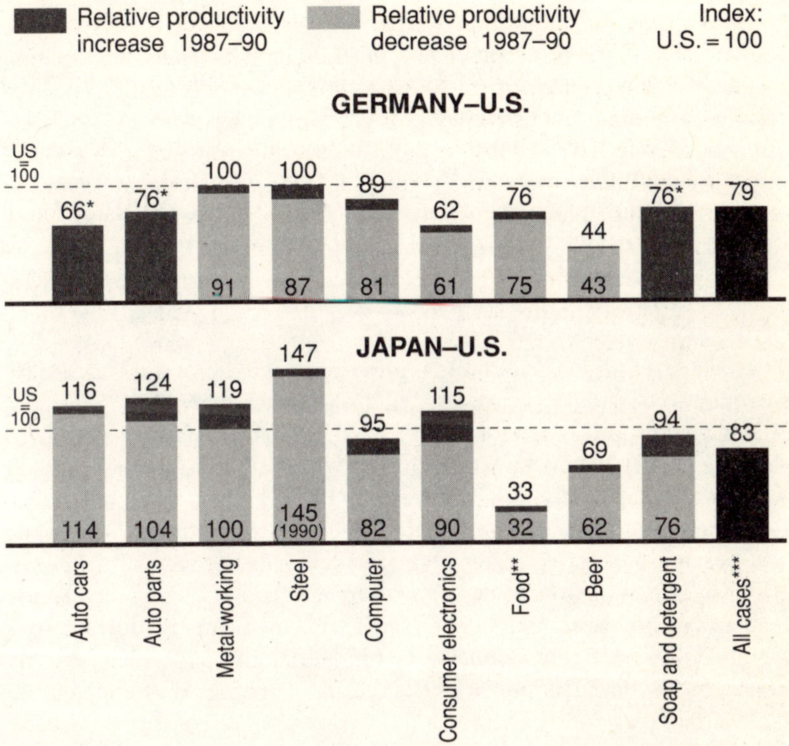

*Only 1990; **Based on shipment; ***Weighted by employment, only 1990

Source: McKinsey Global Institute, *Manufacturing Productivity*, exhibit S-1

If the US has kept its lead over its major competitors, why has it been running a current account deficit over or close to $100 billion annually for more than ten years now? The answer is not because of Japan's unfair trade practices or a general lack of American competitiveness. The deficit is mainly home-made. As long as the savings pool of the American economy is not big enough to finance all investments, the United States is simply forced to import capital goods. Two other reasons increased the trade imbalance during the 1980s: the overvaluation of the dollar for most of the decade, which made exports more, imports less expensive, and the higher growth rates of the US economy compared to its trading partners especially in Europe and South America. However, it has largely gone unrecognized that the trade deficit has declined as a percentage of America's global trade from 24 per cent in 1987 to 8 per cent in 1992. In the same period US exports rose, in volume, by an annual average of 8.6 per cent.[30] Japan managed only 2.3 per cent and Germany 1.7 per cent.[31] America's foreign trade position is in a far better shape than the conventional view presumes.

'The rumors about my death have been premature,' Mark Twain once joked. The same is true for the United States, especially after the 1980s. Although America faces economic problems – the budget deficit and the low savings rate – it has taken on structural challenges better than most industrial countries. Particularly seen from the year 1993, with Europe and Japan in their worst recessions since World War II, the state of and the prospects for the American economy look pretty bright.

Clinton's new agenda

The analysis of the main accusations raised against Reaganomics has shown that they do not hold much water. The 1980s may not have brought a new golden age for America, but neither have they been the abysmal decade as the critics have charged. Such a finding undermines the economic rationale for Clinton's break with the past. Yet for political purposes the President has to keep this image alive, not only because it won him the election but also because it constitutes the common ideological ground of the shaky coalition extending from trade unionists to industrialists within the Democratic party. Not for nothing did he repeat this theme in his address to the Democratic Leadership Council – an influential group of public officials of the party – on 3 December 1993: 'We are reversing economic policies that were in place for twelve years.'[32]

However, breaking with Reaganomics does not explain the essence of Clinton's new economic policies. In his 1992 campaign he successfully capitalized on Bush's inability to lay out a coherent strategy for overcoming the recession. Therefore, it was much more important for Clinton to convince the voters that he had a blueprint for economic growth than to come up with specifics of a new concept. Although the campaign outline *Putting People First* offered a medley of ideas,[33] Clinton was able to put everything in the context of his main economic message: government can initiate the rebuilding of the American economy and thereby strengthen its position in the international marketplace. This conviction has guided Clinton through the first year of his term in both domestic and foreign economic policies; but what are the details of Clintonomics?

Domestic economic policy

In general, President Clinton and his economic advisers are much more skeptical about the self-healing powers of the market than their predecessors, and see it as the task of the government to intervene in the market and correct its results. Concretely this means, as the latest OECD report on the American economy has put it, that Clinton wants to

> work actively towards the realization of such aims as overcoming the trend to an increase in income inequality, speeding up the creation of jobs, and raising investment to improve productivity and to support the growth of real income.[34]

The new President has tried to achieve this by higher government investments in infrastructure and education, financial support for high technology projects, and a reduction of the federal deficit.

On paper, this is a consistent concept. However, in reality it has two flaws. First of all, it rests on a wrong assessment of the roots of the problems, as the analysis of the main charges against Reaganomics has demonstrated. So, for example, the McKinsey study has compellingly shown that neither technological backwardness, nor unsatisfactory worker's skills nor a lack in investment are the main causes why the US lags behind in some industries compared with its main competitors.[35] Secondly, the political implementation of such a program is extremely difficult. A look at the fate of his main economic initiatives in his first year in office supports this skeptical view.

Investment program. So far, Clinton's attempt to shift government spending from 'consumption' to 'investment' has not been overly successful. To begin with his proposed $16 billion stimulus package was defeated by a Republican filibuster in the Senate in the spring of 1993. Then the $140 billion new investment spending that the President wanted in his budget for fiscal year 1994 fell victim to pressures from Congress to reduce the deficit.[36] Eventually, the legislature approved $11.5 billion. In his 1995 budget he has tried again to stress investment expenditures, especially for education, job-training, infrastructure, environment projects, employment programs, and a national information highway. But since revenues will not rise dramatically, under the 1993 ceilings for discretionary spending Clinton will have to kill pet programs of many Congressmen and Senators to finance his proposals. Among them will be such items as mass transportation subsidies, low-income heating assistance, community development block grants, repair and modernization aid for public housing.[37] Given the fact that in 1993 the President was not able to put through his campaign pledge to abandon the subsidies for honey producers, the prospects for doing away with 115 congressional pork-barrel programs – over and above that in a midterm election year – appear pretty slim.

Support for high technology. Based on the premise that the US is no longer competitive in many sectors of high technology, the Clinton administration wants to invest more heavily in civilian and dual-use technology projects. Yet, statistics show that publicly financed research-and-development (R&D) activities increase productivity less than those privately financed. This is due, not only to the high share of public monies which goes into the defense sector, but also to the strong influence of Congress on the distribution of the funds for civilian research which leads to all kinds of techno-pork programs.[38] The bureaucracy has also not yet proven its ability to forecast the sectors that will show high growth rates in the future, let alone critical technologies.[39]

Reduction of the budget deficit. During the presidential campaign the budget deficit was not at the top of Clinton's agenda. Only under public pressure, mainly created by the independent candidate Ross Perot, did Clinton address the problem. His plan to cut the deficits by $500 billion over four years won a narrow victory in Congress. However, this figure exaggerates the consolidation efforts because the reference level was pretty arbitrarily chosen. Like Reagan and Bush before him Clinton decided to travel the easy road: neither meaningful spending cuts nor a substantial increase in revenues was implemented. The much heralded BTU-tax, which was supposed to tax energy consumption, was given up without much fight when it met resistance in Congress. The tax hike on high incomes is more a political symbol than a new source for revenues, and the middle class remained basically untouched. The decline of the deficit from over 5 per cent in 1992 to 4 per cent in 1993 and a predicted 3.5 per cent in 1994 resulted from a combination of lower interest payments for the debt, less than anticipated costs for the S&L bailout, and higher revenues as the economy picked up. On the background of these figures Clinton, in his first State of the Union Address, declared that consolidation of the budget was achieved. However, the structural deficit was not seriously tackled and remains high.

Foreign economic policy

Under Clinton government is supposed not only to fix the domestic side of the economy but also to strengthen America's position in the international marketplace. With the National Economic Council (NEC) of similar stature to the National Security Council (NSC), the President created a new institution to link more effectively internal and external economic policies.[40] This is more than just an organizational change. It expresses a fundamental shift in attitude towards international trade. The chairwoman of the influential Council of Economic Advisers (CEA), Laura D'Andrea Tyson, advised in her latest book an 'aggressive unilateralism' on questions of market access for American manufacturers. She also argued that Section 301 of the US trade law and its temporary Super 301 variant are effective and necessary means to reduce foreign market barriers and increase competition.[41] In early March 1993 Clinton followed this advice and revived Super 301.

In his first fourteen months in office 'free' and 'managed' traders have more or less balanced each other, but the scale is tilting towards the latter. Although Clinton managed to get NAFTA passed in Congress and the Uruguay round of the GATT concluded, with his tenacious adherence to a result-oriented trade agreement with Japan he risks a trade war. The real reasons for the bilateral trade deficit lie in macroeconomic factors, concretely in the massive undersaving of the American economy, and cannot be cured by an aggressive trade strategy.

Conclusions

From the analysis of the last thirteen years of American economic policy several conclusions can be drawn:

(1) The Reagan era has not been as bad a time as many critics argue. All the main macroeconomic indicators – Gross National Product, inflation, unemployment – show that in a historic and an international comparison the 1980s were a decade a bit better than average. Under Reagan, American business has begun a restructuring process which puts it years ahead of its main competitors. The US leads in most of the young industries that are likely to grow fastest in the future – from multimedia, biotechnology, microprocessors, to software.[42] Reaganomics may not have caused this development, but at least it did not stand in its way. This is no minor accomplishment.

(2) So far, Clinton's economic policies have not yet proven to offer a serious counter-concept to Reaganomics. Despite his rhetorical break with the past, in practice he stresses a piecemeal microeconomic approach. To some degree, this reflects Clinton's belief that productivity and investment can only be improved by many little structural reforms. Yet it also results from the brutal reality of the financial crisis in Washington. As the economy is vanishing, three years into a moderate upswing, as the number one topic on the American political agenda[43] Clinton has declared his program to rebuild the economy completed. Therefore, he will focus on social challenges like health-care and welfare reforms.

(3) There is little evidence over the last twenty years that federal policy, as against special conditions, ever produced a trend toward long-term economic change. Reaganomics has not done it, Clintonomics will not do it. Or, as economist Paul Krugman has sarcastically phrased it: 'the U.S. economy is so huge, and the sins of economic policy are so comparatively venial, that Americans can afford to behave irresponsible [sic!] for a long

time'.[44] However, this does not mean economic policy is thrown back to agnosticism. Anything that increases savings and investment, intensifies competition, and makes public policy more predictable needs to be supported. In helping to achieve these goals, government has a mixed record at best.

Notes

1. For their valuable comments on earlier drafts I am indebted to Bert Bilski and Viola Schenz.
2. W. J. Clinton, *A Vision of Change for America* (US Government Printing Office, Washington, DC: 1993), p. 5.
3. *President Clinton's Economic Plan: Historic Deficit Reduction, Economic Growth and Jobs* (Allied Printing, Washington, DC: 1993), p. 2.
4. All data taken from *Economic Report of the President/The Annual Report of the Council of Economic Advisers* (US Government Printing Office, Washington, DC: 1992).
5. L. Thurow, 'The budget catastrophe and the big lie behind it', *Washington Post*, national weekly edition, 15–21 October 1990, p. 23.
6. The term was coined by economist Herbert Stein in April 1976 (H. Stein, *Presidential Economics: The Making of Economic Policy from Roosevelt to Reagan and Beyond* (Simon and Schuster, New York: 1984), p. 241). A favorable assessment is given by P. C. Roberts, *The Supply-Side Revolution: An Insider's Account of Policymaking in Washington* (Harvard University Press, Cambridge, Mass.: 1984).
7. For an insight account of the dilemma between economic rationality and political necessities, see D. Stockman, *The Triumph of Politics* (Harper and Row, New York: 1986).
8. See, for example, B. M. Friedman, *Day of Reckoning: The Consequences of American Economic Policy Under Reagan and After* (Random House, New York: 1988); D. Barlett and J. Steele, *America: What Went Wrong?* (Andrews and McMeel, Kansas City: 1992).
9. Among them R. B. McKenzie, *What Went Right in the 1980s* (Pacific Research Institute for Public Policy, San Francisco: 1994).
10. See M. N. Baily, G. Burtless, and R. E. Litan, *Growth with Equity: Economic Policymaking for the Next Century* (Brookings Institution, Washington, DC: 1993), p. 21.
11. For a more thorough discussion of the roots for the slowdown of productivity growth see S. Bierling, 'Zur Lage der US-Wirtschaft', *Aus Politik und Zeitgeschichte* 44 (1992), pp. 35–42, here pp. 40–1.
12. P. Krugman, *The Age of Diminished Expectations: U.S. Economic Policy in the 1990s* (MIT Press, Cambridge, Mass. and London: 1991), p. 22.
13. See P. Starobin, 'Unequal shares', *National Journal* (hereafter *NJ*), 11 September 1993, pp. 2176–9, here p. 2178. See also C. E. Steuerle, *The Tax Decade* (Urban Institute, Washington, DC: 1992).

14. Brookings Institution, *International Trade and American Wages in the 1980s: Giant Sucking Sound or Small Hiccup?* (Brookings Institution, Washington, DC: 1993).
15. There is also a bright spot in this picture. The earning gap between males and females is narrowing, even though women continue to earn less than men.
16. For a discussion of the question of how the deregulation movement gained the upper hand in Congress and the administration, see M. Derthick and P. J. Quirk, *The Politics of Deregulation* (Brookings Institution, Washington, DC: 1985).
17. See McKenzie, *What Went Right in the 1980s*, p. 319.
18. Ibid., p. 328.
19. For a brief overview of the history of the S&L industry, see M. A.Robinson, *Overdrawn: The Bailout of American Savings* (Penguin Books, New York: 1991).
20. See 'The end of deregulation', *International Herald Tribune* (hereafter *IHT*), 15 August 1989, p. 4.
21. See D. P. Calleo, *The Bankrupting of America: How the Federal Budget Is Impoverishing the Nation* (William Morrow, New York: 1992), pp. 99ff.
22. The best account of Reagan's budget politics is to be found in J.White and A. Wildavsky, *The Deficit and the Public Interest: The Search for Responsible Budgeting in the 1980s* (University of California Press, Berkeley and Los Angeles: 1989).
23. Quoted in M. Reese, 'Goodbye balanced budget', *Newsweek*, 16 November 1981, p. 34.
24. See the subtitle of his book *The Bankrupting of America*.
25. R. Pindyck and A. Dixit, *Investment Under Uncertainty* (Princeton University Press, Princeton, NJ: 1994).
26. See P. Starobin, 'Weak link', *NJ*, 29 January 1994, pp. 231–4.
27. For a thorough discussion of the decline thesis, see J. S. Nye, *Bound to Lead: The Changing Nature of American Power* (Basic Books, New York: 1990), here p. 11.
28. McKinsey Global Institute, *Manufacturing Productivity* (McKinsey Global Institute, Washington, DC: 1993).
29. W. Lewis, 'Competitive exposure drives US productivity gains', *US Policy Information and Texts*, 29 October 1993, pp. 11–13, here p. 11.
30. B. K. Gordon, 'America needs Asia more than it needs Mexico', *IHT*, 11 November 1993, p. 6.
31. 'Ready to take on the world', *Economist*, 15 January 1994, pp. 65–6.
32. '"Long way to go," Clinton admits on economy', *IHT*, 4–5 December 1993, p. 3.
33. B. Clinton and A. Gore, *Putting People First: How We Can All Change America* (Times Books, New York: 1992).
34. Organisation für wirtschaftliche Zusammenarbeit und Entwicklung (OECD), *OECD Wirtschaftsberichte, 1992–1993: Vereinigte Staaten* (OECD, Paris: 1993), p. 138 (translation by the author).
35. See S. Nasar, 'Some new readings on competitive edge', *IHT*, 22 October 1993, pp. 1, 4.

36. See W. Schneider, 'What ever happened to Clintonomics?', *NJ*, 26 June 1993, p. 1680.
37. V. Novak, 'The long brawl', *NJ*, 8 January 1994, pp. 58–62, here p. 59. Discretionary spending is frozen at about $540 billion a year through 1998 without any adjustment for inflation according to the 1993 budget package. Nearly half of the amount goes to the Pentagon.
38. OECD, *OECD Wirtschaftsberichte*, p. 109.
39. See B. Lindsey, 'The has-been pundit and the brand new President', *Wall Street Journal*, 25 February 1993, p. A12.
40. See 'Who makes policy?', *Economist*, 8 January 1994, pp. 45–6.
41. L. D'A. Tyson, *Who's Bashing Whom? Trade Conflict in High-Technology Industries* (Institute for International Economics, Washington, DC: 1992), chap. 7.
42. 'Who's sharper now?', *Economist*, 15 January 1994, p. 17.
43. Right after the election 57 per cent named the economy as the most important problem. One year later the number was down to 18 per cent according a *Washington Post*-ABC News poll (see D. Balz, 'Clinton and Democrats are riding high, new poll finds', *IHT*, 4 March 1994, p. 3).
44. P. Krugman, 'US economic policy: repentance will remain hard to sell', *IHT*, 28 March 1990, p. 8.

3

Challenges to the American Political System: the United States in the Post-Cold War Era

Sergio Fabbrini

'Personal presidentialism'

My purpose is to analyse the effects of the current transformation by the international system of the internal institutional pattern of the American governmental system. If it is true that America witnessed the transformation of the *congressional government* of the last century into the *presidential government* of this century primarily for domestic reasons (given the dramatic economic and technological changes the country registered between the two great crises of the 1890s and the 1930s),[1] it is also true that the 'presidential' transformation of the governmental system has been consolidated by the role America came to play in international politics with the beginning of the Cold War at the end of the 1940s.

In other words, competition and conflict with the rival super-power speeded up an ordering of the relationship between the two chief institutions of government, Congress and the presidency, that favored the latter and strengthened the 'personal' component (personal presidency) at the expense of the 'institutional' one (departmental presidency).[2] I call this institutional equilibrium 'personal presidentialism': meaning a governmental system in which the personal presidency has acquired a decision-making predominance in foreign policy, not only vis-à-vis Congress, but also vis-à-vis the departmental sector of the executive. Although that predominance has been questioned in the post-Watergate years and has been more limited in domestic policy making, the paramount centrality of the Cold War Order strongly supported the maintenance of those power hierarchies in the general structure of the policy-making process.

Given this context it is worthwhile inquiring if the end of the Cold War, although it could not have opened the road for a return to old-fashioned congressional government, could have created, instead, favorable conditions for the affirmation of an alternative variant of presidential government, more cooperative in character, with regard to relations between the president, the presidency and Congress. This variant I call 'parliamentary presidentialism'.

The features of the Cold War era

The long era of the Cold War has been a contradictory period from the point of view of American domestic politics. It could not have been otherwise given the features that it came to assume. These can be summarized as follows: (1) confrontation with the USSR has been exclusively geopolitical in character, so that every situation of imbalance in any country in the world was potentially crucial for the USA; (2) because of the geopolitical nature of the confrontation, considerations of national security (based on armed power) have overridden those of national ideology (based on the power of democracy). It thus became necessary to reach compromises even with non-democratic regimes, if these were willing to counteract the influence of the rival super-power; (3) the predominance of considerations of national security – that is, military security – has led to an economic development conditioned by military industry interests.

Each feature has had contradictory effects on domestic politics. The first effect has been a contrast between the open institutions of domestic policy and the closed institutions of foreign policy. This contrast reached proportions that were unusual in pre-World War II American history. The defensive requirements imposed by the threat of the rival super-power justified the progressive centralization of the decision-making processes within the executive. The victory of the presidency over Congress, and that of the president and his personal presidency over the departmental presidency, came about because each was able to ensure the most rapid response to the threat in question.

Hence the paradox: on the one hand the strengthening of the presidency after World War II was made possible by its progressive democratization to the point that it achieved almost a 'plebiscitary character'. On the other, because of this strengthening of the presidency, its internal decision-making processes have become increasingly impermeable to the checks and balances of the constitutional system.[3] In short, the Cold War generated a sort of 'informal crisis management regime' within the presidency.[4] It became a closed personal presidency standing at the summit of an enormous military and intelligence apparatus, at odds both with the open character of the institutions (from Congress to the political parties) of domestic policy and with the more checkable character of the departmental presidency, although members of the latter presidency, especially if personal friends of the president, have been frequently co-opted into the former.

The second effect has been the contrast between 'republican values' and the 'national interest'. This, however, was nothing new in the history of the United States. I need only cite the much-discussed ambivalence of Jefferson.[5] As a political thinker Jefferson vehemently rejected the European theory of *raison d'état* with its double corollary that, first, the interests of state override those of civil society and, second, that the requirements of external conflict may justify the abandonment of domestic legality. Subsequently, however, when Jefferson became President, he was equally vehement in his pursuit of a statist and expansionist foreign policy which had little in common with humanitarian principles. The Cold War, however, exacerbated this conflict to the point that it created, on the wave of the military intervention in Vietnam, an unprecedented cleavage in the country's national identity.

The third and final effect has been the conflict between considerations of worldwide military supremacy and economic independence. In its long century-and-a-half of albeit only relative isolationism, the United States acquired the reputation of being the country that most efficiently conjugated technological development with economic progress. The Cold War progressively undermined this equilibrium:[6] first, because the resources available for economic development were progressively absorbed by the country's international military expansion; second, because it proved often difficult to utilize the technological innovations of the military sector in the civil manufacturing system. The budget, and especially the trade deficit of the 1980s, showed the largely negative effects of that equilibrium on economic development.

With the second half of the 1960s American politics was marked by conflicts provoked by one or the other of the features of the Cold War. If the Vietnam War brought the conflict between 'national interest' and 'democratic values' to the fore, the economic and political difficulties of the 1970s and 1980s increased resistance both against the 'economically wasteful' policy of national security and against the centralized decision-making process of the apparatus created by this policy. Nevertheless, these conflicts could never develop to their fullest extent because they were curbed by the constraints of the Cold War.

Consider the fierce conflict between the presidency and Congress triggered by the Irangate Affair in 1987. Although Congress launched a major onslaught on the imperial aspirations of the presidency, it substantially decided to handle Irangate by separating the responsibility of President Reagan from that of his staff. Congress thus judged the affair in relation to the constraints of the Cold War, not in terms of its own laws. And it did so despite the fact that, in the congressional debate on the affair, Reagan's supporters had advanced the doctrine of the president's 'inherent powers' in matters of foreign policy.[7] That is, that: (a) powers are separated according to principles of institutional 'competence'; (b) the president, as the 'the nation's only organ in its foreign relations' and 'commander-in-chief of the armed forces', enjoys prerogatives that go beyond the powers enumerated by article II of the Constitution; (c) these prerogatives lie at the centre of foreign policy, this having been allegedly ratified by the Supreme Court in its verdict of 1936 (*US v. Curtiss-Wright*). Of course the Democratic majority in the Senate denounced the doctrine in question but Congress was unable to oppose that doctrine successfully. In short, in 1987 international conditions still obstructed the search for a new institutional equilibrium.

The passing of the Cold War

Two years after the Irangate Affair became public, however, these international conditions underwent radical transformation. Between 1989 and 1991 three fundamental changes occurred.[8] First, the collapse of communism removed one of the central pillars of American super-power status: namely that the country represented an ideological bastion against the 'model of society' propagated by the USSR. One should remember that the confrontation between the USA and the USSR did not consist solely of the arms race; it was also, and principally, an ideological conflict.[9] This confrontation would not have assumed the features that it did had it followed the pattern traditionally ascribed to it of a confrontation between 'great powers'.

The dramatic character of the antagonism between the USA and the USSR did not just derive from the fact that each super-power had become vulnerable to nuclear attack by the other; it was also and chiefly because each propounded a vision of the world that was incompatible with that of the other. Once its enemy had disappeared, the United States began to find it increasingly difficult to gain acceptance as the only and authentic interpreter of the model of 'market democracy'. Thus a corollary to the demise of world bipolarism was the appearance of new tensions within the 'old Western bloc'; tensions due in part to the different historical development of that model.

Second, the end of geo-political rivalry changed the order of priorities given to economic and military resources. Economic considerations once again became part of national security strategy. Their marginalization by military considerations had had harmful consequences for the United States: in fact, throughout the long years of the Cold War, the price for American monopoly of military resources within the Western bloc had been a delay in its civil development. In the new context of international competition this delay showed itself to be a constraint on the country's capacity to exert political influence.

That the United States has lost its international economic competitiveness is indisputable. It is difficult to say whether we are faced with the 'decline', albeit relative, of the United States: what is certain is that the Cold War triggered a deep-lying conflict between the imperatives of national security and those of economic independence.[10] From this point of view, the Gulf War gave striking proof of this change. It showed how the United States was unable to sustain its role as a military super-power using its own economic resources. The era of the self-sufficient super-powers is over.[11] And it also showed that, without economic contributions from other countries, the President could not have guaranteed its international interventionism, nor have relied on the support of Congress.

Third, the reduced importance of geo-political strategies brought a historic change to what has been termed the global agenda. The so-called *high policy*, that is, the wide-range military-nuclear strategies, has been increasingly challenged by the *low policy* of narrow-gauge economic-commercial strategies. Thus the heated international conflict over the regulation of nuclear warheads has progressively given way to no less heated negotiation over commercial tariffs and the distribution of import/export quotas for industrial goods. NAFTA is a good case in point. It is at this level that the leading countries of the Western bloc are currently maneuvering to establish their respective powers of international attraction.[12] But, of course, high policy is not only declining in importance, it is also being strategically redefined. Whereas in the Cold War Order high policy was characterized by the strategy of containment, today, in post-Cold War conditions, it will probably shift to a strategy of reassurance.[13]

All that said, nevertheless, even though the world is no longer bipolar, it still continues to need high policy; and, specifically, high policy which does not leave a power vacuum in the international system that can be filled by 'national egoisms fuelled by irresponsible leaders'.[14] But a world that still needs high policy is therefore a world that still needs the United States, since this is the country that has monopolized it in the Western bloc for at least half a century. Here lies the contradiction of the post-Cold War era: not only because a reassurance strategy is difficult to formulate, both in terms of its objectives and in terms of the means by which it is to be pursued, but also because the relation between high and low policy in the new era is open to question. This difficulty was, once again, dramatically highlighted by the Gulf War. In fact, faced for the first time by a situation that fell outside the familiar pattern of the 'advance of Communism', the Bush presidency labored long before it came up with a convincing high policy.[15]

Foreign scenarios

The case of the American presidency is extremely instructive as to the effects exerted by international changes on the behavior of a government institution. The point is that the presidency plays an active role in that relation, via the *interpretation* that the crucial decision-makers, located within it, and primarily the president himself, offer of those changes. Furthermore, in international politics the interpretation of a situation has especial operative validity during periods of transition from one equilibrium to another. It is also by means of this interpretation's activity that institutions function as actors.[16]

It comes as no surprise that the interpretation of international changes after 1989 has sparked a new Great Debate,[17] which has been no less heated than its extraordinary and visionary forerunner promoted by Woodrow Wilson at the end of World War I. The current debate has not been a dramatic and irreconcilable clash between 'isolationists' and 'interventionists'. This dividing line existed, of course, but it was secondary in importance and did little to mobilize public opinion. After all, the world at the beginning of this century was incomparably different from that of the 1990s. Today, the sharpest division has been between two interventionist options deriving from divergent scenarios of the world order in the post-Cold War era.[18]

The first has had a specific name: *unipolarism*. For this interpretation of international politics the United States is destined, for at least a generation, to perform the role of the single world super-power, as the only country able to promote and guarantee a new international order.[19] Neither Germany (and Europe) nor Japan can assume leadership of the international system: undoubtedly economic giants, they are nevertheless political and military pygmies. And perhaps, given the memories they evoke, this is just as well. In any case economic power does not translate linearly into geo-political influence.

Why should the United States be obliged to acknowledge its pre-eminence? It must because the post-Cold War world is anything but pacified. Indeed, a new and serious threat looms on the horizon: the proliferation of the Weapon States, that is, those states small in size but aggressive because they are equipped with weapons of mass destruction. In this regard, the Iraq of Saddam Hussein is a text-book example of the Weapon State because it displays its three distinctive features: (1) Iraq is not a traditional nation-state; (2) it has been able to build a highly developed state apparatus, and therefore military structure, thanks to its enormous earnings from oil production and sales, although these earnings may equally well derive from the production and sale of other prime materials or, more generally, from a relative solid social accord which provides the state with a sufficient broad fiscal base to finance its military aspirations; (3) its extreme hostility against the West provides the necessary ideological-emotive thrust for the forced militarization of society in order to combat the diabolical power of the enemy (i.e. the United States).[20]

If such is the scenario then it is crucial to preserve and relaunch the domestic internationalist consensus that accompanied the Cold War. This consensus is threatened not only by the traditional post-Vietnam liberal isolationists and the 1930s-style conservative isolationists but primarily by those realists who press for a return to a 'normal foreign policy'. These are the unipolarists' adversaries because they nourish the impossible dream of a world which is able to look after itself. In reality, the unipolarists' international stability can only be the outcome of a conscious high policy taken by the United States. The oft-celebrated stability of the nineteenth century, the 'normal times', which allowed the United States to devote itself to the intensive cultivation of its trade, would not have been possible without the British navy.

As regards domestic affairs, this scenario guarantees the continuing predominance of the personal presidency in the management of foreign policy: indeed it justifies the accentuating of such predominance should it prove possible. The unpredictable threat of the Weapons States, unlike the predictable threat of the rival super-power in the old order of the Cold War, can be dealt with by an apparatus of national security capable of swift action, and thus further exempt from constitutional constraints. From the unipolarists' point of view, the Gulf War, on the domestic front, is a positive example of a 'presidential war',[21] one probably without precedent even if one considers the Truman case of 1950, when the United States went to war against North Korea on the basis of a UN resolution rather than a declaration by Congress. It is doubtful whether Truman could have said what Bush said on 18 March 1991: 'It was argued I can't go to war without the Congress. And I was saying, I have the authority to do this.'[22] In short, the Gulf War, for the unipolarists, saw the passage from a presidency which performed an imperial role, although limited to the anti-Soviet bloc, to a presidency acting to safeguard worldwide security (Global Security Presidency).[23]

The second scenario, too, has had a specific name: *multipolarism*; but its internal implications seem much less certain. For this interpretation the end of the Cold War has led to the diffusion of international power by reducing the importance of geo-political strategies.[24] This is beneficial to the United States, which paid an extremely high economic price for world leadership under the previous international order. Of course the end of the Cold War has not coincided with the disappearance of international threats; and for this reason the United States still has an important role to play in guaranteeing the new equilibrium. The point is, however, that these threats are no longer geo-political in scope and that the United States can counter them with strategies inspired as much by its economic needs as by its ideal vocation. American foreign policy should therefore be based on a new set of priorities: low policies of economic development and human rights should take priority over the traditional military high policies.

From this point of view one should talk less of a return to 'normal times' than of a return to a 'normal foreign policy'; one, that is, sustained by diplomacy and trade, by 'example' rather than 'intervention', by 'being' rather than 'doing'. The United States must therefore exert its influence to build regional and international coalitions for security, to revitalize international bodies, beginning with the United Nations, and to encourage the responsible redistribution of military responsibilities and their concomitant economic costs. This is not a scenario of a pacified world; but it is one that does not envisage America as the world's policeman. Once again, the Gulf War has provided an extraordinary example of a conflict in an era of transition: in its foreign affairs, the United States no longer has that room for maneuver that it enjoyed in the past.[25]

Every American international initiative requires the support, first and foremost economic, of other allied countries. New, principally economic, constraints have come into effect. Bush recognized them in the Gulf War, putting together the first international coalition of the post-Cold War era; but he did not want to translate those constraints into a more cooperative relation with Congress on the internal front. According to this scenario, the dilemmas of the 'postmodern presidency' – suffering from a gap not unlike that envisaged by Lippmann in 1945: too many international responsibilities relative to domestic resources – can be overcome by a decisive reduction in the 'imperial overstretch' of a military nature induced by US competition with the USSR.[26]

But, if there is a large consensus among the multipolarists–declinists that American foreign policy is going to reduce its distinctiveness, there are however different views about the role that the United States has to play in the new multipolar scenario. For example, Nitze wishes a role of 'honest broker' in international conflicts.[27] On the contrary, Brzezinski does not exclude the possibility of 'selective global interventions'.[28] This operative disagreement is an expression of a systemic ambiguity of the multipolar scenario. An ambiguity so well described by Nye:

> The distribution of power in world politics has become like a layer cake. The top military layer is largely unipolar, for there is no other military power comparable to the United States. The economic middle layer is tripolar and has been for two decades. The bottom layer of transnational interdependence shows a diffusion of power.[29]

If so, the new inter-governmental arrangement will need to answer to different needs, each requiring an alternative equilibrium between the president, the presidency and Congress.

Internal constraints

The influence of external scenarios on internal institutional arrangements is never unilinear. Between these two there is always an interaction, as the interpretation by the president of the external scenario is constrained by the features of internal foreign policy-making within which he operates. There are three basic features of that foreign policy-making that need to be considered.

First of all, the number of participants has increased: the old and tight-knit foreign policy establishment, located chiefly on the east coast, has been replaced by a new and more diffuse elite of highly ideologized foreign policy professionals with links in the south-west. The number of economic and ideological groups interested in foreign policy has grown enormously, because of the globalization of the economy but also because of the proliferation of international issues ranging from drug trafficking to ethnic conflicts with backwash effects on domestic politics. And, of course, the media play an increasingly important role in defining the order of priorities on the foreign policy agenda.

Second, congressional sub-committees have become more influential in the foreign policy-making process, although the influence of Congress as a unitary institution has declined. This process has its roots in the generation of Watergate congressmen and in the organizational and legislative reforms that they set in train. In fact, democratization/decentralization has led to the formation of powerful sub-committees – supported by the above new groups, protected by specific regulative prerogatives and able to draw on the services of huge specialist staffs and legislative offices – whose jurisdiction has molded itself in relation to the principal areas or sectors of foreign policy. This 'jurisdictional specialization' has increased the effectiveness of individual sub-committees, these being real rivals to the executive's corresponding sector or area agencies. However, this increased effectiveness has rarely (policy towards South Africa and Nicaragua being exceptions) been tied to a more comprehensive foreign policy strategy by Congress as a whole.

Third, the personal presidency increased its strength at the expense of the departmental presidency. This was both because presidents had to combat the 'Communist threat' in the geo-political competition of the Cold War, and because they sought to respond to the assertiveness of congressional committees and sub-committees in foreign policy – especially since the War Powers Resolution of 1973 – through their personal centralization of decision-making. The intensified rivalry between the National Security Council and the State Department for control of foreign policy reflected, in fact, institutional and party-political conflict between the presidency and Congress.

While the appointment of the secretary of state must be approved by the Senate, the national security adviser is a personal appointee of the president.[30] In matters of foreign policy, therefore, it is obvious that the former is sensitive to congressional wishes, while the basic constraint on the latter is the president's wishes. The progressive shift in the 1970s of the decision-making center of gravity in the National Security Council has also been the presidential response to the post-Watergate foreign policy claims of Congress: reducing the influence of the secretary of state also reduces the influence of Congress, and the president gains the upper hand in the struggle between the two government branches that the Constitution solicits 'for the privilege of controlling the country's foreign policy'.

The outcome of all this has been a foreign policy-making where the president is no longer the exclusive actor: an actor, moreover, who has been furtherly constrained, in the period 1968–92, by the characteristics of the institutional conflict between the Democratic Congress and the Republican presidency.[31] Nonetheless, this new context, open with regard to the actors, decentralized with regard to Congress and personalized with regard to the presidency, has not prevented the president from imposing his own priorities over issues deemed crucial by him. Why is that? A decisive factor for the president has been his ability to preserve control over a crucial resource: *the power to define the international crisis*. That is, when post-Vietnam presidents were able to link a specific international crisis with the rivalry of the Cold War, then they were able to secure margins for decision-making maneuvering that the structuring of foreign policy-making would not have permitted. Of course, the president has been able to use that resource to neutralize adversarial resistance (primarily by Congress) when such resistance did not express a consolidated current of opinion. When, however, as in the case of the pro-Contras policy of the Reagan of the second mandate, resistance by Congress reflected a majority opinion among the electorate, then that resource did not work as expected. How will this structure of foreign policy-making affect the internal relations between governmental actors once one of the two interpretations of the post-Cold War order has become dominant?

'Parliamentary presidentialism'?

There is no doubt that, with the Clinton presidency, the interpretation which has became dominant has been the multipolar one. Tonelson writes:

> Phase one of the great debate on the post-Cold War American foreign policy is over. The Clinton administration's proposed fiscal 1994 defense budget makes it clear that, although the president may continue to affirm America's position as a superpower, he has denied the nation the military resources that role requires, even in a world with no Soviet rival. In other word the 'declinists' have won.[32]

If the plausible consequences triggered by that scenario are related to the internal structure of foreign policy-making, there may be a contradictory outcome from their interaction.

In fact, with a return to normality two principal consequences seem plausible. First, the return to economic and humanitarian considerations will mean that an effective cooperation between presidency and Congress must be ensured. The conclusion, with the elections of 1992, of the long era of party-divided government (in which 'separate institutions *competed* for shared powers'),[33] makes that cooperation less difficult to pursue. Second, the return to diplomacy will trigger a new equilibrium between the personal presidency and the departmental presidency, tipped towards the latter. In sum, with the new multipolar scenario, there will be plausible pressures towards a new institutional balance between the two governmental institutions, and within the presidency: that is, pressures towards what I call 'parliamentary presidentialism', in foreign policy as well in domestic policy.

But two important institutional hurdles lie on the road of those plausible consequences. First, if it is true that Congress is urged to play a more active role by the multipolar interpretation of international politics, it is also true that its current institutional structure, with the strong decentralization of its decision-making powers and with the plurality of actors mobilized around its sub-committees, makes it very unlikely that it can profit from the new opportunities.[34] A cooperative presidentialism, especially in foreign policy, implies a legislature sufficiently centralized, in terms of its decision-making capacities, in order to deal, on an equal basis of effectiveness, with an already powerfully centralized executive. Second, if it is true that the departmental presidency is urged to play a more active role by the multipolar interpretation of international politics, it also true that the unipolar international pre-eminence of the country in the military field, with the vested interests of the personal presidency strongly institutionalized within the governmental structure, will try to hamper the thrust for a new balance of power within the executive in favor of its more traditional component.

In conclusion, if the Clinton presidency pursues its multipolar interpretation of the post-Cold War scenario, then there will be plausible pressure towards a sort of 'parliamentary presidentialism'. But given the still open-ended character of that interpretation, it is also plausible to predict a long period of institutional conflict between the presidency and Congress, and within each of them. This may define the new institutional order more coherently within that interpretation, but also help to refine that interpretation in regard to the power relationships which are going to consolidate both between and within the two institutions.

Notes

1. T. J. Lowi, *The Personal President* (Cornell University Press, Ithaca: 1985), chap. 1.
2. By the first one, I mean the president, the White House Office, with the family of 'special assistants', and the Executive Office, with its eleven offices. By the second one, I mean the fourteen departments with their secretaries. On this, see J. Hart, *The Presidential Branch* (2nd ed.; Pergamon Press, New York: 1987).
3. To the point that, immediately after Clinton's election, L. V. Sigal has written: 'The new president will need to restore constitutional checks and balances after decades of Cold War erosion that culminated in the Iran-contra and Iraqgate scandals' ('The last Cold War election', *Foreign Affairs* 72 (Winter 1993), p. 9).
4. J. L. Gaddis, 'Toward the post-Cold War order', *Foreign Affairs* 70 (Spring 1991), p. 117. The same conclusion is reached by T. Draper, 'Reagan's junta', *New York Review of Books,* 29 January 1987, pp. 5, 8–10, 12, 14.
5. R. W. Tucker and D. C. Hendrickson, 'Thomas Jefferson and American foreign policy', *Foreign Affairs* 69 (Spring 1990), pp.135–56.
6. S. P. Huntington, 'Coping with the Lippman gap', *Foreign Affairs* 66 (1988), pp. 453–77.
7. Minority Report of the Congressional Committees Investigating the Iran-contra Affair, in Congressional Joint Committees, *Report of the Congressional Committee Investigating the Iran-contra Affair* (US Government Printing Office, Washington, DC: 1987).
8. L. Berman and B. W. Jentleson, 'Bush and the post-Cold War world: new challenges for American leadership', in C. Campbell and B. Rockman (eds), *The Bush Presidency: First Appraisals* (Chatham House, Chatham: 1991), pp. 93–128.
9. W. Pfaff, 'Redefining world power', *Foreign Affairs* 70 (Winter 1991), pp. 34–48.
10. P. Kennedy, *The Rise and Fall of the Great Powers: Economic Change and Military Conflict from 1500 to 2000* (Random House, New York: 1989).
11. R. Rose, *The Postmodern President* (2nd ed.; Chatham House, Chatham: 1991).
12. R. D. Hormats, 'The roots of American power', *Foreign Affairs* 70 (Summer 1991), pp. 132–49.
13. M. Mandelbaum, 'The Bush foreign policy', *Foreign Affairs* 70 (Winter 1991), pp. 5–22.
14. J. Joffe, 'Entangled forever', in E. R. Wittkopf (ed.), *The Future of American Foreign Policy* (2nd ed.; St. Martin's Press, New York: 1994), p. 41.
15. Berman and Jentleson, 'Bush and the post-Cold War world', pp.117–18.
16. J. G. March and J. P. Olsen, *Rediscovering Institutions* (The Free Press, New York: 1989), chap. 3.
17. W. G. Hyland, 'American new course', *Foreign Affairs* 69 (Spring 1990), pp. 1–12.
18. 'At bottom the great issue we face is not between isolationism and

internationalism, but the way in which we conceive our international responsibilities and the methods to carry them out' (D. C. Hendrickson, 'The renovation of American foreign policy', *Foreign Affairs* 71 (Spring 1992), p. 59).

19. C. Krauthammer, 'The unipolar moment', *Foreign Affairs* 70 (Winter 1991), pp. 23–33; Joffe, 'Entangled forever'.
20. Although not explicitly unipolarist, the latest article by Samuel P. Huntington shares the world vision of the unipolarists, with its conflict between 'the West and the Rest'. Huntington writes: 'The West (has) to maintain the economic and military power necessary to protect its interests in relations to these (rival) civilizations' ('The clash of civilizations?', *Foreign Affairs* 72 (Summer 1993), p. 49).
21. In fact, 'Again and again Bush practically ignored Capitol Hill as he made his decisions (on the Gulf crisis). While the administration spoke positively of consultation with Congress, it engaged only in notification – and usually after the fact … In the six months of the gulf crisis, Democratic leaders of the Senate and House of Representatives had less influence upon Bush White House than Margaret Thatcher, who resigned as British prime minister in November 1990, or Prince Bansar bin Sultan, the Saudi Ambassador to Washington' (D. Gergen, 'America's missed opportunities', *Foreign Affairs* 71 (Winter 1992), p. 7).
22. *Weekly Compilation of Presidential Documents*, 8 March 1991 (US Government Printing Office, Washington, DC), p. 284.
23. The unipolarists 'cite the Gulf War as proof: only the United States could have organized the coalition and prosecuted the war' (W. G. Hyland, 'The case for pragmatism', *Foreign Affairs* 71 (Winter 1992), p. 44).
24. Among others, see Mandelbaum, 'The Bush foreign policy'.
25. Hyland writes that the multipolarists 'cite the Gulf War to reach an opposite conclusion [to that of the unipolarists]: that the United States could organize the coalition only through the cooperation of a diverse collection of powers' ('The case for pragmatism', p. 44).
26. Kennedy, *The Rise and Fall of the Great Powers*, p. 515.
27. P. H. Nitze, 'America: an honest broker', *Foreign Affairs* 69 (Fall 1990), pp. 1–14.
28. Z. Brzezinski, 'Selective global commitment', *Foreign Affairs* 70 (Fall 1991), pp. 1–20.
29. J. S. Nye, 'What new world order', in Wittkopf (ed.), *The Future of American Foreign Policy*, p. 54.
30. T. C. Sorenson, 'The President and the Secretary of State', *Foreign Affairs* 66 (Winter 1988), pp. 231–48.
31. N. W. Polsby, 'The evolution of an American establishment: Congress, the President, and the contemporary foreign policy community', University of California at Berkeley, Institute of Governmental Studies, mimeo. J. Hart agrees with Thomas Mann that, since Watergate, 'foreign policy is losing its distinctiveness as a domain of presidential responsibility and the trend toward congressional involvement in foreign policy is irreversible' ('President and Prime Minister: convergence or divergence?', *Parliamentary Affairs* 44 (1991), p. 223).

32. A. Tonelson, 'Superpower without a sword', *Foreign Affairs* 72 (Summer 1993), p. 166.
33. C. O. Jones, 'The separated Presidency: making it work in contemporary politics', in A. King (ed.), *The New American Political System* (2nd ed.; The AEI Press, Washington, DC: 1990), pp. 1–28.
34. 'The effect [of the reforms of the 1970s] was not exactly as envisaged ... The authority of the party leadership may have been strengthened, but the weakening of the dominance of the committee chairmen fragmented power in Congress. In short, the reforms of the 1970s generated almost as many problems as they had sought to overcome', C. J. Bailey, 'Congress and legislative activism', in G. Peele, C. J. Bailey, and B. Cain (eds), *Developments in American Politics* (Macmillan, London: 1992), p. 127.

4

The End of Electoral Realignment and the Deadlock of American Democracy

Stefano Luconi

The last few years have witnessed a debate over the alleged decadence of the United States as a world superpower which has also involved the concept of American democracy.[1] In particular, scholars have addressed the question of whether the United States can still offer itself as a model to promote liberal democracy and political pluralism abroad, and some of the answers have been in the negative.[2]

According to Samuel Huntington, the 'two-turnover test' – namely the principle of two changes of government through free elections – is a viable criterion by which to measure the consolidation of democracy in developing countries. In his opinion when, in a post-totalitarian or in a post-authoritarian regime, citizens can vote out of power their first two freely elected governments this gives evidence that their political system is really committed to democracy.[3] However, in the early 1990s, when Huntington elaborated his theory, it seemed that the United States itself could hardly meet such a test. Before Clinton's victory, after almost a quarter of a century of Republican control of the presidency, and with a congressional incumbency rate above 90 per cent, it could easily be argued that an electoral turnover was a rather remote prospect in the United States. After all, the awareness that, from 1980 through 1990, an average of 95 per cent of US representatives who tried to retain their seats in Congress managed to win re-election has led one scholar to remark that 'there was a bigger turnover in the old Soviet Politburo'.[4]

The purpose of this paper is to assess the implications for the concept of democracy of the rise and fall of the realignment perspective of voting behavior in contemporary US politics. Broadly defined, a realignment is a long-term turnabout in the existing power relationships between the two major parties that produces a new majority party and determines a sharp alteration in the political agenda. It results from the persistence of a new polarization of voters, following a massive shift of partisan allegiance in association with an unusual intensity in political conflict and a relevant increase in voter turnout.[5]

As such, realignments should characterize any two-party system. Yet the realignment theory has been elaborated in the United States, and applied to explain patterns of electoral change almost exclusively in that country, with only a few exceptions concerned primarily with the transformations in the balance of party strength in Great Britain.[6] Moreover, according to several scholars, by bringing about a cyclical displacement of both the dominant party and the entrenched interests it represents, realignments have become not only a main feature of the American party system but also the device that makes democracy work in the United States. The realignment perspective implies that, even under conditions of social or economic crisis, Americans do not resort to revolution but to the ballot, because the political system in itself holds the means of satisfying the claims of those groups that are out of power.[7]

In that scenario, elections ensure rotation in government at remarkably regular intervals of time and political minorities can rise to majority status, and thereby shape the direction of public policy, building up coalitions of voters. Indeed, the core of the realignment theory is the concept that American parties are constituent parties, namely heterogeneous coalitions of social, geographical and ideological components that compromise among their conflicting demands to gain a majority at the polls. Thus, the real counterforce to oligarchic control of special interests on American society is the existence of all-inclusive parties that can accommodate groups previously excluded from the decision-making process.[8]

The systemic elaboration of the realignment theory dates back to the early post-war years.[9] Therefore it clearly reflects the legacy of Franklin D. Roosevelt's successful attempt to prevent a radicalization of the mass unrest resulting from the Depression, and to ensure social stability in times of harsh partisan conflict, by forging a stable coalition of unionized workers, organized farmers and first- and second-generation immigrants, as well as by integrating new cohorts of young and ethnic voters into the American political system.[10] It is hardly by chance that one of the pioneer definitions of realignment has been offered as an introduction to Basil Rauch's early interpretation of the New Deal.[11]

Although the realignment perspective dominated the literature on American parties until very recently, scholars have nonetheless challenged the idea that the New Deal was a correct exemplification of the patterns which have determined the course of political events in the United States, at least in the twentieth century. In particular, they have argued that the mobilization of voters in the 1930s was only a short-term reversal of a steep decline in turnout that, after having characterized American elections since the turn of the century, surfaced again in the mid 1960s. They have also maintained that the strong partisan identification that the New Deal witnessed was at odds with a secular trend toward a rise in ticket-splitting, and an increase of people's dissatisfaction with political parties, which have both re-emerged in the last few decades.[12]

Even more troubling has been the failure to identify a post-war realignment.[13] Since the average frequency of realignments was approximately

30 to 40 years,[14] by the late 1960s the American party system should have been ready for a post-New Deal redistribution of partisan support and the establishment of a new durable polarization of voters. Indeed Kevin Phillips has held that the 1968 elections saw the birth of a conservative majority which superseded the Roosevelt coalition and its later revitalizations.[15] Yet, receiving 43.4 per cent of the popular vote, Nixon was a minority president, and Phillips has had to resort to arithmetic acrobatics in order to corroborate his own thesis. Only by adding the Republican vote to the Wallace vote could Phillips argue that the election of Nixon resulted from a realignment of American voters toward the GOP.[16] Moreover, in spite of Humphrey's defeat, the Democratic party maintained a majority in both the Senate and the House of Representatives.

Divided government characterized the party system during the following 24 years. Even if the GOP dominated presidential elections, winning four contests out of five before 1992, the Democratic party never lost its hold on the House of Representatives and was in the minority in the Senate only between 1981 and 1986. The Democrats also resisted the Republican tide at the state level, enjoying large pluralities in state legislatures and governorships, notwithstanding an increase in interparty competition in that sphere.[17]

This scenario conflicted with the traditional realignment perspective, because pre-war realignments had been characterized by single party control of both Congress and the presidency, and at least the New Deal saw some synchronization between national and state electoral outcomes.[18] Therefore, the failure of the GOP to penetrate below the presidential level has forced scholars to qualify assertions that the United States experienced a Republican realignment over the last quarter of a century, even in the face of Reagan's 1984 landslide.[19]

It is quite significant that the first relevant divergence of political events from the pattern outlined in the realignment perspective was the 1968 presidential election. Johnson's full term witnessed an eruption of social unrest and turmoil that questioned the very principles underlying the realignment theory. The Watts riot – which more than coincidentally broke out less than a week after the President had signed into law the Voting Rights Act to prevent disfranchisement of blacks in the South – undermined the idea that minority groups refrained from violence because they had the possibility of fulfilling their goals and triggering changes in US society by casting their ballots.

Moreover, the 1968 election campaign also challenged the notion of constituent parties. As a result of both the rejection of anti-war planks on the floor of a tumultuous Democratic convention in Chicago and the beating of pacifist insurgents outside the convention hall, a component of the liberal coalition felt that the Democratic party no longer had any room to represent their positions, and a number of the McCarthy and Kennedy potential voters failed to turn out on election day.[20]

Insulation of radicals affected also the right wing of the political spectrum. Phillips has suggested that the Republican party could consolidate its own majority status by exploiting southern backlash to Democrats' growing advocacy of civil rights legislation.[21] Yet, as Donald Strong has remarked for Alabama, disenchanted Democrats who had supported Wallace did not join the GOP after the collapse of the American Independent party because their stand for state rights did not fit identification with another nationally organized party that had never pledged officially for southern racial traditions.[22] Even in the 1980s, when the GOP won stable majorities in presidential elections in the South, the voters of that region usually split their ballots to support Democrats for Congress and state legislatures.[23] The most striking instance of that behavior occurred in the 1988 elections, when Bush and Quayle carried Texas, but that state re-elected Bentsen, Dukakis' running mate for vice-president, to the Senate.[24]

Realignment theorists have clearly conceptualized an anti-Downsian explanation for party behavior. According to Downs, since the great bulk of the electorate is moderate, in a two-party system vote-maximizing motives compel parties to converge toward the center and subdue sharp programmatic differences.[25] Conversely, it was the very ideological polarization between the two major parties that brought about realignments. Tension between Republican-conservative and Democratic-liberal traditions has underlain the course of democracy in the United States.[26]

Yet, after Goldwater had so exacerbated the line of partisan cleavage that he suffered one of the most devastating repudiations in the history of US elections – with only few exceptions among which McGovern's 1972 candidacy was the leading example – parties have tended to straddle the fence on the most divisive problems and to pose false choices or 'non-issues' in election campaigns, dodging people's real concerns.[27] It has been argued that even Reagan had to disguise his own ideological extremism during the 1980 campaign in order to defeat Carter.[28] Indeed, the 1980 presidential contest was not perceived as an ideological election. According to polls, in August 1980 only 40 per cent of Americans thought that there were 'important differences' between the Democratic and the Republican party, and as few as 11 per cent of Reagan's supporters voted for him because he was 'a real conservative'.[29] Reagan further moderated his ideological stance for re-election purposes in 1984.[30]

The need for a middle-of-the-road position has received particular emphasis in campaign strategies, especially in the last few years when parties and presidential candidates have endeavored either to keep or win back the votes of the conservative Democrats who strayed to Reagan.[31] As both Republicans and Democrats appealed to the same cohort of the eligible electorate, a growing number of potential voters – especially among the poor and the working class – felt confined to the sidelines of the political debate or even excluded from it, and no longer found a party that advanced their goals or addressed their concerns. Participation in elections seemed more and more meaningless and, consequently, voter turnout dropped dramatically.[32] In 1988 it reached the lowest level since 1924 in presidential contests, when only 50.2 per cent of the eligible population voted. That year, for the first time since the end of World War II, the actual number of voters even declined from that of the previous presidential election, shrinking from more than 92.5 million people to about 91.5 million.[33] With Michael Dukakis stressing technocratic competence and playing down ideology, even liberals could hardly believe they had a champion to side with in 1988.[34]

Blurring ideological differences aimed purposely at making it easier for voters to cross party lines and cast their ballots for a party they recently did not identify with. However, this further contribution to the weakening of partisan attachments was apparently the death-blow for the realignment theory. After previous challenges to the constituent nature of American parties and to the role of elections as tension-managing devices, even the idea of the persistence of the partisan orientations of the electorate seemed groundless. As a result, in some analyses, a dealignment thesis has superseded the realignment theory as a more reliable model to account for current developments in the American party system.

Stability in voting behavior characterizes realignments to such an extent that even cyclical changes in the party balance of power are supposed to influence election outcomes for an average third of a century. Conversely, volatility of the lines of partisan cleavage is the main feature of dealignment. In this view, after the final collapse of the New Deal order in the late 1960s under the pressure of both the Vietnam war and civil rights issues, a new majority party failed to emerge because of the fluidity of voters' alignment. In the face of people's growing dissatisfaction with parties, evaluation of officeholders' performances has replaced partisan loyalty as the key determinant of voting. Consequently, far from reflecting traditional patterns of voting behavior or establishing new long-term trends, presidential contests have become a sort of referendum on the public record of the incumbent administration which are completely insulated from any previous and following vote and, thereby, determine a highly transitory polarization of the electorate.[35]

Commentators have sometimes remarked that the realignment theory suggests a discontinuous and intermittent operating of democracy. Although citizens can always exercise a potential control over government by casting their ballot on election day, they exert their power only when they enter the active electorate or at times of crisis, when they switch their previous partisan allegiance to create a new majority and oust the dominant party. After casting their first ballot or shifting their partisan orientation, the great bulk of voters retain their new party identification somewhat passively until another major crisis arises. Between periods of realignment, therefore, consistency in loyalty to either party regardless of ever changing political circumstances ends up by limiting people's sovereignty. Conversely, in a phase of dealignment voters play a continuous and apparently more active role in the democratic process because the assessment of officeholders' record is a constant of every election.[36]

Yet, the persisting decline in turnout, which is associated with the alienation of citizens from the party system in the current dealignment, offers a greater challenge to American democracy than actual voters' relative unconcern for policy-making performances in the interim between realignments. The dealignment perspective highlights a plebiscitarian working of American politics. While decisions are taken from above, the capacity of people to influence policy-making has been confined to supporting or rejecting the executive record as a whole in referendum-like elections. Indeed, it seems that pluralism is in deep trouble. With a growing number of members of neglected or under-represented groups refusing to participate in elections because of the apparent lack of viable options between parties and candidates, there are also fewer chances of accommodating minorities' claims and displacing dominant interests and their spokespersons. In particular, the rising influence of lobbyists, fund-raisers and other elites without any popular mandate has matched the progressive erosion of the political representation of those potential voters who are underprivileged economically and socially.[37]

Moreover, in the face of an increasing decay in turnout, decision-making has shifted from the voting booth to institutions outside the electoral sphere. The federal judiciary and mass media have become common vehicles for waging political battles. Parties rely on prosecutions, investigations and revelations to achieve their goals rather than pursuing their own aims through the mobilization of voters. Therefore, since neither prosecutors nor journalists are elected officials, ordinary people's sovereignty and their control over public choices have further diminished.[38]

As Schattschneider pointed out more than thirty years ago, a large base of political participation is the essential condition for democracy.[39] Since citizens express their allegiance to the existing political system by casting their ballots on election day, voting abstention implies a delegitimization of the political system itself.[40] However, it has also been suggested that, especially in Western countries, eligible voters fail to go to the polls because they are content with the *status quo* and feel no need for change. Viewed this way, nonvoting would reflect the stability of the political system.[41] Nonetheless, it does not seem that this hypothesis can account for recent turnout trends in the United States. Actually, those cohorts that have shown lower voter participation since the 1960s – the poor, the unemployed, blacks and Hispanics – are also the most economically and socially disadvantaged groups and, thereby, the least likely to be pleased with existing conditions in US society.[42] Holding registration requirements responsible for abstention is also misleading. Participation has decreased significantly even in states that eased registration procedures, which provides further evidence that nonvoting results primarily from potential voters' lack of motivation because of declining competitiveness between parties.[43] For instance, according to a recent study, the largest group of individuals who failed to cast their ballots in the 1990 senatorial races remained at home out of dissatisfaction with the options at stake in the contests.[44]

On the eve of the 1990 mid-term elections, realignment die-hard theorist Kevin Phillips suggested that the Republican presidential cycle which had begun in 1968 was in its late middle age, and that, therefore, the stage of American politics was set for an era of Democratic dominance. In his opinion, the Democratic party could regain its majority status if it managed to cash in on the middle-class backlash to the Republican economic policies that had been benefiting the well-off at the expenses of the bulk of American society since the Reagan years.[45] With economy as the paramount issue in the 1992 campaign, Clinton's victory could apparently corroborate Phillips' thesis.[46]

Yet, it seems at least doubtful that the outcome of the 1992 election reversed the previous trend toward the dealignment of the American party system and witnessed a realignment of voters toward the Democratic party.[47] Actually, receiving only 43 per cent of the popular vote makes Clinton a minority president, and his election resulted primarily from voters' negative assessment of the performance of the Bush administration in relation to the economy.[48] Moreover, even before the Republican landslide in the 1994 mid-term elections – which early impressionistic accounts have regarded as being the beginning of a new Republican era in US politics – a sizeable number of defeats of Democrats at the polls in 1992 and 1993 had already undermined the theory that Clinton's success arose from a Democratic realignment.[49]

Indeed, the new partisan alignment of the electorate in the 1992 presidential contest was so volatile that, for instance, in spite of the president-elect's campaign efforts on behalf of the Democratic candidate, Republican Paul D. Coverdell defeated Democratic incumbent Wyche Fowler, Jr. in a runoff for the US Senate in Georgia only three weeks after Clinton had carried that state.[50] Likewise, Republican Christine Todd Whitman turned Governor Jim Florio out of office in New Jersey in November 1993, notwithstanding Clinton's victory in that state one year earlier.[51]

Also, the outcome of all of the other four nationally spotlighted elections after the 1992 presidential contest – namely the races for US senator in Texas, for governor in Virginia, and for mayor in Los Angeles and New York – went against the Democratic party. In particular, voters' early disenchantment with the new president marked Republican Kay Bailey Hutchinson's landslide over interim Democratic Senator Bob Krueger in a runoff in Texas in June 1993 to fill the vacancy created in the Senate after Bentsen's appointment as Treasury secretary. Indeed, although Clinton had lost Texas by only 3 per cent in 1992, Hutchinson won the seat that Democratic Bentsen had held for 22 years with 67 per cent of the votes – the largest Republican majority in Texas history – after making her opposition to Clinton's tax package the paramount issue of hercampaign.[52]

Besides reaffirming the character of elections as referenda with a highly transitory influence on voters' partisan cleavage, the 1992 election also witnessed the persistence of citizens' alienation from politics. Turnout failed to increase by more than 5 per cent even if voter participation could profit by the presence on the ballot of an anti-establishment candidate such as Perot, who appealed specifically to the potential electorate exhibiting discontent with the two-party system. Perot's centrism was unable to convey any idea of empowering under-represented groups and, thereby, to mobilize their lukewarm potential voters. Perot fared poorly among minorities, as 94 per cent of his supporters were non-Hispanic whites.[53]

Moreover, despite a vociferous shift toward conservative values at the Republican convention, and cosmetic advocacy of minority rights by the Democratic party, the 1992 election did not reflect an ideological polarization. Less than one-fifth of the participating electorate cared about family values or abortion, while nearly two-thirds of those who cast their ballots were concerned with the economy, unemployment and the federal deficit.[54]

A former chairperson of the Democratic Leadership Council – a bailiwick of conservative Democrats who had planned to win back the presidency by distancing their own party from liberalism – Clinton ran a moderate campaign that targeted the middle class by stressing economic growth. The Democratic program also pledged to limit welfare payments to two years, emphasized its opposition to racial quotas for employment and never mentioned affirmative action while discussing civil rights. Overlooking such liberal issues as racial justice was central to Clinton's strategy, probably because, throughout the 1980s, the so-called 'Reagan Democrats' had misinterpreted conventional Democratic themes like equal opportunities and fairness as an attempt to favor blacks to the detriment of whites.[55] In order to reassure that pivotal cohort of moderate voters, Clinton also made a point of separating himself from the black leadership. For instance he exploited the case of Sister Souljah, a rap singer who had reportedly encouraged blacks to kill whites instead of killing one another, in order to castigate Jesse Jackson's National Rainbow Coalition for having invited her to one of its conferences. Clinton even scheduled his appearances at Afro-American meetings late enough to prevent their coverage in the evening news.[56]

The strengthening of the centrist stand of the Democratic party in 1992 further undermined the constituent feature of American parties and contributed to keep marginal groups away from the polls. Jesse Jackson's failure to start another campaign for the Democratic presidential nomination provides an outstanding example that coalition parties have become an endangered species in the United States. In both 1984 and 1988 Jackson launched a rainbow movement of blacks, Hispanics and other minorities. Addressing the concerns of the 'dispossessed' and bargaining with Democratic nominees – in particular Dukakis – for his own support, Jackson contributed to keeping alive the constituent nature of the Democratic party and to getting out the votes of downtrodden groups, especially the blacks.[57] Tangible signs of the persistence of an all-inclusive vocation within the Democratic party as late as 1988 were the decision to reduce the influence of super-delegates to grant Jackson more chances of success in future bids for the presidential nomination, as well as the addition of new seats to the Democratic National Committee in order to accommodate his supporters into the party hierarchy. The Jackson forces were also allowed to participate in the drawing up of the 1988 Democratic platform, which, for instance, led Democrats to declare South Africa a terrorist state and to ask for comprehensive economic sanctions against it.[58]

In contrast, Clinton made Jackson no offers to secure his support in 1992, and turned down Jerry Brown's request to barter his endorsement for the inclusion in the Democratic platform of calls for both a $100 limit on campaign contributions and a ban on electoral financing from political action committees.[59] By refusing to make concessions to radical vote-getters like Jackson and Brown, Clinton tried to reassure the moderates that he had not fallen prey of interest groups within his own party. Yet, following his suburban-oriented campaign, voter turnout dropped among blacks. They made up 10 per cent of the active electorate in 1988, but only 8 per cent in 1992. Likewise, with a share of only 3 per cent of participating voters, Hispanics remained an under-represented minority in the electorate.[60]

Herbert Agar has argued that parties can play a major role in mending divisions within American society. In his opinion the key to reconciling antagonizing points of view, and preventing disruptive conflicts, is straddling divisive issues and avoiding strong ideological or programmatic commitment.[61] Agar has assumed that the participating electorate reflects the different components of society, which is not the case of the current dealignment. Therefore, if drawing middle-of-the-road platforms can help to pacify a shrinking cohort of active voters, it also contributes to the discouragement of participation among a growing number of citizens who perceive the convergence of parties upon the center as a progressive dying out of the role of the ballot as a series of viable alternatives to make real choices. As Downs has maintained, in a two-party system the shift of both major parties toward the center causes abstention among extremist voters.[62]

In conclusion, while both Republicans and Democrats persist in pursuing the votes of the middle class through suburban-oriented programs, the party system has fewer and fewer possibilities of integrating the underrepresented and marginal groups that place themselves on the fringes of the political spectrum. Rather, it promotes their further marginalization from the decision-making process. As a result, the increasing estrangement of Americans from politics threatens not only the legitimacy of the system but also the possibility of turning dissent into consensus and forging democracy in the voting booth. It seems hardly by chance that the 1992 riot in Los Angeles coincided with the waning of Jackson's political influence and the tendency of other Afro-American politicians to downplay racial issues in order to appeal to moderate whites.[63]

Notes

1. Milestones in this controversy are P. Kennedy, *The Rise and Fall of the Great Powers: Economic Change and Military Conflict from 1500 to 2000* (Random House, New York: 1989), pp. 665–92 and J. S. Nye, Jr., *Bound to Lead: The Changing Nature of American Power* (Basic Books, New York: 1990). For other contributions to that debate see also S. P. Huntington, 'The US — decline or renewal?', *Foreign Affairs* 67 (Winter 1988–9), pp. 76–96; H. R. Nau, *The Myth of America's Decline: Leading the World Economy into the 1990s* (Oxford University Press, New York: 1990); P. Kennedy, *Preparing for the Twenty-First Century* (Random House, New York: 1993), pp. 290–325; Z. Brzezinski, *Out of Control: Global Turmoil on the Eve of the Twenty-First Century* (Charles Scribner's Sons, New York: 1993).
2. See, e.g., G. H. Quester, 'America as a model for the world', *PS: Political Science and Politics* 23 (1991), pp. 658–9; T. R. Gurr, 'America as a model for the world? A skeptical view', ibid., pp. 664–7; G. T. Allison, Jr. and Robert P. Beschel, Jr., 'Can the United States promote democracy?', *Political Science Quarterly* 107 (1992), pp. 81–98.
3. S. P. Huntington, *The Third Wave: Democratization in the Late Twentieth Century* (University of Oklahoma Press, Norman: 1991), pp. 266–8.
4. M. R. Hershey, 'The congressional elections', in G. M. Pomper (ed.), *The Election of 1992: Reports and Interpretations* (Chatham House, Chatham, NJ: 1993), p. 159.
5. The literature on realignment is boundless. For two recent review and bibliographic essays, see J. Zvesper, 'Party realignment: a past without a future?', in R. Williams (ed.), *Explaining American Politics: Issues and Interpretations* (Routledge, London: 1990), pp. 167–86; H. F. Bass, Jr., 'Background to debate: a reader's guide and bibliography', in B. E. Shafer (ed.), *The End of Realignment? Interpreting American Electoral Eras* (University of Wisconsin Press, Madison: 1991), pp. 141–78.

6. I. Crewe, 'Prospects for party realignment: an Anglo-American comparison', *Comparative Politics* 12 (1980), pp. 379–400; P. Williams, 'Review article: party realignment in the United States and Britain', *British Journal of Political Science* 15 (1985), pp. 97–115. For attempts to apply the concept of realignment to elections in other countries outside the United States, see R. J. Dalton, S. C. Flanagan, and P. A. Beck (eds), *Electoral Change in Advanced Industrial Democracies: Realignment or Dealignment?* (Princeton University Press, Princeton, NJ: 1984).
7. L. G. McMichael and R. J. Trilling, 'The structure and meaning of critical realignment: the case of Pennsylvania, 1928–1932', in B. A. Campbell and R. J. Trilling (eds), *Realignment in American Politics: Toward a Theory* (University of Texas Press, Austin and London: 1980), p. 21; W. D. Burnham, *The Current Crisis in American Politics* (Oxford University Press, New York: 1982), p. 10; P. F. Galderisi and M. S. Lyons, 'Realignment past and present', in Idem et al. (eds), *The Politics of Realignment: Party Change in the Mountain West* (Westview Press, Boulder, Colo. and London: 1987), p. 4; K. Phillips, *Boiling Point: Democrats, Republicans, and the Decline of Middle-Class Prosperity* (Random House, New York: 1993), p. 59.
8. T. J. Lowi, 'Party, policy, and constitution', in W. N. Chambers and W. D. Burnham (eds), *The American Party Systems: Stages of Political Development* (Oxford University Press, New York: 1967), pp. 238–76; W. D. Burnham, *Critical Elections and the Mainsprings of American Politics* (Norton, New York: 1970), pp. 9–10; S. M. Lipset (ed.), *Emerging Coalitions in American Politics* (Institute for Contemporary Studies, San Francisco: 1978); J. R. Petrocik, *Party Coalitions: Realignment and the Decline of the New Deal Party System* (University of Chicago Press, Chicago and London: 1981); P. Kleppner, 'Critical realignments and electoral systems', in Idem et al., *The Evolution of American Electoral Systems* (Greenwood Press, Westport, Conn. and London: 1981), pp. 3–4, 9–10.
9. S. Lubell, *The Future of American Politics* (Harper and Row, New York: 1952); V. O. Key, Jr., 'The future of the Democratic party', *Virginia Quarterly Review* 52 (1952), pp. 161–5; Idem, 'A theory of critical elections', *Journal of Politics* 17 (1955), pp. 3–18.
10. J. M. Allswang, *The New Deal and American Politics: A Study in Political Change* (Wiley, New York: 1978); K. Andersen, *The Creation of a Democratic Majority 1928–1936* (University of Chicago Press, Chicago and London: 1979); G. H. Gamm, *The Making of New Deal Democrats: Voting Behavior and Realignment in Boston 1920–1940* (University of Chicago Press, Chicago and London: 1989); L. Cohen, *Making a New Deal: Industrial Workers in Chicago 1919–1939* (Cambridge University Press, New York: 1990).
11. As Rauch has pointed out, few laws govern the cyclical development of American political history through 'peaceful revolutions ... made by voting into power new administrations which abandon the policies of their predecessors and turn the nation toward new goals'. In particular, 'when an administration comes to represent the interests of only one major sectional-class group ... the groups whose needs have been neglected by such an administration will sooner or later unite to form a new coalition

capable of winning electoral majorities; ... within a coalition the most powerful single interest tends in the course of time to dominate the others, and to abandon their policies in favor of exclusive devotion to his own. Therewith the cycle is complete and the stage is set for its repetition': B. Rauch, *The History of the New Deal 1933–1938* (Creative Press, New York: 1944), pp. 1, 6.

12. W. D. Burnham, 'The changing shape of the American political universe', *American Political Science Review* 59 (1965), pp. 7–28; Idem, *Critical Elections*, pp. 91–134; A. King (ed.), *The New American Political System* (American Enterprise Institute, Washington, DC: 1978); P. Kleppner, *Who Voted? The Dynamics of Electoral Turnout 1870–1980* (Praeger, New York: 1982); J. H. Silbey, 'Beyond realignment and realignment theory: American political eras, 1789–1989', in Shafer (ed.), *The End of Realignment?*, pp. 3–23.
13. E. C. Ladd, 'Like waiting for Godot: the uselessness of realignment for understanding change in contemporary American politics', *Polity* 22 (1990), pp. 511–25, later reprinted in Shafer (ed.), *The End of Realignment?*, pp. 24–36.
14. W. D. Burnham, 'Party systems and the political process', in Chambers and Burnham (eds), *The American Party Systems*, pp. 287–8.
15. K. Phillips, *The Emerging Republican Majority* (Arlington House, New Rochelle: 1969).
16. Theoretically, the rise of third parties is related to a major shift of partisan allegiance. Disregard in the policies of the two major parties for certain minorities leads those groups whose interests have been overlooked to pursue their own goals through third parties. Yet, only after either major party appropriates minorities' claims, do third-party issues contribute to alter traditional patterns of voting behavior. Therefore the emergence of a third party is a mere proto-realignment phenomenon. It occurs before, not at the same time as an electoral realignment, as Phillips has instead suggested for 1968. Indeed, according to realignment theory, third parties work as half-way houses for voters breaking away from either major party to join the other. See, e.g., D. MacRae, Jr. and J. A. Meldrum, 'Critical elections in Illinois', *American Political Science Review* 54 (1960), pp. 669–70, 675–7; C. Sellers, 'The equilibrium cycle in two-party politics', *Public Opinion Quarterly* 29 (1965) p. 27; Burnham, *Critical Elections*, pp. 27–31; D. A. Mazmanian, *Third Parties in Presidential Elections* (Brookings Institution, Washington, DC: 1974), p. 139; J. L. Sundquist, *Dynamics of the Party System: Alignment and Realignment of Political Parties in the United States* (2nd ed.; Brookings Institution, Washington, DC: 1983), pp. 244–52. Furthermore, George Wallace's role in boosting the switch of Southern voters toward the Republicans is at least doubtful. Actually, after carrying five states for the American Independent party in 1968, Wallace reverted to his former Democratic allegiance to be re-elected governor of Alabama in 1970 and to wage an early-crippled campaign for the Democratic presidential nomination in 1972.
17. J. L. Sundquist, 'Needed: a political theory for the new era of coalition government in the United States', *Political Science Quarterly* 103 (1988), pp. 613–35; M. P. Fiorina, 'An era of divided government', ibid. 107 (1992),

pp. 387–410; Idem, *Divided Government* (Macmillan, New York: 1992); M. Moakley (ed.), *Party Realignment and State Politics* (Ohio State University Press, Columbus: 1992); and review essays by D. W. Brady, 'The causes and the consequences of divided government: toward a new theory of American politics?', *American Political Science Review* 87 (1993), pp. 189–94 and D. McKay, 'Review article: divided and governed? Recent research on divided government in the United States', *British Journal of Political Science* 24 (1994), pp. 517– 34.

18. W. D. Burnham, J. M. Clubb, and W. H. Flanigan, 'Partisan realignment: a systemic perspective', in J. H. Silbey, A. G. Bogue, and W. H. Flanigan (eds), *The History of American Electoral Behavior* (Princeton University Press, Princeton, NJ: 1978), pp. 45–77; D. W. Brady, *Critical Elections and Congressional Policy Making* (Stanford University Press, Stanford: 1988).
19. B. Ginsberg and M. Shefter, 'A critical realignment? The new politics, the reconstituted right, and the election of 1984', in M. Nelson (ed.), *The Election of 1984* (Congressional Quarterly Inc., Washington, DC: 1985), pp. 1–25; P. Abramson, 'The 1984 Elections and the Future of American Politics', in Idem, J. H. Aldrich, and D. W. Rhode, *Change and Continuity in the 1984 Elections* (rev. ed.; Congressional Quarterly Inc., Washington, DC: 1987), pp. 281–305; P. A. Beck, 'Incomplete realignment: the Reagan legacy for parties and elections', in C. O. Jones (ed.), *The Reagan Legacy: Promise and Performance* (Chatham House, Chatham, NJ: 1988), pp. 145–71.
20. Sundquist, *Dynamics of the Party System*, pp. 380–1.
21. Phillips, *The Emerging Republican Majority*, pp. 468–73.
22. D. S. Strong, 'Alabama: transition and alienation,' in W. C. Havard (ed.), *The Changing Politics of the South* (Louisiana State University Press, Baton Rouge: 1972), p. 471.
23. R. P. Steed, L. W. Moreland, and T. A. Baker (eds), *The 1984 Presidential Election in the South: Patterns of Southern Party Politics* (Praeger, New York: 1986); Beck, 'Incomplete realignment', pp. 166–7.
24. For a recent overview of the dynamics of the party system in the South, see Andrew Appleton and Daniel S. Ward, 'Party transformation in France and the United States: the hierarchical effect of system change in comparative perspective', *Comparative Politics* 26 (1993), pp. 77–82, 87–95.
25. A. Downs, *An Economic Theory of Democracy* (Harper and Row, New York: 1957), pp. 114–41.
26. A. J. Reichley, *The Life of the Parties: A History of American Political Parties* (Free Press, New York: 1992).
27. E. J. Dionne, Jr., *Why Americans Hate Politics* (Simon and Schuster, New York: 1991).
28. L. Gray, 'Il problema dei partiti politici americani', in R. Tierski (ed.), *Gli Stati Uniti fra primato e incertezza* (Il Mulino, Bologna: 1983), pp. 219, 235–8.
29. First percentage from a survey conducted by CBS News/*New York Times*, 2–7 August 1980, as quoted by E. C. Ladd, 'The brittle mandate: electoral dealignment and the 1980 presidential election', *Political Science Quarterly* 96 (1981), p. 4; second percentage from a *New York Times* exit poll, as quoted by W. D. Burnham, 'The 1980 earthquake: realignment, reaction,

or what?', in T. Ferguson and J. Rogers (eds), *The Hidden Election: Politics and Economics in the 1980 Presidential Campaign* (Pantheon Books, New York: 1981), pp. 109–10.

30. A. M. Schlesinger, Jr., *The Cycles of American History* (1st English ed.; André Deutsch, London: 1987), p. 313. For a study emphasizing the relative moderatism of Reagan's presidency in terms of policies and popular support, see L. M. Schwab, *The Illusion of a Conservative Reagan Revolution* (Transaction Publishers, New Brunswick, NJ: 1991).
31. For the 1988 campaign, see M. R. Hershey, 'The campaign and the media', in G. M. Pomper (ed.), *The Election of 1988: Reports and Interpretations* (Chatham House, Chatham, NJ: 1989), pp. 78–83, 85–8; M. Duffy and D. Goodgame, *Marching in Place: The Status Quo Presidency of George Bush* (Simon and Schuster, New York: 1992), pp. 24–7.
32. F. F. Piven and R. A. Cloward, *Why Americans Don't Vote* (2nd ed.; Pantheon Books, New York: 1989), pp. vii–viii; M. J. Avey, *The Demobilization of American Voters: A Comprehensive Theory of Voter Turnout* (Greenwood, New York: 1989); Dionne, Jr., *Why Americans Hate Politics*.
33. C. Smith (ed.), *The '88 Vote* (Capital Cities-ABC, New York: n.d.).
34. W. D. Burnham, 'The Reagan heritage', in Pomper (ed.), *The Election of 1988*, p. 27; W. E. Leuchtenburg, *In the Shadow of FDR: From Harry Truman to Bill Clinton* (Cornell University Press, Ithaca: 1993), pp. 257–9.
35. S. Lubell, *The Hidden Crisis in American Politics* (Norton, New York: 1971), p. 278; E. C. Ladd with C. D. Hadley, *Transformation of the American Party System* (2nd ed.; Norton, New York: 1978); Ladd, 'The brittle mandate', pp. 1–25; M. P. Fiorina, *Retrospective Voting in American National Elections* (Yale University Press, New Haven: 1981); E. C. Ladd, 'On mandates, realignments, and the 1984 presidential election', *Political Science Quarterly* 100 (1985), pp. 1–25; Idem, 'The 1988 elections: continuation of the post-New Deal system', ibid. 104 (1989), pp. 1–18; M. P. Wattenberg, *The Rise of Candidate-Centered Politics: Presidential Elections of the 1980s* (Harvard University Press, Cambridge, Mass.: 1991); H. D. Clarke and M. Suzuki, 'Partisan dealignment and the dynamics of independence in the American electorate, 1953–88', *British Journal of Political Science* 24 (1994), pp. 57–77.
36. R. J. Trilling and B. A. Campbell, 'Toward a theory of realignment: an introduction', in Campbell and Trilling (eds), *Realignment in American Politics*, p. 4; A. J. Lichtman, 'The end of realignment theory? Toward a new research project for American political history', *Historical Methods* 15 (1982), pp. 183–4.
37. T. B. Edsall, 'The changing shape of power: a realignment in public policy', in S. Fraser and G. Gerstle (eds), *The Rise and Fall of the New Deal Order 1930–1980* (Princeton University Press, Princeton, NJ: 1989), pp. 269–93.
38. B. Ginsberg and M. Shefter, *Politics by Other Means: The Declining Importance of Elections in America* (Basic Books, New York: 1990).
39. E. E. Schattschneider, *The Semi-Sovereign People: A Realist's View of Democracy in America* (Holt, Rinehart and Winston, New York: 1960), p. 112.
40. G. M. Pomper, *Elections in America: Control and Influence in Democratic Politics* (Dodd, Meade & Company, New York: 1970), p. 246; W. H. Riker

and P. C. Ordeshook, *An Introduction to Positive Political Theory* (Prentice Hall, Englewood, NJ: 1973), p. 63; R. E. Wolfinger and S. J. Rosenstone, *Who Votes?* (Yale University Press, New Haven: 1980), p. 7; R. A. Teixeira, *The Disappearing American Voter* (Brookings Institution, Washington, DC: 1992), pp. 101–5.

41. S. M. Lipset, *Political Man: The Social Bases of Politics* (2nd ed.; Johns Hopkins University Press, Baltimore: 1981), p. 185.

42. T. E. Cavanagh, 'Changes in American voter turnout, 1964–1976', *Political Science Quarterly* 96 (1981), pp. 53–65; H. J. Gans, *Middle Class Individualism: The Future of Liberal Democracy* (Free Press, New York: 1988), pp. 73–4; Piven and Cloward, *Why Americans Don't Vote*, pp. xi, 160–4, 204–5; P. J. Davies, *Elections USA* (Manchester University Press, Manchester: 1992), p. 25; S. Verba et al., 'Race, ethnicity and political resources: participation in the United States', *British Journal of Political Science* 23 (1993), pp. 461–3.

43. M. P. Wattenberg, 'From a partisan to a candidate-centered electorate', in A. King (ed.), *The New American Political System* (2nd ed.; American Enterprise Institute, Washington, DC: 1990), pp. 154–5; S. E. Bennett, 'The uses and abuses of registration and turnout data: an analysis of Piven and Cloward's studies of nonvoting in America', *PS: Political Science and Politics* 23 (1990), pp. 166–71.

44. L. Ragsdale and J. G. Rusk, 'Who are nonvoters? Profiles from the 1990 Senate elections', *American Journal of Political Science* 37 (1993), pp. 735, 740, 744–5.

45. K. Phillips, *The Politics of Rich and Poor: Wealth and the American Electorate in the Reagan Aftermath* (Random House, New York: 1990).

46. A. Grant, 'The 1992 US presidential election', *Parliamentary Affairs* 46 (1993), pp. 239–54.

47. Skepticism has been expressed, among others, by J. LaPalombara, 'What to expect from President Clinton', *Relazioni Internazionali* 57 (1993), pp. 8–10; E. C. Ladd, 'The 1992 vote for President Clinton: another brittle mandate?', *Political Science Quarterly* 108 (1993), pp. 1–28; G. M. Pomper, 'The presidential election', in Idem (ed.), *The Election of 1992*, pp. 150–1; Michael Nelson, 'Conclusion: some things old, some things new', in Idem (ed.), *The Elections of 1992* (CQ Press, Washington, DC: 1993), p. 183.

48. In particular, the swing from the Republican to the Democratic party that occurred between 1988 and 1992 was as low as 6 per cent nationwide. In as many as thirty states the swing was below 2 per cent (D. Butler, 'The United States elections of 1992', *Electoral Studies* 12 (1993), p. 187).

49. D. Goodgame, 'Right makes might', *Time International*, 21 November 1994, p. 28; S. V. Roberts, 'Sea of change', *US News & World Report*, 21 November 1994, p. 39. For a non-academic and hasty interpretation of the outcome of the 1992 presidential election as a Democratic realignment, see L. I. Barrett, 'A new coalition for the 1990s', *Time*, 16 November 1992, pp. 47–8.

50. *New York Times*, 26 November 1992, p. A20; B. Lockerbie and J. A. Clark, 'Georgia: a state in transition', in R. P. Steed, L. W. Moreland, and

T. A. Baker (eds), *The 1992 Presidential Election in the South: Current Patterns of Southern Party and Electoral Politics* (Praeger, Westport, Conn. and London: 1994), pp. 44–8.

51. *New York Times*, 4 November 1993, pp. A1, B8.
52. Ibid., 7 June 1993, p. A1.
53. Ladd, 'The 1992 vote for President Clinton', p. 22.
54. Election day exit poll conducted by Voter Research and Surveys, in *Newsweek*, special election issue, November–December 1992, p. 10. For an analysis of the 1992 Republican convention, see G. Wills, 'The born-again Republicans', *New York Review of Books*, 24 September 1992, pp. 9–14.
55. B. Clinton and A. Gore, *Putting People First: How We Can All Change America* (Times Books, New York: 1992), pp. 63–6, 164–5; A. Hacker, 'The blacks and Clinton', *New York Review of Books*, 28 January 1993, p. 14; T. R. Fraizer, 'Liberalism becomes a four-letter word', *Radical History Review* no. 55 (1993), p. 180; W. C. Berman, *America's Right Turn: From Nixon to Bush* (Johns Hopkins University Press, Baltimore: 1994), pp. 159–60; T. B. Edsall and M. D. Edsall, *Chain Reaction: The Impact of Race, Rights, and Taxes on American Politics* (Norton, New York: 1991), pp. 163–4, 181–4, 225–7.
56. J. W. Germond and J. Witcover, *Mad as Hell: Revolt at the Ballot Box, 1992* (Warner Books, New York: 1993), pp. 292–303; C. O'Clery, *America, A Place Called Hope?* (O'Brien Press, Dublin: 1993), pp. 50–4; W. C. McWilliams, 'The meaning of the election', in Pomper (ed.), *The Election of 1992*, pp. 203–4; B. Woodward, *The Agenda: Inside the Clinton White House* (Simon and Schuster, New York: 1994), pp. 40–1.
57. S. D. Collins, *The Rainbow Challenge: The Jackson Campaign and the Future of US Politics* (Monthly Review Press, New York: 1986); A. Kopkind, 'The Jackson moment', *New Left Review* no. 172 (1988), pp. 83–91. After Jackson's 1984 registration drive, black turnout in the primaries of that year was the highest ever, with a record increase of 103 per cent in New York State, 82 per cent in Alabama, 43 per cent in Florida and 38 per cent in Pennsylvania over 1980: P. Gurin, S. Hatchett, and J. S. Jackson, *Hope and Independence: Black's Response to Electoral and Party Politics* (Russell Sage Foundation, New York: 1989), p. 175. Even Adolph L. Reed, Jr., who has questioned Jackson's voter registration capacities, has nonetheless acknowledged that Jackson's candidacy played a major role in stimulating a remarkable increase in black turnout between 1980 and 1984: *The Jesse Jackson Phenomenon: The Crisis of Purpose in Afro-American Politics* (Yale University Press, New Haven: 1986), pp. 17–20.
58. G. M. Pomper, 'The presidential nominations', in Idem (ed.), *The Election of 1988*, p. 52; I. Derbyshire, *Politics in the United States: From Carter to Bush* (Chambers, London: 1990), p. 131; S. J. Wayne, *The Road to the White House, 1992: The Politics of Presidential Elections* (St Martin's Press, New York: 1992), pp. 97, 149.
59. Germond and Witcover, *Mad as Hell*, pp. 338–42. See also L. S. Maisel, 'The platform-writing process: candidate-centered platforms in 1992', *Political Science Quarterly* 108 (1993), p. 680.
60. Data from Hacker, 'The blacks and Clinton', p. 14; S. M. Lipset, 'The significance of the 1992 election', *PS: Political Science and Politics* 26 (1993),

p. 12. In addition, Charles S. Bullock has estimated that black turnout in the Democratic primaries in the Southern states that voted on the so-called Super Tuesday fell by 25% between 1988 and 1992 because Jackson was not on the ballot: 'Nomination: the South's role in 1992 nomination politics', in Steed, Moreland, and Baker (eds), *The 1992 Presidential Election in the South*, p. 20.

61. H. Agar, *The Price of Union* (2nd ed.; Houghton Miffin Company, Boston: 1966), pp. 688–91.
62. Downs, *An Economic Theory of Democracy*, pp. 118–19.
63. The most outstanding case is that of former Virginia Governor L. Douglas Wilder, who, incidentally, was the only Afro-American to run for the 1992 Democratic presidential nomination, but withdrew even before a single vote was cast in the primaries. See A. J. Schexnider, 'The politics of pragmatism: an analysis of the 1989 governatorial election in Virginia', *PS: Political Science and Politics* 23 (1990), pp. 154–6; R. C. Smith, 'Recent elections and black politics: the maturation or death of black politics?', ibid., pp. 160–3. For Wilder's brief presidential campaign, see Germond and Witcover, *Mad as Hell*, pp. 106–8; R. J. Barilleaux and R. E. Adkins, 'The nominations: process and patterns', in Pomper (ed.), *The Elections of 1992*, pp. 38–9.

5

Freedom, Race and Citizenship in American History

Eric Foner

In 1993 Governor Pete Wilson of California, a state in the grip of economic recession and experiencing a massive population influx from Asia and Latin America, proposed to deny American citizenship to children born in the United States to illegal residents.[1] Although evidently unaware that his proposal would require abrogation of the Constitution's Fourteenth Amendment, the governor did, at least, draw attention to the fact that citizenship and nationality are once again topics of intense public debate – a result of the upsurge of ethnic, religious, and linguistic particularism in Europe and the Third World and the ever-increasing visibility of the multicultural character of the United States. The latest in a long line of American statesmen to substitute a nickname or diminutive for their actual first name in hopes of creating a false impression of folksy populism, Pete Wilson is also not the first politician to blame America's problems on an alien invasion or to propose to redefine American nationality along racial and ethnic lines. There is nothing new, at least in the United States, about bitter conflicts over who should and should not be a citizen.

Perhaps the intensity of these debates arises from the tension between the universal principles of what is sometimes called the American Creed and the need to define national identity. From the time of independence, American political culture, unlike that of other nations, has been predicated on abstract verities that ostensibly apply to all mankind – the inalienable rights enumerated in the Declaration of Independence, the universal rationality and propensity for self-improvement taken for granted by classical economics. Our *raison d'être* as a nation rests on principles that are universal, not parochial. Yet the process of defining nationality is inherently exclusionary. Nationalism always involves defining a community or people in contradistinction to outsiders. No matter how wide the 'circle of we', most people on earth will remain excluded from it. It is now almost obligatory to refer to Benedict Anderson's celebrated definition of the nation as a state of mind, 'an imagined political community', a construction or invention rather than a timeless entity. The nation's borders are as much intellectual as geographic. One needs to add, however, that the process of imagining is itself contentious and ultimately political. Who constructs the community, who has the power to enforce a certain definition of the nation, will determine where the boundaries of inclusion and exclusion lie. Rather than being permanently fixed, moreover, national identities are inherently unstable, subject to continuing efforts to draw and redraw their imagined borders. 'The history of freedom', a scholar of British history has recently written, 'is really the history of controversies over its constructions and exclusions'. The same may be said of citizenship.[2]

In a society resting, rhetorically at least, on the ideal of equality, the boundaries of the imagined community take on extreme significance. Within the cognitive border, Americans have long assumed, civil and political equality of some kind ought to prevail; outside its perimeter, equality is irrelevant. The more rights are enjoyed within the circle of citizenship, the more important the boundaries of inclusion and exclusion become. Since citizenship implies the ability to enjoy the full benefits of American freedom, 'who belongs?' has long been the central question of American nationality.[3]

From the foundation of the American nation, of course, the existence of slavery constituted not simply the most vivid contradiction to America's professed ideals, but the most impenetrable boundary of citizenship itself. Already deeply-entrenched in the Southern states by the time of the American Revolution, slavery helped to shape the identities, the sense of self, of all Americans, giving citizenship a powerful exclusionary dimension. The value of American citizenship, as Judith Shklar has argued, derived to a considerable extent from its denial to others. The Constitution's very language revealed that three distinct populations co-existed on American soil. One was the Indians, dealt with as members of separate nations and not counted in apportioning representation in Congress. The Constitution divided the non-Indian population into 'people' and 'persons', a seemingly innocuous distinction which, in fact, reflected enormous differences in status and rights. 'We the people', according to the preamble, created the Constitution and, presumably, the nation itself. Later in the document, however, reference is made to 'other persons', apparently existing outside the political community. These 'persons', of course, are slaves (although the word itself is studiously avoided). By leaving the fate of slavery to the individual states and mandating that the condition adheres to those who escape to a jurisdiction where slavery has been abolished, the Constitution virtually guarantees the future continuation of bondage. Slaves, as Edmund Randolph later wrote, were 'not ... constituent members of our society', and the language of liberty and citizenship did not apply to them.[4]

What of those within the 'circle of we?' The word citizen appears in four places in the original Constitution – in articles elaborating the qualifications for the President and members of Congress and in the comity clause requiring each state to accord citizens of other states 'all the privileges and immunities of citizens of the several States'. Nowhere does the original Constitution define who in fact are citizens of the United States, or what privileges and immunities they enjoy. It is left to the individual states to determine the boundaries of citizenship and citizens' legal rights.

Nothing in the Constitution limits the rights of citizens according to race, sex, or any other accident of birth. The Constitution does, however, empower Congress to create a uniform system of naturalization, and the laws passed in the 1790s to implement this provision offered the first legislative definition of the boundaries of American nationality. The very effort to establish a uniform naturalization procedure marked a break with the traditions of Britain, where until 1844 only a private Act of Parliament could confer citizenship upon a foreigner. Americans, however, thought of their country as a refuge for those fleeing the tyranny of the Old World, an 'asylum for mankind', as Thomas Paine put it so memorably in *Common Sense*. Yet slavery rendered blacks all but invisible to those imagining the American community. When the era's master mythmaker, Hector St John Crèvecoeur, posed the famous question, 'What then is the American, the new man?', he answered: 'a mixture of English, Scotch, Irish, French, Dutch, Germans, and Swedes ... He is either a European, or the descendant of a European'. This at a time when fully one-fifth of the American population (the highest proportion in our entire history) consisted of Africans and their descendants.[5]

The naturalization law of 1790 confirmed this racialized definition of American nationality. With no debate, Congress restricted the process of becoming a citizen to 'free white persons', a provision already included in the naturalization requirements of several Southern states, and a good illustration of how slavery, from the beginning, helped to define the American way. This limitation lasted a long time. For eighty years, only white immigrants could become naturalized citizens. Blacks were added in 1870, but not until the 1940s did most persons of Asian origin become eligible. Only in the last quarter of the nineteenth century were groups of whites barred from entering the country and becoming citizens. Beginning with prostitutes, convicted felons, lunatics, polygamists, and persons likely to become a 'public charge', the list of excluded classes would be expanded in the twentieth century to include anarchists, communists, and the illiterate. But for the first century of the republic, virtually the only white persons in the entire world ineligible to claim American citizenship were those unwilling to renounce hereditary titles of nobility, as required in an act of 1795.[6] The two groups excluded from naturalization – European aristocrats and non-whites – had more in common than might appear at first glance. Both were viewed as deficient in the qualities essential for republican citizenship – the capacity for self-control, rational forethought, and devotion to the larger community. These were precisely the characteristics that Jefferson, in his famous comparison of the races in *Notes on the State of Virginia*, claimed blacks lacked, partly due to natural incapacity and partly because the bitter experience of slavery had (quite understandably he felt) rendered them disloyal to the nation. Jefferson still believed black Americans should eventually enjoy the natural rights enumerated in the Declaration, but they should do so in Africa or the Caribbean, not the United States. For him, as for many of his contemporaries, the concept of politics as an arena where citizens left behind self-interest in pursuit of common goals implied the desirability of a homogenous citizenry whose common experiences, values, and innate capacities made the idea of a public good realizable.[7]

Blacks formed no part of the imagined community of Jefferson's republic. But no dream of 'colonizing' the entire black population outside the United States could negate the fact of the black presence. Whether free or slave, their status became increasingly anomalous as political democracy (for white men) expanded in the nineteenth century along with an insistently self-congratulatory rhetoric celebrating the United States as a 'empire of liberty', a unique land of equality and democracy. Indeed, in a country which lacked more traditional bases of nationality – long-established physical boundaries, historic, ethnic, religious, and cultural unity – America's democratic political institutions themselves came to define nationhood. Increasingly, the right to vote became the emblem of American citizenship – if not in law (since suffrage was still, strictly speaking, a privilege rather than a right, subject to regulation by the individual states) then in common usage and understanding. Noah Webster's *American Dictionary* noted that the term 'citizen' had, by the 1820s, become synonymous with the right to vote. In America, unlike Europe, 'the people' ruled, and the 'public' itself was essentially defined via the ballot. Hence, who was and was not included as part of 'the people' took on increasing importance. Suffrage, said one advocate of democratic reform, was 'the only true badge of the freeman'. Those denied the vote, said another, were 'put in the situation of the slaves of Virginia'.[8]

Various groups of Americans, of course, stood outside this boundary. Dealt with by treaties and assumed, as a legal fiction, to be citizens of other nations, Indians were not generally held to be citizens of the United States even though certain statutes contemplated this possibility for those who left their tribes and received land allotments from the federal government. Women's citizenship was something of an open question. Free women were certainly members of the imagined community called the nation; indeed according to the prevailing ideology of separate spheres they played an indispensable role in the training of future citizens. The common law subsumed women within the legal status of their husbands. But courts generally (although not always) held that married women had a civic status of their own. They could be naturalized if immigrating from abroad, and a native-born American woman did not automatically surrender her nationality by marrying a foreigner. Not until 1907 did Congress, alarmed by massive immigration, require American women who married aliens to take the nationality of their husbands, a provision that remained on the statute books until the 1930s.[9]

In the nineteenth century, however, the public arena was very much a male preserve; indeed as democracy expanded, participation in politics became a defining characteristic of American manhood. In both law and social reality, women lacked the essential qualification of political participation – the opportunity for autonomy: whether the propertied independence of the republican tradition, which enabled men to devote themselves to the public good, or the personal independence deriving from ownership of one's self and one's labor, celebrated in the emerging liberal ethos. Women were also widely believed (by men) to be naturally submissive, by definition unfit for independent-minded citizenship. Nature itself, said a delegate to Virginia's constitutional convention of 1829, had pronounced on women an 'incapacity to exercise political power'. The democratic citizen was emphatically a male head of household, and it was rarely noticed that without women's work in the domestic sphere few men would have enjoyed the freedom to take part in the political arena.[10]

If women occupied a position of subordinate citizenship, non-whites were increasingly excluded from the imagined community altogether. Slaves, of course, were by definition outside the 'circle of we', and, in the South, in the words of a Georgia statute, free blacks were 'entitled to no right of citizenship, except such as are specifically given by law'. Apart from the ability to possess property, few indeed were given. The North's black community on the eve of the Civil War numbered a mere 220,000, or about one per cent of the region's population. Yet as the nineteenth century progressed this tiny group was subjected to increasing discrimination in every phase of its life. In most Northern states blacks were barred from public schools, denied access to public transportation, excluded from places of public accommodation, and prohibited from serving on juries and in state militias. The position of Northern blacks, said Frederick Douglass, was 'anomalous, unequal, and extraordinary ... Aliens we are in our native land'. Over a century later, Malcolm X would say much the same thing with his customary directness. 'Being born here in America doesn't make you an American. Why, if birth made you an American, you wouldn't need any legislation ... They don't have to pass civil rights legislation to make a Polack an American.' Malcolm X's point was that despite prejudice against white immigrants, they were always viewed as potential citizens. Almost as soon as they landed on these shores, alien men became entitled to legal equality, and eligible to vote.[11]

Democracy for whites, however, expanded hand in hand with deterioration in the status of free blacks. In 1800, no Northern state restricted the suffrage on the basis of race. Most black men were poor, but those able to meet property qualifications could vote alongside whites. Between

1800 and 1860, however, every state that entered the Union, with the single exception of Maine in 1821, restricted the suffrage to white males. Moreover, as property qualifications for whites were progressively eliminated, blacks' political rights became more and more constrained. In 1821, the same New York Constitutional Convention that removed property requirements for white voters raised the qualification for blacks to $250 – a sum beyond the reach of nearly all the state's black residents. Sixteen years later, Pennsylvania revoked African-Americans' right to vote entirely. By 1860, only five states, all in New England, allowed blacks to vote on the same terms as whites. In effect, race had replaced class as the major line of division between men who could vote, and thus be regarded in popular usage as citizens, and those who could not.[12]

Were blacks citizens of individual states or of the nation? Despite the naturalization law's exclusion, there seemed no way to deny the citizenship of native-born free blacks. Citizenship, however, was increasingly believed to confer a variety of rights that most whites did not wish to see blacks enjoy. The federal government treated them as, in effect, resident aliens, generally refusing requests from free blacks for American passports. Most Northern states appear to have recognized the citizenship of free blacks, but at the price of severing, in their case at least, the tie between citizenship and anything resembling civil and political equality. The logical peculiarities of the situation were revealed in the political crisis of 1819–21, when Missouri sought admission to the Union with a constitution establishing slavery and excluding free blacks from the state. As a number of Northern Congressmen pointed out, this latter provision blatantly violated the comity clause forbidding each state to discriminate against citizens of other states. If Massachusetts recognized blacks as citizens, how could Missouri exclude them? Southerners responded, in effect, that whether or not individual states recognized free blacks as citizens, the comity clause applied only to whites. In the end a compromise was reached, whereby Congress ordered Missouri not to prohibit citizens of other states from entering, without defining who such citizens were. Almost immediately, the issue resurfaced when, in the wake of the Denmark Vesey conspiracy, South Carolina decreed that black seamen arriving in Charleston would be imprisoned until their vessels were ready to depart – another violation of the comity clause, which Massachusetts protested to no avail.[13]

Not until 1857 did the Supreme Court offer a definitive answer to the question of black citizenship. By then, four Northern states had adopted the same disputed rule as Missouri, prohibiting all blacks from entering their territory. In the Dred Scott decision, Chief Justice Roger B. Taney announced that no black person could be a citizen of the United States. It was, ironically, because the definition of citizenship mattered so much that Taney felt constrained to produce his complex argument excluding blacks. America was a land of equality, he insisted, with only one class of citizens – 'members of the sovereignty', equally entitled to their 'liberties and rights'. States could treat blacks in any way they chose, but no state could introduce 'a new member' into the national political community. Blacks, the Chief Justice went on, had not formed part of the 'people' who created the constitution, and had, in the eyes of the founders, been 'considered as a subordinate and inferior class of beings ... They had no rights which the white man was bound to respect'.[14]

The relationship between inclusion and exclusion, between the expanding rights of white citizens and the deteriorating condition of blacks, was symbiotic, not contradictory. As the substance of citizenship expanded and Americans' rhetoric grew ever more egalitarian, a fully developed racist ideology gained broad acceptance as the explanation for the boundaries of nationality. Unlike republicanism, in which the citizen is or ought to be willing to sacrifice private interests in the pursuit of the common good, nineteenth-century liberalism seemed more comfortable with the actual diversity of needs, experiences, and interests of a heterogeneous population. But liberalism contained its own thrust toward homogeneity. The liberal citizen is guided by rational self-interest. Yet were all human beings capable of disciplined self-governance? If not, then nature itself – inborn incapacity, rather than human contrivance – explained the exclusion of blacks from citizenship rights. Of course, as John Stuart Mill once asked, 'was there ever any domination which did not appear natural to those who possessed it?' Yet Mill himself argued, in his great work *On Liberty*, that the right to self-government applied 'only to human beings in the maturity of their faculties'. Entire 'races' of less than 'civilized' people lacked the capacity for rational action essential to democratic citizenship.[15]

Mill's view was widely shared in the United States. Perhaps this was inevitable in a nation whose economic growth depended in large measure on the labor of black slaves and whose territorial expansion involved the dispossession of one non-white people, the Indians, and the conquest of the lands inhabited by another, the Mexicans. The rhetoric of racial exclusion suffused the political language. Only the Caucasian race, insisted John C. Calhoun, possessed the qualities necessary for 'free and popular government ... Ours, sir, is a government of the white race'. This sentiment was not confined to the South. Much the same idea was expressed by Stephen A.Douglas in his debates with Abraham Lincoln: 'I believe this government was made on the white basis. I believe it was made by white men for the benefit of white men and their posterity for ever, and I am in favor of confining citizenship to white men ... instead of conferring it upon negroes, Indians, and other inferior races'. Although Whigs tended to be somewhat more open to the possibility that non-whites could be assimilated into the political nation, they too, were attracted to the idea of racial and cultural homogeneity and to the idea that Anglo-Saxon

Protestantism was the unique seedbed of American freedom. Even as this focus on 'race' – in the nineteenth century an amorphous category amalgamating ideas about culture, history, religion, and color – helped to solidify a sense of national identity among the diverse groups of European origin that made up the free population, it drew ever more tightly the lines of exclusion of America's imagined community. Gone was the idea of liberty and self-government as universal human rights, for only some peoples were 'fit' to enjoy the blessings of freedom or capable of governing themselves.[16]

This racialized definition of citizenship and American nationality was challenged, of course, by abolitionists, black and white, in the years before the Civil War. The antislavery crusade insisted on the 'Americanness' of slaves and free blacks and repudiated not only slavery but the racial boundaries that confined free blacks to second-class citizenship. Drawing on eighteenth-century traditions of natural rights, the Declaration of Independence, and the perfectionist creed of evangelical religion, abolitionists sought to define the core rights to which all Americans, regardless of race, were entitled. In so doing, they pioneered the idea of a national citizenship whose members enjoyed equality before the law protected by a beneficent national state. Revising Crèvecoeur, Ralph Waldo Emerson wrote of America's destiny as the forging of a 'new race' amalgamating not only Europeans, but 'Africans' and 'Polynesians' as well. Although far less egalitarian in their racial views than most abolitionists, Republicans in the 1850s also insisted that America's professed creed was broad enough to encompass all mankind. While hardly a proponent of black suffrage or equality before the law, for example, Lincoln explicitly rejected Douglas's race-based definition of liberty, insisting that the basic rights enumerated in the Declaration of Independence applied to all peoples, not merely Europeans and their descendants.[17]

Thus, the crisis of the Union, among other things, was a crisis of the meaning of American nationhood, and the Civil War a crucial moment in which key elements of the language of politics were reconstituted and their outer boundaries redefined. The struggle for the Union produced a consolidation of national loyalties and of the national state itself. Inevitably, it propelled to the forefront of public discussion the question, 'who is an American?' 'It is a singular fact', Wendell Phillips wrote in 1866, 'that, unlike all other nations, this nation has yet a question as to what makes or constitutes a citizen.'[18]

Four decades earlier, during Spanish America's wars of liberation, José de San Martín had proclaimed that the empowerment of the nation state demanded a uniform definition of citizenship, rendering previous divisions and exclusions obsolete: 'In the future the aborigines shall not be called Indians or natives; they are children *and citizens* of Peru and they shall be known as Peruvians.' In the United States, too, the state-building process itself, coupled as it was with the destruction of slavery and the enrollment of 200,000 black men in the Union Army, threw into question earlier definitions of nationality. The 'logical result' of black military service, one Senator observed in 1864, was that 'the black man is henceforth to assume a new status among us'. Indeed, emancipation and the raising of black soldiers were themselves crucial moments in the wartime process of state-building, which, by their very nature, linked the rise of national power with the vision of a national citizenry whose equal rights were enjoyed regardless of race. Even before the death of slavery, the Lincoln administration effectively abrogated the Dred Scott decision by explicitly affirming the citizenship of free blacks. This stance was strongly seconded by Francis Lieber, at the time perhaps America's leading political scientist, who advised Attorney General Edward Bates that there could be 'not even a shadow of a doubt' that blacks were entitled to citizenship. As for Dred Scott, wrote Lieber, 'I execrate that opinion from the bottom of my soul'.[19]

By the beginning of Reconstruction most Republicans were agreed on two principles: 'the national citizenship', as one newspaper put it, 'must be paramount to that of the State', and the emancipated slaves were entitled to the basic rights of American citizens. Precisely how to define these rights became the focus of the political struggles of early Reconstruction. Before the war, Republicans like Lincoln had insisted that the principles of 'free labor' – the right to pursue a calling and earn a living without encountering onerous discrimination, opportunity for social advancement, and command over the 'fruits of one's labor' – differentiated the free society of the North from the slave South. The destruction of slavery fixed free labor principles as a central element of American freedom. Free labor formed the basis of the first statutory definition of American citizenship, the Civil Rights Act of 1866, which declared all persons born in the United States (except Indians) national citizens and spelled out rights they were to enjoy equally without regard to race – the ability, essentially, to compete in the marketplace, own property, and receive equal treatment before the law. States could not deprive an individual of these basic rights; if they did so, state officials would be held accountable in federal court.

'American citizenship must mean something', the measure's author, Senator Lyman Trumbull, told the Senate, and in constitutional terms, the Civil Rights Act represented the first attempt to spell out the consequences of emancipation and define, in Trumbull's words, 'the inherent, fundamental rights' of American citizens. Soon afterwards, Congress approved the Fourteenth Amendment, placing in the Constitution the definition of citizenship as birth on American soil or naturalization, and prohibiting states from abridging any citizens' 'privileges and immunities' or denying them 'equal protection of the law'. This broad language opened the door for future Congresses and the federal courts to breathe substantive meaning into the guarantee of legal equality.[20]

The Civil Rights Act and Fourteenth Amendment said nothing about the suffrage – this remained a privilege, to be regulated by the states, not a fundamental right of citizens. Black spokesmen bitterly resented this exclusion, and in their newspapers, conventions, and public speeches put forth persistent claims for full recognition of their membership in the political community. The country's very democratic ethos made their exclusion all the more onerous. In a democracy, said Frederick Douglass, to be denied the vote was 'to brand us with the stigma of inferiority'. 'To say that I am a citizen to pay taxes ... obey laws ... and fight the battles of the country, but in all that respects voting and representation, I am but as so much inert matter ... is to insult my manhood,' he added. In 1867, spurred by the insistent demands of African-Americans and deep dissatisfaction with the results of President Andrew Johnson's Reconstruction policy, Congress enfranchised black men in the South. Two years later, it approved the Fifteenth Amendment, barring any state from making race a qualification for voting.

'The great Constitutional revolution ... ', declared Republican leader Carl Schurz, 'found the rights of the individual at the mercy of the States ... and placed them under the shield of national protection.' Transcending boundaries of race and region, the statutes and Amendments of Reconstruction broadened the boundaries of freedom for all Americans, requiring that the states respect the fundamental individual liberties that the Bill of Rights had protected against infringement by the federal government. Indeed it was precisely because they represented so striking a departure from the previous traditions of American law that these measures aroused such bitter opposition. 'We are not of the same race', declared Indiana Senator Thomas Hendricks, 'we are so different that we ought not to compose one political community'. Federal definition of the citizens' rights and civil and political equality for black Americans, declared President Johnson, violated 'all our experience as a people'. His veto messages sought to resurrect the racial boundaries of nationality that Congress had abandoned. History demonstrated, Johnson insisted, that only 'white men' possessed the 'peculiar qualities' that equipped them for democratic self-government. As for blacks, neither 'mentally' not 'morally' were they fit for American citizenship.[21]

Reconstruction Republicans rejected this reasoning, and insisted that blacks now formed part of the national community. But their universalism, too, had its limits. In his remarkable 'Composite Nation' speech of 1869, Douglass condemned prejudice against immigrants from China, insisting that America's destiny was to serve as an asylum for people 'gathered here from all corners of the globe by a common aspiration for national liberty'. Any form of exclusion, he insisted, contradicted the essence of democracy. A year later, Charles Sumner, the Senate's leading Radical, moved to strike the word 'white' from naturalization requirements.

Senators from the Western states objected vociferously. They were willing to admit blacks to citizenship, but not persons of Asian origin. Sumner's measure, remarked Republican Senator Cornelius Cole of California, 'would kill our party as dead as a stone'. In the end, instead of eliminating 'white', Congress added people of African descent to those eligible for citizenship via naturalization. The racial boundaries of nationality had been redrawn, not eliminated.[22]

Nor did Reconstruction policy makers make any effort to expand the definition of citizenship rights to incorporate women. Congress intended to overturn the nation's racial system, but to leave its system of gender relations intact. Like race, claimed the postwar women's movement, sex was an 'accident of the body', an illegitimate basis for legal discrimination. Reconstruction, declared Olympia Brown, offered the opportunity to 'bury the black man and the woman in the citizen'. Yet slavery's denial of blacks' family rights – including the right to the man to stand as head of the household and represent his family in political society – had been among abolitionism's most devastating indictments of the peculiar institution. Even as feminists sought to reform the institution of marriage to make it more egalitarian, Republicans – including many former slaves – saw emancipation as restoring to blacks the natural right to family life, in which men would take their place as heads of the household and women would return to the domestic sphere from which slavery had unnaturally removed them.[23]

As is well-known, the feminist effort to gain legal equality and the right to vote fell on deaf ears in Congress. In its representation clause, the Fourteenth Amendment for the first time introduced the word 'male' into the Constitution, producing a bitter schism between advocates of blacks' rights and those demanding woman suffrage. When women tried to employ the Amendment's expanded definition of citizenship to press their own rights, they found the courts singularly unreceptive. In 1872, the Supreme Court upheld an Illinois law barring women from practicing law; woman, said Justice Bradley, was confined by nature to the 'domestic sphere' and restricting her occupational opportunities did not, therefore, violate the principles of free labor or the equal rights of citizens. In *Minor v. Happersett*, the Court rejected the claim that the right to vote was intrinsic to citizenship. Citizenship, declared Chief Justice Morrison Waite, was compatible with disenfranchisement; it meant 'membership of a nation and nothing more'.[24]

Virtually no Republican lawmakers, in fact, had intended, in rewriting the Constitution, to invalidate discrimination based on gender. The language of the Fifteenth Amendment clearly left the door open for suffrage distinctions based on grounds other than race – a sign that in law, citizenship still did not necessarily encompass the right to vote. But the Court's argument in cases involving women constituted a step in the progressive narrowing of the boundaries of citizenship, a narrowing soon extended to other groups as well. With the end of Reconstruction, the egalitarian impulse faded from national life, and the imagined community was reimagined once again. The Supreme Court progressively restricted the rights protected under the Fourteenth Amendment and did nothing when, beginning in the 1890s, one Southern state after another stripped black citizens of the right to vote.

The 'failure' of Reconstruction strongly reinforced the racist thinking that came to dominate American culture in the late nineteenth century, fueling the conviction that blacks were unfit for self-government. 'A black skin', Columbia University political scientist John W. Burgess would write at the turn of the century, 'means membership in a race of men which has never of itself succeeded in subjecting passion to reason, and has never, therefore, created any civilization of any kind.' The retreat from the post-war ideal of color-blind citizenship was also reflected in the resurgence of racial Anglo-Saxonism linking patriotism, xenophobia, and an ethnocultural definition of nationhood in a renewed rhetoric of racial exclusiveness. This language was now applied by scientists and sociologists not only to nonwhites but to groups of whites whose growing numbers alarmed self-proclaimed defenders of America's racial and cultural heritage. 'Lower races' – a term that often included the urban poor, the insane, and immigrants from Southern and Eastern Europe – were said to be impulsive and emotional, and to lack the capacity for abstract reasoning, much as Jefferson had described blacks a century before. The idea that many immigrants, like blacks, were representatives of 'servile' races unfit for democratic citizenship legitimated renewed efforts to narrow the boundaries of nationhood. The Exclusion Act of 1882 prohibited for ten years the further entry of immigrants from China and forbade courts to naturalize those already here. Renewed in 1892, the law was made permanent a decade later. In 1921 and 1924, in a fundamental break with the tradition of open entry for whites except for specifically designated classes of undesirables, Congress imposed the first sharp numerical limits on European immigration, establishing a nationality quota system that sought to ensure that new immigrants would forever be outnumbered by descendants of the old and that within a generation the foreign born would cease to be a major factor in American life. Until well after World War II, applicants for immigration visas were required to declare their 'race', even if this meant nothing more, in fact, than being Dutch or French.[25]

By the early twentieth century, with black disfranchisement in the South, the exclusion of Asians from entering the country, and the broad segmentation of immigration and labor markets along racial, ethnic, and gender lines, the boundaries and substantive content of American citizenship had again been severely curtailed. Not until our own time would a great mass movement reinvigorate the ideas of the Reconstruction era and erase, permanently, one hopes, the second-class legal status of blacks, even as nationality quotas for immigration fell by the wayside. The triumph of a far more inclusionary vision of American nationality reflected not so much the unfolding of the immanent logic of the American Creed as a set of specific historical circumstances – the discrediting of racialist ideologies by the struggle against Nazism; the advent to positions of power in the political and academic worlds of the children and grandchildren of the new immigrants; the consolidation of a trade union movement committed in principle and, to some extent, in reality, to racial and ethnic inclusiveness; the deployment of the ideal of America as an asylum for freedom as a weapon in the Cold War; the rise of the civil rights movement; and, last but not least, a rapidly expanding economy that appeared able to absorb new waves of immigrants. Today, some of these conditions retain their potency while others have already faded into history. It seems safe to predict that in the twenty-first century, the boundaries of citizenship and the definition of American nationality will remain, as they have been throughout US history, sources of social contention and political struggle.

Notes

1. *Los Angeles Times*, 10 August 1993.
2. D. A. Hollinger, 'How wide the circle of the "We"? American intellectuals and the problem of the ethnos since World War II', *American Historical Review* 98 (1993), pp. 317–37; B. Anderson, *Imagined Communities: Reflections on the Origin and Spread of Nationalism* (rev. ed.; Verso, London: 1991), p. 6; I. C. Fletcher, 'Rethinking the history of working people: class, gender, and identities in an age of industry and empire', *Radical History Review* 56 (1993), p. 85.
3. K. L. Karst, *Belonging to America: Equal Citizenship and the Constitution* (Yale University Press, New Haven: 1989), pp. 2–3.
4. J. N. Shklar, *American Citizenship: The Quest for Inclusion* (Harvard University Press, Cambridge, Mass.: 1991), pp. 15–16; E. Randolph, *History of Virginia*, ed. A. H. Shaffer (University of Virginia Press, Charlottesville: 1970), p. 253.
5. J. C. D. Clark, *The Language of Liberty 1660–1832: Political Discourse and Social Dynamics in the Anglo-American World* (Cambridge University Press, Cambridge: 1993), p. 53; Y. Arieli, *Individualism and Nationalism in American Ideology* (Harvard University Press, Cambridge, Mass.: 1964), pp. 72–3; W. D. Jordan, *White Over Black: American Attitudes Toward the Negro, 1550–1812* (University of North Carolina Press, Chapel Hill: 1968), pp. 336–41.
6. J. H. Kettner, *The Development of American Citizenship 1608–1870* (University of North Carolina Press, Chapel Hill: 1978), pp. 214–46; R. M. Smith, '"One united people": second-class female citizenship and the American quest for community', *Yale Journal of Law and the Humanities* 1

(1989), p. 246n.; E. P. Hutchinson, *Legislative History of American Immigration Policy 1798–1965* (University of Pennsylvania Press, Philadelphia: 1981), pp. 65–6, 309, 405–42.

7. T. Jefferson, *Notes on the State of Virginia* (Harper and Row, New York: 1964), pp. 132–7; J. O. Appleby, *Without Resolution: The Jeffersonian Tensions in American Nationalism* (Oxford University Press, Oxford: 1992), pp. 17–18, 23–4.
8. Arieli, *Individualism*, p. 24; R. J. Dinkin, *Voting in Revolutionary America: A Study of Elections in the Original Thirteen States 1776–1789* (Greenwood Press, Westport, Conn.: 1982), pp. 266–7; N. Webster, *An American Dictionary of the English Language* (2 vols.; Converse, New York: 1828); W. B. Scott, *In Pursuit of Happiness: American Conceptions of Property from the Seventeenth to the Twentieth Century* (Indiana University Press, Bloomington, Ind.: 1977), pp. 76–8; M. D. Peterson (ed.), *Democracy, Liberty, and Property: The State Constitutional Conventions of the 1820s* (Bobbs-Merrill, Indianapolis: 1966), pp. 60–1.
9. Kettner, *Citizenship*, pp. 291–3; L. K. Kerber, 'The paradox of women's citizenship in the early republic: the case of *Martin vs. Massachusetts*, 1805', *American Historical Review* 97 (1992), pp. 51–3; Smith, '"One united people"', p. 253; V. Sapiro, 'Women, citizenship, and nationality: immigration and naturalization policies in the United States', *Politics and Society* 13 (1984), pp. 1–26.
10. C. Smith-Rosenberg, '"Domesticating virtue": coquettes and revolutionaries in young America,' in E. Scarry (ed.). *Literature and the Body: Essays on Population and Persons* (Johns Hopkins University Press, Baltimore: 1988), p. 161; Peterson, *Democracy, Liberty, and Property*, pp. 293–4; J. R. Gunderson, 'Independence, citizenship and the American Revolution', *Signs* 13 (1987), pp. 59–77.
11. H. McGary and B. E. Lawson, *Between Slavery and Freedom: Philosophy and American Slavery* (Indiana University Press, Bloomington: 1992), p. 10; L. F. Litwack, *North of Slavery: the Negro in the Free States 1790-1860* (University of Chicago Press, Chicago: 1961); D. W. Blight, *Frederick Douglass's Civil War: Keeping Faith in Jubilee* (Louisiana University Press, Baton Rouge: 1989), p. 13; G. Breitman (ed.), *Malcolm X Speaks* (Merit, New York: 1965), p. 25.
12. R. J. Cottrol and R. T. Diamond, 'The Second Amendment: toward an Afro-Americanist reconsideration', *Georgetown Law Journal* 80 (1991), p. 334.
13. Kettner, *Citizenship*, pp. 311–23; Litwack, *North of Slavery*, pp. 35–6, 50–53; *Annals of Congress*, 16th Congress, 2nd Session, pp. 549, 1134–6.
14. Karst, *Belonging to America*, pp. 44–5; J. R. Pole, *The Pursuit of Equality in American History* (2nd ed.; University of California Press, Berkeley: 1993), pp. 182–4.
15. S. M. Okin, *Women in Western Political Thought* (Princeton University Press, Princeton: 1979), p. 215; R. Bellamy, *Liberalism and Modern Society: A Historical Argument* (Pennsylvania State University Press, University Park, Pa.: 1992), pp. 25–8; D. F. Ericson, *The Shaping of American Liberalism: The Debates Over Ratification and Slavery* (University of Chicago Press,

Chicago: 1993), pp. 12–20; U. S. Mehta, 'Liberal strategies of exclusion', *Politics and Society* 18 (1990), pp. 427–30.

16. R. Horsman, *Race and Manifest Destiny: The Origins of American Racial Anglo-Saxonism* (Harvard University Press, Cambridge, Mass.: 1981), pp. 208–9; P. M. Angle, *Created Equal? The Complete Lincoln–Douglas Debates of 1858* (University of Chicago Press, Chicago: 1958), pp. 111–12; R. M. Smith, 'The "American Creed" and American identity: the limits of liberal citizenship in the United States', *Western Political Quarterly* 41 (1988), pp. 233–5.
17. W. E. Nelson, *The Roots of American Bureaucracy, 1830–1900* (Harvard University Press, Cambridge, Mass.: 1982), pp. 42–52; S. N. Katz, 'The strange birth and unlikely history of constitutional equality', *Journal of American History* 75 (1988), p. 753; M. M. Gordon, *Assimilation in American Life: The Role of Race, Religion, and National Origin* (Oxford University Press, New York: 1964), p. 117; R. F. Basler (ed.), *The Collected Works of Abraham Lincoln* (9 vols.; Rutgers University Press, New Brunswick: 1953–5), II, p. 405.
18. E. Foner, *Reconstruction: America's Unfinished Revolution, 1863–1877* (Harper and Row, New York: 1988), p. 258.
19. Anderson, *Imagined Communities*, pp. 49–50; Foner, *Reconstruction*, p. 8; Cottrol and Diamond, 'Second Amendment', p. 243; Francis Lieber to Edward Bates, 25 November 1862, Francis Lieber Papers, Huntington Library.
20. R. J. Kaczorowski, 'To begin the nation anew: Congress, citizenship, and civil rights after the Civil War', *American Historical Review* 92 (1987), p. 53; Foner, *Reconstruction*, pp. 243–4, 256–8; *Congressional Globe*, 39th Congress, 1st Session, p. 1757.
21. P. S. Foner (ed.), *The Life and Writings of Frederick Douglass* (4 vols.: International Publishers, New York: 1950–5), IV, p. 159; Blight, *Douglass's Civil War*, p. 192; F. Bancroft (ed.), *Speeches, Correspondence and Political Papers of Carl Schurz* (6 vols.; Putnam's, New York: 1913), I, pp. 487–5; Foner, *Reconstruction*, pp. 250, 279; L. Cox and J. H. Cox (eds), *Reconstruction, the Negro, and the New South* (University of South Carolina Press, Columbia, SC: 1973), pp. 92–3.
22. P. S. Foner and D. Rosenberg (ed.), *Racism, Dissent, and Asian Americans from 1850 to the Present* (Greenwood Press, Westport, Conn.: 1993), pp. 223–7; Cornelius Cole to Olive Cole, 5 June, 5 July 1870, Cornelius Cole Papers, University of California, Los Angeles.
23. E. C. DuBois, 'Outgrowing the compact of the Fathers: equal rights, woman suffrage, and the United States Constitution, 1820–1878', *Journal of American History* 74 (1987), p. 846; *Congressional Globe*, 38th Congress, 2nd Session, 193, p. 215; A. D. Stanley, 'Conjugal rights and wage labor: rights of contract in the age of emancipation', *Journal of American History* 75 (1988), p. 480.
24. Smith, '"One united people"', pp. 260–2; N. Basch, 'Reconstructing female citizenship: *Minor* v. *Happersett*' in D. G. Nieman (ed.), *The Constitution, Law, and American Life: Critical Aspects of the Nineteenth-Century Experience*, (University of Georgia Press, Athens, Ga.: 1992), pp. 52–66.

25. J. W. Burgess, *Reconstruction and the Constitution, 1866–1876* (Scribner's, New York: 1902), pp. 44–5, 133, 244–6; Smith, '"American Creed"', pp. 233–6; G. Mink, 'The lady and the tramp: gender, race, and the origins of the American welfare state', in L. Gordon (ed.), *Women, the State, and Welfare* (University of Wisconsin Press, Madison: 1990), pp. 96–100; N. L. Stepan, 'Race and gender: the role of analogy in science', *Isis* 77 (1986), pp. 261–77; A. Saxton, *The Indispensable Enemy: Labor and the Anti-Chinese Movement in California* (University of California Press, Berkeley: 1971), pp. 177–8; J. Higham, *Strangers in the Land: Patterns of American Nativism, 1860–1925* (Rutgers University Press, New Brunswick: 1955), pp. 311–29; Pole, *Idea of Equality*, p. 285n.

6

From Boas to Geertz: American Anthropology and the Historical Construction of Cultural Identity

Alessandra Lorini

As in 1903 the African-American scholar W. E. B. Du Bois prophetically wrote that 'the problem of the twentieth century is the problem of the color line', we might well argue, with Henry Louis Gates Jr. (today's chairperson of the African-American studies program at Harvard), that the problem of the twentieth-first will be the problem of ethnic differences. It is true, as Gates argues, that no one could have predicted that the hottest issues dominating academic and popular discourse in the United States in the final decade of the twentieth century, in the aftermath of the fall of the apartheid in South Africa, the dissolution of Soviet Union, and the horrors that ethnic hatred has produced in ex-Yugoslavia, would be the matter of cultural pluralism in school curricula and its relation to 'American' national identity.[1]

Why is there a debate over national self-definition? Why is the question of 'Who Are We?' so dramatized in contemporary public opinion?

Among those who have raised the issue of a present danger of cultural fragmentation is the liberal historian Arthur Schlesinger Jr. In his widely debated *The Disuniting of America: Reflections on a Multicultural Society*, Schlesinger argues that the United States is in danger of losing its national identity because of the actions of the most extreme supporters of specific groups opposed to the whole society. Schlesinger accepts the fact that 'American identity will never be fixed and final'. But what he is afraid of is the breaking of those 'bonds of cohesion' of the American republic built on 'common ideals, common political institutions, common language, common culture, common fate'. What constitutes American nationality in Schlesinger's view are 'the great unifying Western ideas of individual freedom, political democracy, and human rights'. I agree with Schlesinger that American history cannot be reconstructed 'as social and psychological therapy whose primary purpose is to raise the self-esteem of children from minority groups'.[2] As the director of Afro-American studies at Princeton Cornel West has remarked, Afrocentrism, the latest form of black nationalism, can only offer a compensatory and consolatory history. Afrocentrism, as the theorizing of a single 'African Cultural System' that connects emotionally all people of African descent and claims the African origin of civilization 'is a gallant yet misguided attempt to define an

African identity in a white society perceived to be hostile', as 'it reinforces the narrow discussions about race'.[3]

In this perspective, Martin Bernal's *Black Athena* is central to the raging controversy over multiculturalism and Afrocentrism. As an attempt to overturn a major historical paradigm – the Caucasian Greek foundations of Western civilization – by considering the contributions of African and Semitic people as fundamental to Western culture, *Black Athena* challenges the foundations of 'our identity'.[4] Yet, whether Athena was 'black' or 'white' is significant only in the context of racist thought. It is this aspect that Afrocentrists have used to make claims for 'black' superiority. Thus, in today's incandescent debate about 'Who Are We?', Bernal's work is not taken as a brilliant and debatable investigation on who the ancient Egyptians were, but on who we think we are now. Among those liberal intellectuals who reject both the idea of monolithic and homogeneous Western values and narrowly ethnic claims, Gates argues that 'rather than mourning the loss of some putative ancestral purity, we can recognize what's valuable, resilient, even cohesive in the hybrid and variegated nature of our modernity'. One can agree with him that '"the humanities" has *not* meant the best that has been thought by all human beings; rather "the humanities" has meant the best that has been thought by white males in the Greco-Roman, Judeo-Christian traditions'. Gates' answer to those who are concerned about the 'fragmentation of humanistic knowledge', is what he calls the 'decentering of the humanities' as 'the study of the possibilities of human life in culture'. He urges us to get away from 'the paradigm of disciplinary essentialism: imagining the boundaries of disciplines as hermetic, imagining our architectures of knowledge as natural or organic'.[5] I would argue that this is a call for cultural studies to produce interdisciplinary knowledge in a post-ethnic perspective. By offering broad definitions of culture, contemporary anthropology is at the center of cultural studies which are constructed on the issue of 'partiality' that feminist theorizing has raised.[6]

Feminist theorizing has unravelled the role of gender in cultural representations. Gender is a way of thinking about sexual difference in particular and difference in general. As Joan Scott has explained, by stressing the relational aspect of gender it is possible to think in terms of different gender systems and the relations of those to other categories such as race or class or ethnicity. As the category of gender is extended to the issue of differences within difference, the unitary meaning of the category 'women' is challenged. If there are so many differences of class, race, ethnicity and sexuality, is there a common identity for women?[7] Furthermore, how is knowledge of difference produced, legitimated and disseminated? How are identities constructed and in what terms? Hence the issue of partiality as it emerges in the debate over the historical, political construction of identities and self/other relations: gendered positions make all accounts of, or by, other people inescapably partial.[8] Consequently, one can expect cultural studies to offer only non-neutral, incomplete and partial truths.[9] As Joyce Appleby in her 1992 presidential address to the OAH Conference put it: 'No scientifically based, objective model exists to guide our curiosity. We and the cultural milieus in which we think determine historical significance.'[10]

How can the truth of cultural accounts be evaluated? Is knowledge separable from ideology? As Joan Scott observes, so-called traditional historians present themselves as the guardians of the discipline by establishing a difference between 'history' and 'ideology': history would be knowledge gained through neutral investigation, and ideology would be knowledge distorted by considerations of interest. But women's history, according to Scott, 'throws open all the questions of mastery and objectivity on which disciplinary norms are built'.[11] Thus, partiality, non-neutrality, and difference are analytical terms that help reformulate the issues of cultural fragmentation and common ground in today's debate over national identity. The cultural critic Hayden White has pointed out that historians attempt to explain the past by bringing in different paradigms of the form that a valid explanation may take. Whereas for some historians explanation 'represents the result of an *analytical* operation which leaves the various entities of the field *unreduced* either to the status of general causal laws or to that of instances of general classificatory categories', for other historians 'the individual entities of the field are revealed at the end of the analysis to be related to one another ... explanation strives not for *dispersion*, but for *integration*, not for *analysis*, but for *synthesis*'.[12] The avalanche of information that the last two generations of social and cultural historians have recovered about the past of ordinary people is certainly analytical, and therefore 'fragmented'. This production cannot be reduced to 'a coherent national narrative'. As Joyce Appleby observes, 'aspects of American past have emerged that do not fit into the celebratory account of the nation's origins'.[13] Hence the contemporary debate on 'Who Are We?' as a search of a cultural and national identity in post-Cold War America.

In his discussion of American culture in the post-Cold War era the historian Christopher Thorne argued that the definition of 'the Other' to define America and Americanism has been the unifying factor throughout American history. Once 'the Other' is defined, an effort has always been made, born in part out of domestic insecurities, to remake 'the Other' into a likeness of Americans. This has been a predominant characteristic of American political culture, something that Michel Foucault would have called 'a regime of truth'.[14] According to Thorne, defining 'the Other' coincides with the construction of national identity around the major idea that US ideals and socio-economic paradigms have universal relevance, and that people in the world want to be like the Americans. It is a self-celebratory image, an identity that is claimed, proclaimed, elaborated as a counterpoint of a devalued Other.

What is the cultural process of 'devaluating the Other'? Who are 'the Others' in the post-Cold war period? These are questions that contemporary anthropologists are raising.

According to Clifford Geertz, the anthropologist most quoted by historians, the end of colonialism dramatically altered the nature of the social relationship between those who ask and look, the ethnographers, and those who are asked and looked at, a distant tribe. The change of the moral context in which ethnographical acts took place in the 'Colonial Encounter', makes some anthropologists feel that the end of imperialism is the end of anthropology as a science. According to Geertz, the question of 'Who Are *We*' seems more compelling at the beginning of the twenty-first century. It is, perhaps, Geertz concludes, 'the need to turn the External Other of the Colonial Encounter, into Internal Others on whose differences our identity is built'. Although distant from Geertz's interpretive approach, James Clifford, a post-modernist anthropologist, expresses a similar view on the way contemporary anthropology is looking at 'the Others'. The terms of the Colonial Encounter defined 'Others' as primitive, tribal, preliteral, non-historical. Today anthropologists investigate the new urban communities and problematic traditional identities in contemporary society. According to Clifford, anthropology is now 'rediscovering cultural difference within the cultures of the West'.[15] Does the turning of the 'External Other' of the 'Colonial Encounter' into 'Internal Others' create a new ethnographic paradigm?

At the beginning of the nineteenth century anthropologists were still studying external others who were separated from Western civilization by space. Their field became a kind of non-history, since it dealt with societies which were thought to be unchanging, or at best slowly moving, societies which could not have history because they had no chronology. During the first half of the nineteenth century, anthropology concerned itself with 'archaic' civilizations and the customs of 'the primitives'. Given the absence of datable documents and events out of which a chronology could be established, anthropologists reconstructed the laws of social development through the comparative method. The classification system Victorian comparativists used was based on analytical units of customs, manners, morals and institutions thought to be universal. As it was commonly thought that progress was self-evident, everywhere the process of change was from simple to complex, from irrational to rational, and from superstition to enlightenment. As systems of colonial control rested on knowledge, anthropology was to provide that knowledge.

While the sphere of interest of historians through the nineteenth century increasingly became the nation states, anthropologists were relegated to the study of colonial peoples.[16] But, by the 1920s, British and American anthropologists had radically turned away from the comparative studies of the nineteenth century. For the American school that Franz Boas founded, the object of anthropology became the construction and reconstruction of the uniqueness of individual cultures in relation to their histories, and the search of mechanisms through which these cultures were transmitted. Accordingly, field-work that is the direct, first-hand observation of native peoples became the hallmark of anthropologists.[17]

Boas was a Jewish German physicist who made the United States his country in 1887.[18] As he progressively turned from maths and physics to ethnology and anthropology, Boas came to value the unique potentials of each individual and believe that the object of his science was the enlightenment of humanity.[19] As he himself left Germany because of the anti-liberal and anti-Semitic climate of the time, Boas had a profound distaste for racism and any kind of prejudice, and his liberal views coincided with those of his contemporary American progressives who recognized human dignity as the essential quality of mankind, and experienced, at the same time, similar intellectual conflicts and contradictions.[20] The Black leader W. E. B. Du Bois, for example, found in Boas' anthropology a scientific support to his battle for the political and civil rights of black people. On the other hand, Boas' active contribution to the foundation of the inter-racial National Association for the Advancement of Colored People opened a fruitful alliance between black and Jewish intellectuals in the common battle against racism and anti-Semitism.[21]

Boas argued against the ethnocentric nineteenth-century version of cultural evolution as a uniform series of stages from savagery to Victorian England, and the assumption that all existing forms of culture were to be evaluated in terms of their similarity to the most highly evolved culture. As early as 1896 Boas made a definitive break with 'the view of by far the greater number of living anthropologists', namely, 'the working of the uniform laws governing the human mind'. Although he agreed 'that certain laws exist which govern the growth of human culture, and it is our endeavor to discover these laws', he did not agree with the conclusion that 'there is one grand system according to which mankind has developed everywhere'. Boas contrasted, instead, the 'comparative method' of evolutionism with the 'historical method'. He argued that the former 'has been remarkably barren of definite results', and believed 'it will not become fruitful until we renounce the vain endeavor to construct a uniform systematic history of the evolution of culture'.[22] As he was convinced that 'all the nations of modern times, and those of Europe not less than those of other continents, are equally mixed; and the racial purity on which European nations like to pride themselves does not exist',[23] the two fundamental questions that his anthropological research led to were 'why are the tribes and nations of the world different, and how have the present differences developed'.[24]

Boas' views, however, did not became popular until the 1920s. Although he was entrusted in 1908 by the United States Immigration Commission with an investigation of the physical characteristics of foreign immigrants, his findings on physical changes in the new environment did not affect the bias of immigration restrictionists.[25] Boas measured several thousands of immigrants and their children, mainly Eastern European Jews and Southern Italians in New York City. His findings were very radical, as he established the primacy of environment in influencing physical differences by using the cephalic index, a measure that had been considered a stable parameter, immune from the environment. According to Boas, changes in the bodily shape of Eastern European Jewish and Southern Italian children in New York, who tended to grow taller and live longer than their parents or former compatriots, emphasized the plasticity of human types. He also found it reasonable to infer that the fundamental traits of the human mind were subject to change in a new environment.[26] Boas' research aimed at defeating nativistic sentiments that pushed immigration restrictionism and eugenics measures. Many eminent politicians such as Theodore Roosevelt and Henry Cabot Lodge shared mainstream scientific beliefs on the undermining of 'racial purity' by 'smaller-brain races', such as the new immigrant groups and colored people, who were held incapable of progress.

Boas' views on racial equality and contemporary immigration issues were systemized in *The Mind of Primitive Man* (1911). He hoped he could help Americans to develop a greater tolerance for forms of civilization different from their own, and to look at 'foreign races' with sympathy as they could be a great asset to the country when given fair opportunities.[27] Accordingly, Boas defined a 'double standard of cultural evaluation' that his students elaborated in the following decades: a 'universalistic' one that allowed him to criticize his own society, and a 'relativistic' one that enabled him to defend cultural alternatives.[28] He thus established a new scientific paradigm by showing that differences in physical appearances did not lead to any significant difference in mental abilities or social skills. The existence of observable and undeniable differences had to be explained, Boas argued, with different historical and not biological experiences.

Although Boas' views were rather well known among American social scientists, they did not become mainstream thought for two decades at least. In 1916 a book published by Madison Grant, a wealthy amateur naturalist of the New York Museum of Natural History, entitled *The Passing of the Great Race*, popularized the view that the nordic branch of the white race was the greatest, that the black race was the most inferior, and that Italians, Spaniards, Greeks were less desirable than nordic people, and that the Jews were very undesirable:

> The new immigration ... contained a large and increasing number of the weak, the broken and the mentally crippled of all races drawn from

> the lowest stratum of the Mediterranean basin and the Balkans, together with hordes of the wretched, submerged populations of the Polish Ghettos. Our jails, insane asylums and almshouses are filled with this human flotsman and the whole tone of American life, social moral and political has been lowered and vulgarized by them.[29]

The popularity of Grant's book was due to the anxiety the war had unleashed about foreigners, America's 'Internal Others'. One of the inspirers of restrictionist policies, Grant was asked by a congressional commission to act as an expert to elaborate anti-immigration laws.[30] Boas answered Grant's book by arguing that

> homogeneous populations do not exist anywhere in the world. A greater or less amount of heterogeneity has always been observed, and heterogeneity in our modern civilization, at least, is always connected with social stratification. In a heterogenous population like that of the United States the difficulties in the way of determining a direct relation between selective influences and bodily form are almost unsurmountable.[31]

Apparently, society, not heredity, was the key.[32] Once the 'one grand scheme' of evolutionism was rejected, the multiplicity of cultures which took the place of the cultural stages of savagery, barbarism, and civilization were no more easily brought within one standard of evaluation than they were within one system of explanation. Later Boas admitted that he found difficult to define progress in ethical terms, and even more difficult to discern 'universally valid' progress in social organizations, 'for what we choose to call progress depends upon the standards chosen'.[33]

At the turn of the century it was how evolutionism was interpreted and constructed into a race ideology that gave a scientific language to racism and made it appear an objective form of knowledge that supported white supremacy. This was particularly true at a time of mass immigration that made northern American cities the most culturally heterogenous and fragmented. Nevertheless foreign immigrants could become Americanized by perceiving their 'whiteness' when confronted with the growing number of black southern immigrants who moved North to flee segregation and lynching mobs.

Boas' new scientific paradigm was constructed around his subjective antiracist views. Following his lead, his students Ruth Benedict and Margaret Mead, among others, constructed their 'External Others' to grasp a heterogeneous American society and its 'Internal Others'.

Ruth Benedict, first a student and then a colleague of Franz Boas at Columbia, in her *Patterns of Culture* (1934) held a liberal, pluralist vision, responding to the dilemmas of a modern American society. The ethnographic stories she and Margaret Mead told were explicitly linked to a context in which diverse values were struggling, with an apparent breakdown of established traditions.

According to Clifford Geertz, Benedict's writing about other societies is an example of 'a sort of Aesopian commentary on one's own. For an American to sum up Zunis, Kwakiutl, Dobu, or Japanese, whole and entire, is to sum up Americans, whole and entire, at the same time'.[34]

Benedict developed Boas' anthropology into her own approach in which 'culture wholeness became her disciplinary idea'.[35] Influenced by Jung, by the Gestalt psychologists, and by her readings of German philosophers of history such as Spengler and Dilthey, Benedict's key idea was that each culture is configurated or integrated around one or a few dominant drives, themes or patterns. She argued that each culture selects from material available to be borrowed, as well as from the creative productions of its own members, and reinterprets the materials it chooses to incorporate. At the beginning of her *Patterns of Culture* (1934), which was translated in two dozen languages and sold about two million copies, she observed that 'modern existence has thrown many civilizations into close contact, and at the moment' – she regretted to report – 'the overwhelming response to this situation is nationalism and racial snobbery.' She remarked that the 'cultural basis of race prejudice is a desperate need in present Western civilization'. She made very clear that there had never been a time in history 'when civilization stood more in need of individuals who are culture-conscious, who can see objectively the socially conditioned behavior of other people without fear and recrimination'. Her concept of 'cultural patterns' was based on dominant personality traits that societies followed from which their differences emerged. Consequently, individual behavior was shaped by society. However, not all individuals were endowed with the same permeability to socially constructed norms of behavior and did not conform. Hence these individuals, according to the standards of their society, were thought to be insane or pathological. But in another culture, in which different personality traits were dominant, those insane or pathological behavior might be admired.[36]

In Benedict's writings the alien was portrayed as the familiar in order to criticize contemporary American society. In her article on 'The uses of cannibalism', as Michel de Montaigne did in 1580 in his famous essay *Des Cannibales*, Benedict provokingly examined ancient ritualistic practices of cannibalism that enabled tribes 'to derive the most intense emotional satisfaction from the death, even the accidental death of a solitary enemy'. She found those practices harmless when compared to modern wars.[37]

'Extravagant otherness' as self-critique – the main trope in Benedict's writing – continued in Benedict's most famous work, *The Chrysanthemum and the Sword*. According to Geertz this popular book is a forced march through cultural difference:

> Japan comes to look, somehow, less and less erratic and arbitrary while the United States comes to look, somehow, more and more so … and the enemy who at the beginning of the book is the most alien we have ever fought is, by the end of it, the most reasonable we have ever conquered.

Benedict dismantled American exceptionalism by confronting it with a more exceptional and spectacularized 'Other' – the Japanese – within the intellectual-political milieu of World War II. The people around her, Geertz observes, were 'scholars in uniform' in the quest of 'national character'. Geertz concludes his interpretation of Benedict's work by criticizing what he calls an 'activist social science', of which *The Chrysanthemum and the Sword* is an example of 'science-without-tears policy tract'.[38]

Benedict's skeptical view of American culture that most liberals had at that time, made possible the acceptance of her sympathetic understanding of Japanese culture. Consequently, as her student Margaret Mead remarked,

> It was the kind of book that colonels could mention to generals and captains to admirals without fear of producing an explosion against 'jargon', the kind of book it would be safe to put in the hands of congressmen alert to resist the 'schemes of long-haired intellectuals'.[39]

Like her teachers Franz Boas and Ruth Benedict, Margaret Mead held a liberal and pluralist vision, and raised her ethnographical questions about 'External Others' with the moral perspective of offering pedagogical answers to complex changes in culturally heterogeneous American society.

Mead became well known with the publication of *Coming of Age in Samoa* (1928) that made a strong statement in support of cultural explanation for differences in human behavior. By contrasting the 'primitive' and the 'modern', Mead constructed Samoa as a mirror of American self-criticism. This heuristic contrast implied a relationship between 'We' (Western culture) and 'the Others' (namely what a monolithic Western culture defined as outside of itself), as Mead wrote in the introduction.[40] This self-referential character of primitivism allowed Westerners such as Mead to question their own cultural identities and the future of their societies. Again, it was America's self-scrutiny that stimulated the cultural contrast. In fact, at the end of Mead's text Samoa looked like an answer to what Mead perceived as the cultural neurosis of American adolescents. Samoa was represented as the alter-ego of the perceived cultural chaos of the West. She contrasted 'a simple, homogeneous primitive civilization, a civilization that changes so slowly that to each generation it appears static, and a motley, diverse, heterogeneous modern civilization'.[41]

The anthropologist's self-absorption in her own society produced a narrative in which 'the Other' was constructed in general terms. To put it another way, the ethnographer's voice was not a 'dialogical' one – to use

Mikhail Bakhtin's concept – as it was ambivalently self-absorbed in a monologue with her own culture. In fact, Mead's narrative seldom utilized direct quotations. The other was called 'the Samoans', an assumed unity of non-Westerners to reflect on Western concerns. This posture of neutral observation consented Americans to see themselves as a composite, heterogenous nation of immigrants.[42] Mead did describe specific Samoans in her text, but only as examples of observations she was making and not as active participants in the construction of her account. Through her monologues Mead gave frequent descriptions of 'typical' daily activities in Samoa. The ethnographer's voice appeared as having total vision and knowledge of a generalized 'Other' constructed as a mirror to produce a message of moral and political meaning for her own society.

Clifford Geertz has criticized this 'activist social science' for reducing complexities into a political tract. But then, how can the relationship between observer and the observed be managed in Geertz's terms?

In the opening essay of *The Interpretation of Cultures*, Geertz argues that cultural analysis needs 'thick description', that is, a deep level of description that is able to distinguish a meaningless reflex – a twitch or a blink, for example – from the wink, a consciously employed communicative device. According to Geertz, thick description examines public behavior for what it says rather than what it does. It is a reading of the symbolic content of the action, interpreted as a sign. Accordingly, Geertz's concept of culture is essentially semiotic. He believes, with Max Weber, 'that man is an animal suspended in webs of significance he himself has spun'. Consequently, Geertz takes culture 'to be those webs, and the analysis of it to be therefore not an experimental science in search of law but an interpretive one in search of meaning'.[43] Only thick description fulfils the object of Geertz's ethnography: 'a stratified hierarchy of meaningful structures.' Anthropological research is not merely observational but is an interpretative activity. Ethnography is thick description, as doing ethnography is like reading a manuscript. Geertz's semiotic concept of culture implies that culture is public because meaning is. Culture, then, 'is not a power, something to which social events, behaviors, institutions, or processes can be causally attributed; it is a context, something within which they can be intelligibly – that is, thickly – described'. Then, if ethnography is thick description and the anthropologists are those who do it, they have the power of 'scientific imagination' that is, to bring the readers of their writings in touch with the lives of strangers.[44]

The cultural historian Natalie Davis has actually conversed with the lived worlds of the past in her *The Return of Martin Guerre*. In her work history is 'historical imagination', that is, the re-imagining of the past while recovering it. As Davis was writing her history of local motivations, values, and feelings of a sixteenth-century French community, she was also assisting in the production of a film by the same title. The film script made Davis work with actors whose goals were to re-enact and re-experience a lived community. As Davis puts it, 'Writing for actors raised new questions about the motivations of people in the sixteenth century ... I felt I had my own historical laboratory, generating not proofs, but possibilities.'[45] Davis is aware that what she offered was in part her invention, a re-imagination of the already imagined, a reconstruction of the imagination of historical subjects. And cultural history as historical imagination is as intrinsically incomplete as Geertz's cultural analysis. 'The real is as imagined as the imaginary,' as Geertz puts it.[46] And this is more so the more deeply cultural analysis goes. Natalie Davis is aware, however, of the hazards of drawing upon anthropology for an historian:

> We consult anthropological writings not for prescriptions, but for suggestions; not for universal rules of human behavior, but for relevant comparisons ... Indeed, the impact of anthropology on my own historical reflection has been to reinforce my sense not of the changeless past, but of the varieties of human experience.[47]

Similarly, the British historian Edward P. Thompson found the anthropological impulse

> in locating new problems, in seeking old problems in new ways, in an emphasis upon norms or value systems and upon rituals, in attention to expressive functions of forms of riot and disturbance, upon symbolic expressions of authority, control and hegemony.[48]

Yet Thompson insisted that the methodology of symbolic anthropology should include historical change and contexts, and repeatedly denied the possibility of subsuming historical behavior to a set of universal laws or overarching theories.[49] Both Thompson and Davis, one could argue, are mainly interested in giving voice to the masses of people whose history has for generations remained unwritten, and their emphasis on the role of culture as a mediator of social relationships and structures has to be understood as their conviction of people's capacity to construct their own cultural identity through communities.[50]

From this perspective, Geertz's thick description, as he uses it, for example, in his often-quoted essay 'Deep play: notes on the Balinese cockfight', does not offer any understanding of historical change. The historian William Roseberry has argued that from Geertz's description, the Balinese cockfight is not related 'to political processes of state formation and colonialism', and does not explain the significant change this form of 'deep play' has gone through time. In other words, Roseberry argues, cockfighting is presented as having a single universal significance for the whole society.[51] 'Ideally thick description', historian Ronald Walters has remarked, 'says something about society. In practice, it often describes reality as a drama in which the focus is upon symbolic exchanges, not social consequences.'

In fact, thick description leads to 'brilliant readings of individual situations, rituals and institutions. It does not require saying how "cultural texts" relate to each other or to general processes of economic and social change'.[52] Perhaps the most serious criticism of Geertz's thick description comes from the anthropologist Vincent Crapanzano who cannot see in 'deep play' any understanding of the Balinese from their point of view. Crapanzano argues that Geertz establishes an opposition between the observers (Geertz and his wife as professional anthropologists) and the Balinese who live in their little world. Whereas Geertz and his wife are cast since the opening section of 'deep play' as individuals, the Balinese are generalized, as Margaret Mead did with the Samoans. Geertz, in Crapanzano's view, engages in a dialogue with his reader in a way that he does not engage with the Balinese who remain 'cardboard figures':

> There is only the constructed understanding of the constructed native's constructed point of view. Geertz offers no specifiable evidence for his attributions of intention, his assertion of subjectivity, his declarations of experience. His constructions of constructions of constructions appear to be little more than projections, or at least blurrings, of his point of view, his subjectivity, with that of the native, or, more accurately, of the constructed native.[53]

Geertz's human animal is suspended in 'webs of significance' (culture), and is inherently a-historical. But cultures, as another critic of Geertz has argued, 'are webs of mystification as well as signification. We need to ask who *creates* and who *defines* cultural meanings, and to what ends'. In other words, Geertz is silent 'on the way cultural meanings sustain power and privilege'. In fact, symbolic anthropologists in the name of interpretive detachment do not consider the political consequences of cultures as ideologies: 'Where feminists and Marxists find oppression, symbolists find meaning.'[54] A call for reconciliation has come from George Marcus and Michael Fischer: they argue that a bridge should be built:

> between the advances in the study of cultural meaning achieved by interpretive anthropology, and the concerns of ethnographers to place their subjects firmly in the flow of historic events and the long-term operation of world political and economic systems.[55]

How to build this bridge? I would argue that this bridge is the dialogical language of a post-ethnic perspective that problematizes culturally constructed identities by exploring and giving recognition to diversity.

The political philosopher Charles Taylor has placed the relationship between identity and recognition within the dialogical character of human life. Following Mikhail Bakhtin's explorations on inner dialogicality, identity depends on one's negotiation through dialogue with others.[56] Taylor argues that modern preoccupation with identity and recognition is the consequence of the collapse of traditional social hierarchies based on the notion of honor against which the notion of 'dignity of human beings' has emerged. With the move from honor to dignity a politics of universalism based on equal recognition and dignity of all citizens has followed. At the same time, Taylor argues, the development of the modern notion of identity has given rise to a politics of difference: everyone should be recognized for his or her unique identity. Are these opposite trends reconcilable? How do we evaluate different identities? What we need, in Taylor's view, is a 'fusion of horizons' by developing new vocabularies of comparison in order to articulate these differences:

> [A] real judgment of worth suppose a fused horizon of standards ... that we have been transformed by the study of the other, so that we are not simply judging by our original familiar standards. A favorable judgment made prematurely would be not only condescending but ethnocentric. It would praise the other for being like us.[57]

A serious problem with much of the politics of multiculturalism is that the demand for favorable judgments is paradoxically homogenizing as it implies that the standards to make such judgments are already available. Yet these standards are those of North Atlantic civilization. Furthermore, the enemies of multiculturalism in American academies have perceived the weakness of this demand of equal recognition and have used it as an excuse to answer as Saul Bellow is quoted to have said: 'When the Zulus produce a Tolstoy we will read him.'[58] This answer shows the depths of ethnocentricity. First, there is an implicit assumption that excellence has to take forms familiar to us: the Zulus should produce a Tolstoy. Second, we are assuming that their contribution is yet to be made.

A post-ethnic perspective based on recognition of differences problematizes and historicizes different components of American national identity. According to the African-American writer and Nobel prize winner Toni Morrison, a specific character of American identity is 'American Africanism', which she defines as a 'fabricated brew of darkness, otherness, alarm, and desire that is uniquely American'. The pervasiveness of the presence of blackness in the construction of American identity exists, according to Morrison, in the nation's major struggles:

> The presence of black people is not only a major referent in the framing of the Constitution, it is also in the battle over enfranchising unpropertied citizens, women, the illiterate. It is there in the construction of a free and public school system; the balancing of representation in legislative bodies; jurisprudence and legal definitions of justice. It is there in theological discourse; the memoranda of banking houses; the concept of manifest destiny and the permanent narrative that accompanies (if it does not precede) the initiation of every immigrant into

> the community of American citizens. The presence of black people is inherent, along with gender and family ties, in the earliest lesson every child is taught regarding his or her distinctiveness. Africanism is inextricable from the definition of Americanness – from its origins on through its integrated or disintegrating twentieth-century self.

Morrison does not want dominant Eurocentric scholarship replaced by a dominant Afrocentric scholarship. What she suggests is to unravel what makes intellectual domination possible.[59]

I would argue that language, through which identities are constructed and internalized, makes this domination possible. I would like to take the example that Morrison makes of internalization of the language of domination, by comparing Friday, Daniel Defoe's constructed Other in *Robinson Crusoe*, to Justice Clarence Thomas.

Crusoe's narrative is a success story, one in which a socially, culturally, and biologically handicapped black man, Friday, is civilized and Christianized; he is taught, in other words, to be like a white. Following Morrison's Judge Thomas/Friday metaphor, if one looks at Defoe's story from Friday's point of view rather than Crusoe's, it becomes clear that Friday had a very complex problem. Friday's real problem 'was not to learn the language of repetition, easily, like the parrot, but to learn to internalize it'. Friday progressively 'moves from speaking *with* to thinking *as* Crusoe'. The loss of the mother tongue seems not to disturb Friday, even though he never completely learns the master's:

> He negotiates a space somewhere in between. He develops a serviceable grammar that will never be eloquent; he learns to shout warnings of advancing, also black, enemies, but he can never dare speak *to* these enemies as his master does. Without a mother tongue, without the language of his original culture, all he can do is recognize his old enemies and, when ordered, kill them. Finally, Friday no longer negotiates space between his own language and Crusoe's. Finally, the uses of Crusoe's language, if not its grammar, become his own. The internalization is complete.

According to Morrison:

> both Friday and Clarence Thomas accompany their rescuers into the world of power and salvation. But the problem of rescue still exists: Both men, black but unrecognizable at home or away, are condemned first to mimic, then to internalize and adore, but never to utter one single sentence understood to be beneficial to their original culture, whether the people of their culture are those who wanted to hurt or those who loved them to death.[60]

Possibilities are already available, however, for the construction of cultural common grounds from a post-ethnic/cosmopolitan perspective. As Henry Gates says, in the contemporary world 'Mixing and hybridity are the rule, not the exception.' He reminds us that Duke Ellington, Miles Davis and John Coltrane have influenced the whole world of popular music, not only black musicians. Other black musicians feel comfortable with Mozart as much as with jazz, and others combine Bartok with blues. Black dancers Alvin Aily and Judith Jamison, for example, excel in classic ballet and combine all Western cultural forms with African-American styles to produce performances that were neither, and both. Similarly, in literature black writers such as Jean Toomer, Zora Hurston, Richard Wright, Ralph Ellison, James Baldwin, Toni Morrison and others have always blended forms of Western literature with African-American vernacular and written traditions. One could agree with Gates that African-American culture has been a model of multiculturalism and plurality, and represents the best collective hope 'to forge a new, and vital, common American culture in the twenty-first century'.[61]

Geertz seems to offer a similar perspective when he concludes that:

> ... whatever use ethnographic texts will have in the future, if in fact they actually have any, it will involve enabling conversation across societal lines – of ethnicity, religion, class, gender, language, race – that have grown progressively more nuanced, more immediate, and more irregular. The next necessary thing (so at least it seems to me) is neither the construction of a universal Esperanto-like culture, the culture of airports and motor hotels, nor the invention of some vast technology of human management. It is to enlarge the possibility of intelligible discourse between people quite different from one another in interest, outlook, wealth, and power, and yet contained in a world where, tumbled as they are into endless connection, it is increasingly difficult to get out of each other's way.

The world of separated differences in which previous generations of anthropologists worked has turned into 'one of a gradual spectrum of mixed-up differences'. 'The There's and the Here's, much less insulate, much less well-defined, much less spectacularly contrastive (but not less deeply so) have again changed their nature.'[62]

A post-ethnic/cosmopolitan perspective can be the paradigm of cultural studies whose interdisciplinary partiality and dialogical character make explicit the subjective non-neutrality of the historian, anthropologist, literary critic.

Notes

1. H. L. Gates, Jr., *Loose Canons: Notes on the Culture Wars* (Oxford University Press, New York: 1992), p. xii.
2. A. M. Schlesinger, Jr., *The Disuniting of America: Reflections on a Multicultural Society* (Norton, New York: 1992), pp. 102, 138, 68.
3. C. West, *Race Matters* (Beacon Press, Boston: 1993), p. 4.
4. The 'Aryan model' that Bernal questions, was created by nineteenth-century scholars deeply influenced by racist and anti-Semitic theories. The 'Aryan model' of explanation of the origins of Greek civilization is based on the assumption that Greek civilization is a mixture of local and Indo-European elements; the invading Europeans were white, as were the Greeks. The 'Ancient model' of explanation that Bernal basically accepts in a revised version, gives relevance to the Egyptian and Semitic influences. See M. Bernal, *Black Athena: The Afroasiatic Roots of Classical Civilization* (Rutgers University Press, New Brunswick, NJ: 1987), I.
5. Gates, *Loose Canons*, pp. xvi, 113, 115.
6. Cultural studies blur the boundaries of historical ethnography (Natalie Davis, Carlo Ginzburg), cultural criticism (Hayden White, Edward Said), the critique of hegemonic structure of feeling (Raymond Williams), the study of scientific communities (Thomas Kuhn), the semiotics of exotic worlds (Tzvetan Todorov).
7. J. Scott, 'Women's history', in P. Burke (ed.), *Historical Writing* (The Pennsylvania State University Press, University Park, Penn.: 1991), pp. 56, 57.
8. J. Clifford and G. E. Marcus (eds), *Writing Culture* (The University of California Press, Berkeley, Ca.: 1986), p. 19.
9. Ibid., p. 23.
10. J. Appleby, 'Recovering America's historic diversity: beyond exceptionalism', *Journal of American History* 79 (1992), p. 430.
11. Scott, 'Women's history', pp. 51-2.
12. By paradigm White means 'the model of what a set of historical events will look like once they have been explained': H. White, 'Interpretation in history', in Idem, *Tropics of Discourse* (Johns Hopkins University Press, Baltimore: 1978), p. 63.
13. Appleby, 'Recovering America's historic diversity', pp. 429, 430.
14. C. Thorne, 'American political culture and the end of the Cold War', *Journal of American Studies* 26 (1992), pp. 310, 333.
15. Clifford and Marcus (eds), *Writing Culture*, p. 23.
16. B. S. Cohn, 'Anthropology and history in the 1980s', *Journal of Interdisciplinary History* 12 (1981), pp. 228–30.
17. See G. W. Stocking, Jr., *Observers Observed* (University of Wisconsin Press, Madison: 1984).
18. Franz Boas was born in Minden, Westphalia in 1858. He studied at Heidelberg, Bonn and Kiel where he received his doctorate in 1881. He majored in physics and mathematics and then shifted to physical and cultural geography. Boas made his first trip to the North Pacific Coast in 1886, taught anthropology at Clark University from 1888 to 1892, served

as chief assistant in anthropology at the World Columbian Exposition in Chicago in 1893, worked as Assistant Curator in ethnology and somatology at the American Museum of Natural History in New York, became lecturer in physical anthropology at Columbia University where he was appointed professor in 1899. See L. A. White, 'The ethnography and ethnology of Franz Boas', *Bulletin of the Texas Memorial Museum* 6 (1963), p. 5.

19. See R. Bunzel, 'Introduction', in F. Boas, *Anthropology and Modern Life* (Greenwood Press, Westport, Conn.: 1962), p. 6.
20. See W. Goldschmidt (ed.), *The Anthropology of Franz Boas: Essays on the Centennial of His Birth* (How and Chandler, San Francisco: 1959), p. 2. Boas could not accept the requirement in Bismarck's Germany of declaring religious affiliation in order to hold a scientific position, and found in New York a congenial atmosphere of intellectual freedom. Together with W. E. B. Du Bois, Mary W. Ovington, and other New York intellectuals and reformers, Boas actively participated in the creation of the inter-racial National Association for the Advancement of Colored People. See M. Hyatt, *Franz Boas Social Activist: The Dynamics of Ethnicity* (Greenwood Press, Westport, Conn.: 1990).
21. See A. Meier, *Negro Thought in America, 1880–1915* (The University of Michigan Press, Ann Arbor, Mich.: 1963), pp. 162, 183, 261.
22. F. Boas, 'The limitations of the comparative method of anthropology', *Science* 4 (1896), pp. 901, 904, 905, 908.
23. F. Boas, *Columbia University Lectures, 1907* (Macmillan, New York: 1908), pp. 15, 26.
24. Ibid., p. 7.
25. US Senate, *Reports of the Immigration Commission*, 'Changes in Bodily Forms of Descendants of Immigrants', Senate document no. 208 (Government Printing Office, Washington, DC: 1911), p. 76. Boas and his assistants measured the stature, head length and breadth, bizygomatic diameter, and in some case the weight, of nearly 18,000 persons in New York. All were immigrants or the American-born children of immigrants. Of these, some 5,500 were aged 25 and upward, and the remainder children over the age of four. The largest number were East European Jews (about 6,000) and Bohemians, Sicilians and Neapolitans (about 3,000 of each), with smaller groups of Poles, Hungarians, and Scots. See J. M. Tanner, 'Boas' contributions to knowledge of human growth and form', in Goldschmidt (ed.), *The Anthropology of Franz Boas*, p. 99.
26. Hyatt, *Franz Boas Social Activist*, pp. 107–10; C. N. Degler, *In Search of Human Nature: The Decline and Revival of Darwinism in American Social Thought* (Oxford University Press, New York: 1991), pp. 63–5.
27. F. Boas, *The Mind of Primitive Man* (1913; Macmillan, New York: 1938), p. 278.
28. G. W. Stocking, Jr., 'Anthropology as kulturkampf: science and politics in the career of Franz Boas', in W. Goldschmidt (ed.), *Uses of Anthropology* (American Anthropological Association, Washington, DC: 1979), p. 47.
29. M. Grant, *The Passing of the Great Race* (1916; Arno Press, New York: 1970), pp. 88, 92.

30. Grant's ideas became the principles underlying the Immigration Acts (the 'quota' acts) of 1921 and 1924. See M. Klass and H. Hellman, *The Kinds of Mankind: An Introduction to Race and Racism* (Lippincott, Philadelphia: 1971), pp. 97–8. Boas did not fail to criticize Grant's book and exposed the fallacies on which it was constructed in a book review on the New Republic. He argued that Grant had given a new edition of Gobineau's theory, had made the mistake of analyzing hereditary traits of humanity as a whole, and had not taken into account the influence of environment on local groups. Boas argued that far from being interested in scientific data, Grant intended to propose a eugenistic remedy to the danger the new immigrants would represent to American democratic institutions: F. Boas, 'Inventing a great race', *New Republic*, 13 January 1917, pp. 305–6. Boas's data undermined those of anthropometrists who treated their indexes as constant ratios based on fixed traits. In the urban setting of the New World, round-headed Eastern European Jews became more long-headed, and South Italians, originally long-headed, became more round-headed. Hence the problem of physical variability was not a mere matter of genes, but a result of still unknown differences on the more permanent characteristics.
31. F. Boas, 'Report on an Anthropometric Investigation of the United States', in M. Mead and R. L. Bunzel (eds), *The Golden Age of American Anthropology* (Braziller, New York: 1960), pp. 418–20.
32. 'Heredity may explain a part of the pronounced mental similarities between parents and children; but this explanation cannot be transferred to explain on hereditary grounds the similarity of behavior of entire nations in which the most varied lines occur. These assume their characteristic forms under the pressure of society': F. Boas, *Aryans and Non-Aryans* (Information and Service Associates, New York: 1934), p. 11. Among Boas's students were: A. L. Kroeber, Robert H. Lowie, A. A. Goldenweiser, Paul Radin, Edward Sapir, Ruth Benedict, Margaret Mead, and Melville Herskovitz.
33. Boas came to identify valid progress in social forms as being intimately associated with the advancement of knowledge based on the recognition of a wider concept of humanity: F. Boas, *Anthropology and Modern Life* (Greenwood Press, Westport, Conn.: 1984), p. 228.
34. In Geertz's view ethnographers need to convince their readers not merely that they have truly 'been there', in close contact with the Other, but also that had the readers been there, they 'should have seen what they saw, felt what they felt, concluded what they concluded': C. Geertz, *Works and Lives: The Anthropologist as Author* (Stanford University Press, Stanford, Ca.: 1988), pp. 11, 15, 16.
35. R. Handler, 'Ruth Benedict and the modernist sensibility', in M. Manganaro (ed.), *Modernist Anthropology: From Fieldwork to Text* (Princeton University Press, Princeton, NJ: 1990), p. 172.
36. R. Benedict, *Patterns of Culture* (Houghton Mifflin, Boston: 1934), pp. 19, 15, 255.
37. R. Benedict, 'The uses of cannibalism', in M. Mead, *An Anthropologist at Work: Writings of Ruth Benedict* (Houghton Mifflin, Boston: 1959), pp. 44–8, quoted in Geertz, *Works and Lives*, pp. 104–5.

38. Geertz, *Works and Lives*, pp. 106, 121, 123, 127.
39. Quoted ibid., p. 127.
40. M. Mead, *Coming of Age in Samoa* (William Morrow and Co., New York: 1928), pp. 7–8.
41. Ibid., p. 114.
42. See D. Gordon, 'The politics of ethnographic authority: race and writing in the ethnography of Margaret Mead and Nora Zeal Hurston', in Manganaro (ed.), *Modernist Anthropology*, pp. 146–62.
43. C. Geertz, *The Interpretation of Cultures* (Basic Books, New York: 1973), p. 5.
44. Ibid., pp. 7, 10, 14, 26.
45. N. Zemon Davis, *The Return of Martin Guerre* (Harvard University Press, Cambridge, Mass.: 1983), pp. vii, 5.
46. C. Geertz, *Negara: The Theatre State in Nineteenth-Century Bali* (Princeton University Press, Princeton, NJ: 1980), p. 136.
47. N. Zemon Davis, 'Anthropology and history in the 1980s', *Journal of Interdisciplinary History* 12 (1981), pp. 273, 275.
48. E. P. Thompson, 'Folklore, anthropology, and social history', *Midland History* 1 (1972), p. 248.
49. E. P. Thompson, *The Poverty of Theory and Other Essays* (Monthly Review Press, New York: 1978), p. 25.
50. See S. Desan, 'Crowds, community, and ritual in the work of E. P. Thompson and Natalie Davis', in L. Hunt (ed.), *The New Cultural History* (The University of California Press, Berkeley: 1989), pp. 47–71.
51. W. Roseberry, 'Balinese cockfights and the seduction of anthropology', *Social Research* 49 (1982), p. 1021.
52. R. Walters, 'Signs of the times: Clifford Geertz and historians', *Social Research* 47 (1980), pp. 553, 552.
53. V. Crapanzano, 'Hermes' dilemma: the masking of subversion in ethnographic description', in Clifford and Marcus (eds), *Writing Culture*, pp. 70, 74.
54. R. M. Keesing, 'Anthropology as interpretive quest', *Current Anthropology* 28 (1987), pp. 161–2.
55. G. E. Marcus and M. J. Fischer, *Anthropology as Cultural Critique: An Experimental Moment in the Human Sciences* (The University of Chicago Press, Chicago: 1986), p. 44.
56. C. Taylor, *Multiculturalism and the Politics of Recognition* (Princeton University Press, Princeton, NJ: 1992), pp. 32–3.
57. Ibid., pp. 70–1.
58. Ibid., pp. 42, 71.
59. T. Morrison, *Playing in the Dark* (Harvard University Press, Cambridge, Ma.: 1992), pp. 90, 38, 47, 48, 63, 8.
60. T. Morrison (ed.), *Race-ing Justice, En-gendering Power* (Pantheon Books, New York: 1992), pp. xxiv–xxix.
61. Gates, *Loose Canons*, p. xii.
62. Geertz, *Works and Lives*, p. 148.

7

Identity Politics, Gender Wars and the Cultural Marketplace in the United States

Emory Elliott

The emotionally charged atmosphere generated around many discussions of identity and diversity in the US, indeed in much of the world, is more than a little daunting. In his essay 'The new cultural politics of difference', Cornel West puts the particular situation of the United States into a sweeping, but persuasive, historical context. Assessing what he calls the 'shattering of male WASP cultural homogeneity' in America since World War II, West argues that the extraordinary movement of global decolonization of the mid-twentieth century inspired women and minority groups in America to challenge the established power structure. While provoking 'Intense intellectual polemics and inescapable ideological polarization', West says, 'these [internal] critiques prompted three crucial process that have affected intellectual life in this country. First is the appropriation of theories of postwar Europe'. Second, 'the recovery and revisioning of American history in light of the struggles of white male workers, African Americans, Native Americans, Latino/a Americans, gays and lesbians'. Third, 'the impact of forms of popular culture such as television, films, music videos, and even sports on highbrow, literary culture. The black-based, hip-hop culture of youth around the world is one grand example'. As the consequences of this three-pronged intellectual revolution continue to restructure American thought and culture, West says that we face the danger of 'escalating racial hostility, violence, and polarization in the United States'. In response to this crisis, West urges those who support the interests of minority groups to find sustenance in the 'nourishing powers of subcultures' while resisting 'a narrow closing of ranks' which identity politics may encourage.[1]

A similar mediating strategy informs Henry Louis Gates' recent essay 'Beyond the culture wars: identities in dialogue'. Gates opens by asking: 'What is this crazy thing called multiculturalism?' After excluding sexual and class identities from his definition and pointing out that the media has come to use the term 'multicultural' as a euphemism or code for the more politically threatening word 'multiracial', Gates cautions against the various possible misuses of the concept of multiculturalism. Particularly troubling, he says, is the particular kind of media emphasis on multiculturalism which heightens the level of identity politics by suggesting the necessity of economic competition among diverse groups. As cultural sub-groups seek leverage and resources within the multicultural American society, these groups thereby incur reductive and even racist labels.[2]

Gates finds the very phrase, 'identity politics', to be in itself problematic because it suggests a static social construction while actually both of the terms are in a constant state of flux. He says:

> The point is that identity politics cannot be understood as a politics in the harness of a pregiven identity. The 'identity' half of the catchall phrase 'identity politics' must be conceived as being just as labile and dynamic as the 'politics' half is. The two terms must be in dialogue, as it were, or we should be prepared for the phrase to be revealed as an oxymoron.[3]

Enlisting the work of Isaiah Berlin, Gates voices deep concern over whether expressions of identity politics such as the yearning for 'cultural authenticity' pose 'a greater threat to civil order, and human decency, than does the messy affair of cultural variegation'. 'Let us remember', Gates advises, 'that identities are always in dialogue.'[4]

The calls of scholars such as West, Gates, and Houstin Baker and artists such as Toni Morrison to move beyond identity politics parallel similar expressions which are appearing in works of popular culture. The newest forms of rap music, while not suggesting abandonment of identity politics, are proposing more moderate themes of social healing. Movies such as Spike Lee's *Do the Right Thing* which depicts explosive divisions among working-class Italian Americans, African Americans, and Korean Americans and John Singleton's *Boyz 'N the Hood* in which gang members kill an aspiring black high-school athlete and also threaten to destroy the hopes of two academically talented young African Americans, send powerful messages about the potentially tragic results of identity politics.

But for the time being, these expressions of the problematics of identity politics may be somewhat moot, for massive and very profitable cultural machinery has been put into motion and now appears to be running under its own power. Debates regarding differences dominate the language of media, the courts, the colleges, the government, and the cultural market place. Such events as the Rodney King case and its aftermath, the Clarence Thomas hearings, the Menedez trials, the World Trade Center bombings, the Two Live Crew trials and the 'Gangsta Rap' censorship hearings feed the media frenzy for evidence of the dire social and moral consequences of ethnic diversity.

Prophets of doom, such as Patrick Buchanan and Rush Limbaugh, imagine a future America in which images such as those of the burning of Los Angeles will become standard TV fare as people of various ethnic backgrounds battle one another over urban territories. The question that such fearmongers always leave lurking in the minds of their audiences is how long will it be before the rioters head out for the territories of the walled-in white suburbs. Considerable economic opportunities from marketing firearms and security systems to the sales of newspapers, books, movies, videos, and TV advertising time are generated by such reductive, paranoid, and false projections. In America, a subject this good for business, no matter how distorted and dangerous, will not quickly be contained by facts and reason.

The question before us as researchers and scholars in the humanities is how to bring systematic analysis to a cultural marketplace in such disarray? My purpose here is to sketch out a few of the problems we confront and to suggest what appear to me, at least, to be some productive current directions for discussion.

One problem we face in the United States in regard to the issue of ethnicity is the strong tendency in American culture for everyone, from academics to talk-show viewers, to parse every issue into bi-polar opposites. As Sara Sulerie has said 'we all love to dump on dichotomies, and no self-respecting cultural critic would be caught dead with a binarism, but perhaps our desires exceed the actualities that we are forced to inhabit'. 'Down with either–or. Up with both–and. But is it more easily said than done?'[5] Of course, the media love either/or sound bites and stereotypes because extremism creates controversy which sells. But even academic debates tend to slip into binary configurations.

Those discussing ethnicity and American culture either yearn for continuation of the traditional, though perhaps mythic, melting-pot America where members of minority groups supposedly sought integration, assimilation, and participation in the mainstream, or they envision a new social and cultural mosaic of many divided ethnic subcultures symbolized for some by urban gang group conflicts. Two of the most nuanced and incisive discussions of these complex issues of cultural diversity are the notable formulations of Werner Sollors and Thomas Sowell.

In *Beyond Ethnicity: Consent and Descent in American Culture*, as well as in more recent essays, Sollors argues that the synthesis of diverse national and ethnic identities into an integrated American cultural whole is necessary and probably inevitable. In contrast, Sowell, in his *Ethnic America: A History*, posits a theory of ethnic group resistance to the dominant ideology that is gradually, but never completely, mollified by a process determined by mutual dependence between the larger society and the particular group. Both scholars argue that forms of ethnic identity in America must ultimately be accommodated to values and institutions shared with the dominant ideology. Ethnic cultural differences may be negotiated, but when they serve as social barriers to assimilation, they will gradually be overcome.[6]

Indeed, many facts of demographic change in America contradict apocalyptic prophecies and fail to support the notion of discrete communities unalterably separated by ethnicity and race. Statistics indicate that the population of the United States is no more ethnically diverse today than it was a hundred years ago and may, in fact, even be less so.[7] Statistics also show that the percentage of the current US population born outside the country is smaller than it was at the beginning of this century and that the racial and ethnic diversity of middle class neighborhoods is higher than it has ever been. The opportunities for education and jobs provided after the Civil Rights Movement and continued through affirmative action programs have enabled large numbers of previously excluded people to improve their social status. The rate of interracial marriage has climbed rapidly, and the Census Bureau projects that the country will maintain roughly its present racial proportions well into the next century. Indeed, as the Bush campaign managers and supporters fond to their dismay, the political benefits of exploiting racial and ethnic fears have been cast somewhat into doubt by the last election when, to quote one observer in the *Times Literary Supplement*, 'the Republicans mistakenly imagined that divisive cultural politics would work in this year's campaign'.[8]

In the cultural marketplace, signs of the awareness within American communities of inter-ethnic social blending appear in recent articles in popular magazines such as the African American journal *Ebony* and the mainstream *Newsweek*. A cover of a recent issue of *Newsweek* depicted a computerized composite of a woman's face that is supposed to represent a composite of features of several different ethnic groups.[9] Indeed, in popular culture, indeterminate racial and ethnic identity has become so common that the title of a recent article in *Ebony* magazine asked 'Who's black and who's not?' and its subtitle proclaimed 'New ethnicity raises provocative questions about racial identity'. Accompanied by pictures of family members of several of the article's prime subjects, the essay discusses current actors and singers who do not publicly claim their African heritage. The reporter proclaims that once a black actress begins to achieve success, she 'backs away from black things' and proclaims herself to be 'Indian, Spanish, Irish, and French Creole'.[10]

On the front page of the *Los Angeles Times Sunday Book Review* of 20 February 1994 is the color photo of a red-haired white woman wearing a blue and gold uniform of the DAR with an American eagle on her chest.[11] To the right of her image is a black and white inset of an African American family circa 1942, which we learn later is the 'white' woman's family. The contrasting photographic images is not the only irony figured on the page: the review's title, 'All in the family', invokes in the popular cultural memory the 1960s sitcom of that name which exposed, and perhaps helped to purge or mollify, prejudices of white Americans toward African Americans through humorous, but pointed, learning experiences of the good-hearted but blindly racist Archie Bunker. Beneath the review's heading is the equally ironic title of the book itself, Shirley Taylor Haizlip's *The Sweeter the Juice: A Family Memoir in Black and White*. Invoked is the colloquialism, 'the darker the berry the sweeter the juice', a traditional assertion of the superior sexual desirability of African Americans which rebuked white aspersions regarding black sexuality. Implied in the phrase is that the large numbers of mixed offspring in the South were proof of the contradiction between white denials of the humanity of blacks and the real human desires of individual white men and women for individual people of African descent. The review's subtitle, 'What does color mean if you can chose your race?' underscores a central theme of Haizlip's book which is the absurdity of social and political divisions and tensions that exist even among people of the same families as a result of the polarizing racial attitudes and laws of the United States.

Such border-crossings are now so common in American universities that militant groups struggle to maintain group identities though various rituals such as ethnic dress days, ethnic food days, and other forms of ethnic heritage celebrations. In academic circles, the subject of cultural hybridity has recently become a major topic of research, and in American literature courses, texts that deal with racial 'passing' such as those of Charles Chesnutt and Nella Larsen have become more frequently taught.[12]

Some of the most impressive and intriguing evidence of such cultural and ethnic blending is represented in the current research of the scholar of ethnic studies George Lipsitz. In an unpublished essay entitled 'After the fire is gone: the future of multi-culturalism in Los Angeles', Lipsitz attributes the insurrection not to the Rodney King verdict primarily but to the imbalance of wealth that developed rapidly in America from about 1980 to the present.[13] He also argues that the media has used those events as a grounds for creating the myth of a racially divided society in which ethnic harmony is impossible. To counter this false representation, Lipsitz presents a wealth of historical materials showing how multiculturalism has functioned for generations in the submerged and subversive popular culture of music, dance, speech, and style even when it has been veiled from the dominant society.

Building on the colonial and postcolonial theories of Franz Fanon and others, Lipsitz argues that 'it is through culture that societies arbitrate what is forbidden and what is permitted, who is excluded and who is included, who speaks and who is silenced. People can be imprisoned by stories just as securely and just as surely as they can be imprisoned by iron bars and stone walls'. In fact, Lipsitz says, stories can be more powerful than laws because they can 'make inequitable power relations seem natural and inevitable'. Lipsitz provides many examples of popular artists and entertainers whose lives, identities, and work display extraordinary mixtures of various ethnic heritages. Of his many examples of the many performance artists who have and continue to blend together into musical groups, taking on new names, languages, and styles of dress and speech, the figure of 'L'il Julian' is representative: 'The first Chicano rock and roll star in Los Angeles, [he] was really a Hungarian Jew pretending to be a Chicano singing black music produced by an ethnic Greek who thought of himself as black!'[14]

I do not mean to suggest that ethnicity is no longer an important force in American society or that ethnic identity will not always be a major issue in America. Cultural diversity is represented in movies, TV sitcoms, talk shows, university conferences, and political campaigns. With the decline in the birth rate of the Euro-American population over the last twenty years, and with continued immigration, minority groups will increase in different regions of the United States and their members will continue to struggle against prejudice and injustices of the dominate society and with the internal pressures of double consciousness and nationalist allegiances. And in the struggles over resources and privileges, the established population of whatever hue and pigment will feel threatened by and resentful of newcomers.

But this *is* to say that, in spite of the images of social fragmentation, urban division, and cultural mosaics, those rituals of American national consensus that Sacvan Bercovitch has explored so usefully will continue, for good or ill, to absorb, neutralize, and contain rhetoric of cultural resistance and encourage assimilation and mainstreaming.[15] As Luke Menand has observed in his *TLS* piece entitled 'Being an American: how the United States is becoming less, not more diverse': 'What most of the "identities" aspire to be (with the obvious exception of the small separatist elements that have inevitably become attached to them) are not separate and rival realms of value, but different flavors in the same dish.'[16]

At the same time, given Americans' either/or Manichean, Ramistic, Puritan Calvinist mode of thinking, it is not surprising that American academics on the right and the left are also going to extremes in some of the public discussions of multiculturalism. In the last fifteen years, we have all witnessed and many have participated in the explosion of the literary canon, the humanities curriculum, and the discourses of class, gender, and ethnicity across America. In my view, the results of these developments have been mostly positive. Regretfully, however, instead of clarifying matters for the larger public audience, the spirited debates between such figures as Alan Bloom, E. D. Hirsh, and former NEH Directors William Bennett and Lynn Chaney on the right and by public spokespersons such as Stanley Fish, Jane Tompkins, Houstin Baker, Henry Louis Gates, and Catherine Stimpson and others on the left have confusion and misunderstanding in their wakes.[17]

Instead of viewing this lively intellectual exchange as a healthy airing of important professional differences over matters of research, curriculum, pedagogy, history, and cultural heritage, the media has sensationalized it by giving their audiences sound bites and quick takes which present stark black and white contrasts. We have the reductive image of a battle between the 'solid knowledge' of history and the classics on the one side versus academic chaos of postmodern eclecticism and decaying intellectual standards; great books versus movies and MTV; erudite lectures by rigorously-trained elite professors versus mindless rap sessions led by ageing, but still militant, radicals of the 1960s. While most teachers and scholars have been working responsibly and skillfully to adjust reading lists, courses, and text books in concert with changes in our understanding and interpretations of the past and present, they have been accused as barbaric anti-intellectuals.

In looking at new anthologies and colleges courses in American literature, for example, we should not forget that in 1963 many of us were taught from the *Masters of American Literature* anthology that contained only eight authors who then constituted the canon.[18] I remember how exasperating graduate students in English found it to devise dissertation topics when it seemed that everything had been said about Shakespeare, Milton, Melville, and Faulkner. None of my professors ever suggested that I write a paper, let alone a dissertation, on one of the many women and minority group authors now being intelligently and fruitfully studied by both men and women scholars.

In their enthusiasm to expand the subject of American culture to include contributions from parts of the world other than Europe, however, many professors have met considerable resistance from some students, and even more so from their parents, who feel that faculty have pushed cultural diversity too far. On the whole, such complaints are rare, for the great majority of Americans, unless instigated or manipulated by the special interest groups, recognize the values of taking a broader perspective on America's cultural diversity. In fact, the extraordinary popularity of books by African American, Chicano/a, American Indian, and Asian American authors, as well as of the movies and TV dramas that the books have generated, has helped to identify a parallel market for productions which cash in by attacking the recently popular writers.

There is no question that at the moment identity politics sells and has been selling very well. The millions reaped at the box office by the films *Dances with Wolves*, *Glory*, and *The Joy Luck Club*; the success of movies by African American directors such as Spike Lee, Singleton, and Robert Townsend; and the appearance of several television sitcoms dealing with race and gender relations from The Cosby Show to Murphy Brown provide ample evidence of the profits of diversity. Americans love the new and the exotic, and issues of race and gender are especially hot. Just recently the controversial kiss between the star of the top-rated TV show Rosanne and Muriel Hemingway yielded the highest ratings and marketshare and reportedly prompted only a few phone calls of protest.[19]

So it would seem that we have here a paradox: on the one hand, ethnic diversity and identity politics are ultimately not as divisive to American society as it would at first seem and not as likely to bring on some cultural or political apocalypse as some believe. On the other, multiculturalism is a subject that is having a tremendous effect upon American life at many levels, particularly in the cultural marketplace. If people are so eager to read about, talk about, and view images of issues surrounding race and ethnicity, then how can this be a relatively benign phenomenon? Does such attention lead to resistance and division or to assimilation, or neither? Is there something more going on here that has not yet been fully explored? The answer to this last question is 'Yes', and, as Walt Whitman knew long before Freud and Lacan, the secret force at the core of this and many social mysteries is sex. The ways in which gender issues complicate the identity politics of race and ethnicity have served paradoxically both to heighten an atmosphere of adversity and tension surrounding issues of difference and to generate a tendency toward racial and ethnic assimilation.

Of course, it is a historical cliché that the Women's Movement of the 1830s and 1840s received much of its political energy from the abolition movement with which it was always allied and that some felt then and now that it drew attention away from the anti-slavery efforts. It is also frequently expressed by African Americans of both sexes that the Women's Suffrage Movement between 1885 and 1919, which occurred during the decades of the Lynch Law and the rise of the Ku Klux Klan, channeled reform energies away from racial oppression to advance the interests primarily of white women. It is still a complaint, usually voiced in whispers, of many men of color in the United States that much of the force and many of the benefits the Civil Rights movement of the 1950s and 1960s were redirected by women leaders of the Feminist Movement to yield greater opportunities and advancement for women, especially privileged white women, than for minority people, especially for men of color. The resentments, whether fully justified, have had consequences that are not trivial.

Current gender wars entwined with issues of identity politics include those within the Asian American intellectual communities that have resulted in divisions between Asian American men and women writers, expressed most publicly in the exchanges between Maxine Hong Kingston and Frank Chin. Similar tensions exist within the African American intellectual communities and appear in the writings of African American women novelists such as Alice Walker and Toni Morrison. Within the Mexican American literary community, the work of Gloria Anzaldúa not only explores cultural borderlands but has come to symbolize a declaration of Chicana sexual independence. In each of these three cultural examples, the traditional gender relations – most would say the traditional subordinate relation of women to men – has been challenged in the last twenty-five years especially. The results have been some curious though not altogether surprising collaborations of social brotherhood and sisterhood that cross racial and ethnic lines.[20]

Two recent anecdotes from the experiences of a native observer (me) illustrate that gender antagonisms are not confined to the academy but pervade everyday discourse: in March 1994, my clock radio, which was tuned to a Los Angeles rock station, awakened me with the following banter. First, in a commercial for the African American woman author Terry McMillan's latest mega-blockbuster novel *Waiting to Exhale*, two presumably African American men discuss the merits of the novel as one recommends the book to the other.[21] The reluctant customer complains: 'Those black women writers are always so unfair to black men, and I'm tired of having black men being put down by black women'. The McMillan fan says that her books are different because her portraits of black male characters are fair and balanced. After expressing his amazement, the skeptic agrees to give her work a try. Second, when the 1994 nominations for the Academy Awards were announced, I awakened to a debate between the members of a male–female DJ team over the choices for best picture: 'Why wasn't *The Joy Luck Club* nominated?' asked Kim. 'Because it's a "chick film"', Mark answered. 'Yes, I see now', Kim answered, 'all the films that were nominated were "guy films" – *The Fugitive*, *In the Name of the Father*. All except *The Piano*, the one where the woman doesn't ever speak.' Indeed, with rare exceptions, current movies project images of white male gunfighters, crime fighters, bodyguards, and fire fighters, as male stars such as Harrison Ford and Kevin Costner save and protect, or destroy, ethnic others. Even the ageing Clint Eastwood and Sean Connery collect sexual rewards for their selfless heroism in films brimming with gender politics.

Based on the jingoistic novel by Michael Crichton, the popular film, *Rising Sun*, features the salt-and-pepper team of Wesley Snipes and Connery, who show those Japanese businessmen who's boss. Drawing upon his vast knowledge of Japanese language and culture, the Connery cop patronizes his black partner while also humiliating the Japanese. But the main controversy over the movie focused less on its racism and nationalism than on its sexism. The rape and murder of a white blond woman which is caught on video tape becomes the focus of the repeated male gaze of the men of all three ethnic groups as their investigative replay of the scene enables them, and the audience, to luxuriate in fantasies of violence against women. The movie's denouement, which reveals that the Connery character has taken as a secret lover a much younger Asian woman scientist who briefly assists in the case, not only alludes to similar multi-ethnic conquests in Connery's James Bond flicks of the 1960s but drives home the point of total American white male dominance in the post cold war era.

Similar reassertion of white phallocentric imperialism structures another recent film about the attempted assassination of the President, *In the Line of Fire*. Here Clint Eastwood needles his partner, a beautiful female Secret Service agent, by stating that she got her job because of her gender to which she responds: 'What demographics do you represent?' As the much younger professional is melting into submission under his paternalistic gaze and manly charms, he counters with an ambiguous plea for pity and assertion of male dominance: 'White piano-playing heterosexuals over the age of fifty. There ain't a whole lot of us, but we do have a powerful lobby.' Eastwood's enemy, played by John Malkovich, is also white; but that is only because James Edward Olmos turned down the part saying that 'because movies make such an impact on the public ... [I] did not want the role of a Mexican American trying to assassinate the president'.[22]

The most notorious public display in which gender conflict complicated an issue involving race was the Clarence Thomas confirmation hearing. In her introduction to the collection *Race-ing Justice, En-Gendering Power: Essays on Anita Hill, Clarence Thomas and the Construction of Social Reality*, Toni Morrison concludes that for all of its destructive stereotyping, this episode may have had a positive benefit by airing previously buried, often invisible, gender wars:

> Regardless of political alliances, something positive has already surfaced. In matters of race and gender, it is now possible and necessary, as it seemed never to have been before, to speak about these matters without the barriers, the silences, the embarrassing gaps in discourse. It is clear to the most reductionist intellect that black people think differently from one another; it is also clear that the time for undiscriminating racial unity has passed. A conversation, a serious exchange between black men and women, has begun in a new arena, and the contestants defy the mold. Nor is it as easy as it used to be to split along racial lines, as alliances and coalitions between white and black women, the conflicts among black women, and among black men, during the intense debates regarding Anita's Hill's testimony against Clarence Thomas's appointment prove.[23]

Morrison's analysis of the power of gender over race in this and other issues is borne out by the public opinion polls which show that over 80 per cent of men of all ethnic groups supported Thomas while roughly the same percentage of women supported Hill.[24]

Thus, in one way the case dealt a serious set-back to black unity and identity politics while at the same time, as Morrison argues, it complicated perceptions of about the African American community and perhaps strengthened bonds of brotherhood and sisterhood that cut across racial lines. Just as the bonds of sisterhood that formed across ethnic, racial, and class divisions can, to some degree, reduce the tensions among those women who might otherwise be political opponents, so too may male bonding have the potential for complicating identity politics in potentially productive ways.

There are obvious examples, of course, in the world of sports and in the popular media. Boxing had long served to provide an arena in which ethnic and racial tensions have been released. Since the 1950s, many team sports, such as baseball and American football, have encouraged camaraderie that overcomes racial difference. When projected on the screens of American homes, the images of integrated teams transmit a message of racial harmony and assimilation. In other forms of popular culture, even gangster movies, such as *Bugsy* and *Goodfellas* have present boys and men of various ethnicities, Jewish, Italian, and Irish, joining together in their unsavory pursuits in ethnically and racially mixed brotherhoods.

Even the current cultural wars fit the pattern in which gender division and gender bonding eclipse racial difference. In Los Angeles, recently, the opening of David Mamet's *Oleanna* proved this play to be controversial on more levels than one. Highlighting the issue of the proliferation of sexual harassment cases in academic settings, the play received considerable attention during its New York run because of the powerful gender conflict it depicts: a college professor is confronted in his office by a female student who comes to complain about her grade. During the conference, he sympathizes with her and condescendingly identifies with her feelings of ignorance and marginality, and comforts her with a casual embrace; and he promises to give her an A for the class if she will put aside her anxieties over grades and attend tutorials with him in his office. When she brings a harassment charge against him for seeming to compromise her and for making sexual advances, he and the audience are startled, but his naïveté does not prevent him from losing his job, home, and marriage. In New York, Mamet was berated by feminist critics such as Elaine Showalter for his misogyny,[25] and applauded by male critics such as Jack Kroll who said 'Mamet has sent a riveting report from the war zone between genders and classes, a war that will cause great havoc before it can create a new human order'.[26]

When the play moved to the Mark Taper Forum in Los Angeles, Mamet insisted that the male lead be played by the black actor Lionel Mark Smith even though the student would be played by the white actress Kyra Sedgwick. When the Forum's artistic director protested that putting an African American in that part would make the play inflammatory and illogical (since the character laments that he bears 'the white man's burden'), Mamet sought artistic freedom at the smaller and less central Tiphany Theater.[27] Having seen the play myself, I can testify that the almost entirely white audience seemed much more disturbed by the student's charges against the professor than by the male actor's race. And except for a couple of reviews about the inappropriateness of the 'white man burden' line, there was no racially motivated protest. To my mind, the casting served to underscore the multicultural–masculinist theme that all men who are in positions of authority in today's society, regardless of their color, had better re-think the sexual implications of their words and actions toward women – a main point that many men took away, I believe, from the Thomas–Hill proceedings which may have inspired Mamet's cast substitution.

One of the signatures of Mamet's work is his postmodern dialogue. His characters assault each other with words, interrupting each other and spitting out single words and fragments of sentences in rapid fire bursts. Telephone calls interrupt on-stage conversations generating doubled dialogues with participants both on and off stage. Characters attempt to finish one another's thoughts by completing each other's phrases and sentences. To unaccustomed ears, the jangling rhythms and syncopated timing at first makes the dialogue seem to be an incomprehensible babble or to be spoken in a foreign language. As the words become familiar, the fragmentary expression requires constant interpolation by both the characters and the audience. Here's a typical example from the opening scene of *Oleanna*:

Carol: I'm doing what I'm told. I bought your book. I read your …
John: No, I'm sure you …
Carol: No, no, no. I'm doing what I'm told. It's *difficult* for me. It's *difficult* …
John: … but …
Carol: I don't … lots of the *language* …
John: … please …
Carol: The *language*, the 'things' that you say …
John: I'm sorry. No. I don't think that that's true.
Carol: It *is* true. I …
John: I think …
Carol: It *is* true.
John: … I …
Carol: Why would I … ?
John: I'll tell you why: you're an incredibly bright girl.
Carol: … I …
John: You're an incredibly … you have no problem with the … Who's kidding who?
Carol: … I …
John: No. No. I'll tell you why. I'll tell … I think you're *angry* I …[28]

What emerges from Mamet's jarring and disconcerting exchanges, however, are dramatic explorations of some of the most compelling moral issues of American society. In the case of *Oleanna*, audible gasps throughout the theater during the performance and head-shaking conversations as the audience exits indicate that this fictional skirmish in the gender wars strikes close to home. Part of Mamet's point, however, seems to be that communication through language is the greatest challenge in the effort to mediate problems of difference and identity. When language fails, violence results, as in the climax of *Oleanna* when the angry and frustrated John begins beating Carol.

For most of the men and women in Mamet's audience, the different skin shades of Carol and John become a less significant factor in their relationship as the complexities of their gendered positions, their misperceptions of each other, and their inability to see themselves through the eyes of the Other become central. Even John's line in which he complains of the 'white man's burden', rings with ironic truth: as an aspiring African American male in the academic profession who is trying to support a family and gain economic security, John bears the white man's burden as well. In this instance, he becomes a representative of the white male authority structure against which those on the margins, such as young women, continue to struggle. John's identity as male supersedes his identity as black male.

One of the benefits of American multiculturalism for me is the opportunities I have to talk to men (and I use that term self-consciously for accuracy) from all over the world when I travel in taxis in large cities in America. These experiences enable me to learn of some of the particular experiences of people from Africa, Haiti, China, Bangladesh, Pakistan, Romania, Greece, Russia, Malaysia, Mexico and other countries. Depending upon the length of the ride, I ask them about their families and aspirations.

While my sample is limited and my method quite unscientific, I am always struck at how many have wives who are working at better paying jobs than their own, how much they worry about the dangers of American streets and schools for their children, and how much they are impressing the importance of education upon their children. In New York, especially it seems that a remarkably high percentage of taxi drivers are sending their children to private schools, or are saving to do so. Without using the phrase 'The American Dream', these men tell stories that fit that mythic metanarrative pattern, but often they also share their difficulties of getting along with demanding American women, regardless of their race or ethnicity.

For example, recently an Ethiopian taxi driver explained that he and his African American wife were both struggling to raise a family but that he also wished to help his brother in Ethiopia. He had just sent four hundred dollars to his brother to enable him to buy a truck to start a business, but he dared not tell his African American wife of this extravagance because she would not understand: 'You know how American women are', he confided, 'she thinks that Ethiopians are all lazy and wasteful and that my brother would just waste the money.'

I am not saying that such gender bonding is inherently a positive thing, since I believe that it would be a better world if gender related social and political distinctions did not exist. At the same time, such conversations remind me repeatedly of how much gender identification matters in forming contacts and sympathy across racial and ethnic lines and how the memories that I and each of these drivers have of one another, no matter the role that myth and misperception plays in their formation, function to bridge differences of ethnicity, race, profession and class.

In Mamet's play and in the cultural market place at large the battle lines of the gender wars daily cut across and often take precedence over the borders of ethnic identities. It is apparent how cultural representations of identity politics function more often to complicate and diffuse, if not defuse, the energies of ethnic and racial nationalism at, what Gates calls, 'the sites of contest and negotiation, self-fashioning and refashioning'.[29]

Notes

1. C. West, 'The new cultural politics of difference', in C. McCarthy and W. Crichlow (eds), *Race Identity and Representation in Education* (Routledge, New York: 1992), pp. 16, 22.
2. H. L. Gates, 'Beyond the culture wars: identities in dialogue', in P. Franklin (ed.), *Profession 93* (The Modern Language Association of America, New York: 1993), pp. 6–11.
3. Ibid., p. 9.
4. Ibid., p. 11.
5. S. Sulerie, 'Multiculturalism and its discontents', in Franklin (ed.), *Profession 93*, p. 17.
6. W. Sollors, *Beyond Ethnicity: Consent and Descent in American Culture* (Oxford University Press, New York: 1986); T. Sowell, *Ethnic America: A History* (Basic Books, New York: 1981).
7. L. Menand, 'Being an American: how the United States is becoming less, not more, diverse', *Times Literary Supplement*, 30 October 1993, pp. 3–4.
8. Ibid.
9. *Newsweek*, 13 October 1993, cover.
10. *Ebony* 45 (March 1990), pp. 134–6.
11. 'All in the family', *Los Angeles Times Book Review*, 20 February 1994, pp. 1, 8.
12. On the issue of hybridity, see L. Lowe, 'Heterogeneity, hybridity, multiplicity: marking Asian American differences', *Diaspora* 1 (1991), pp. 29–44 and G. Spivak, *In Other Worlds* (Routledge, New York: 1987).
13. G. Lipsitz, 'After the fire is gone: the future of multi–culturalism in Los Angeles', unpublished manuscript, University of California at San Diego, January 1994, pp. 1–6. I am also indebted to Lipset's essays '"Turning the tapestry around": from literary history to cultural history', unpublished manuscript, University of California at San Diego, December 1993, and 'Facing the music in a land of a thousand faces', *Sunburst* (February 1993), esp. pp. 7, 14.

14. Lipsitz, 'Facing the music', pp. 11, 19.
15. The relation of Bercovitch's work to multiculturalism in contemporary America is examined by S. B. Girgus in 'The new ethnic novel and the American idea', *College Literature* 20 (1993), pp. 57–72.
16. Menand, 'Being an American', p. 4.
17. The relevant works of these authors have been so widely discussed as to need no further citation here.
18. L. Edel (ed.), *Masters of American Literature* (Houghton Mifflin, New York: 1959).
19. This media event received extensive American press coverage during the last two weeks of March 1994.
20. On these issues, see K. K. Cheung, *Articulated Silences: Hisaye Yamamoto, Maxine Hong Kingston, Joy Kogawa* (Cornell University Press, Ithaca: 1993); J. P. Butler, *Gender Trouble: Feminism and the Subversion of Identity* (Routledge, New York: 1990).
21. For discussions of the controversial success of Terry McMillan's novel, see D. Pickney's review of *Waiting to Exhale*, in *New York Review of Books*, 4 November 1993, pp. 33ff. and S. Isaacs' review of the novel in *New York Times Book Review*, 31 May 1992, pp. 12ff.
22. *Press-Enterprise*, Riverside, California, 5 March 1994, p. B-10.
23. T. Morrison, 'Introduction', in Idem (ed.), *Race-ing Justice, En-Gendering Power: Essays on Anita Hill, Clarence Thomas and the Construction of Social Reality* (Pantheon Books, New York: 1992), p. xxx.
24. 'Public tends to believe Thomas', *Los Angeles Times*, 14 October 1991, pp. 1ff.
25. E. Showalter, 'Acts of violence: David Mamet and the language of men', *Times Literary Supplement*, 6 November 1992, pp. 16–17.
26. *Newsweek*, 9 November 1992, p. 65.
27. *Press-Enterprise*, 12 February 1994, p. E-6.
28. D. Mamet, *Oleanna* (Dramatist Play Services, Inc., New York: 1993)
29. Gates, 'Beyond the culture wars', p. 11.

8

Real Americans: Gender and the Defense of the Multicultural Nation

John Bodnar

As her father lay dying in April 1993 Hillary Clinton, in a public address in Texas, stressed the importance of family and the need for caring. The wife of the American President, possibly remembering her relationship with her parents, told her audience that Americans needed a new infusion of love and caring in their social relationships. She claimed that America was facing grave difficulties because its citizens were preoccupied with self-interest and seldom felt part of a larger collective. 'We need a new definition of society', she claimed, '[that] makes us feel part of something bigger than ourselves'.[1]

The image of a powerful woman using concepts like love and caring to stem a perceived threat to the viability of the nation reflected how much American society had changed since the end of World War II. During and after the war powerful male warriors stood as cultural symbols that defended the nation and its families. The public memory of the war effort had venerated heroic soldiers in the creation of the Iwo Jima war memorial in Washington and in popular films like the *Sands of Iwo Jima* (1949). Actor John Wayne became the emblem of the patriotic American warrior who placed duty above self-interest and led marines in a bloody assault against the Japanese. With Hillary Clinton, however, the public role of saving the nation and the definition of a real American moved from the masculine to the feminine.[2]

John Wayne's role made him the foremost box office star in the United States in the early 1950s. Hillary Clinton's public performances, however, earned her equal measures of praise and scorn. Speakers at the Republican National Convention in August 1992 found fault with the influence she exerted on her husband's campaign and media critics called her 'Lady Macbeth', a woman of consuming ambition who dominated her spouse and was contemptuous of traditional female functions.[3] Because of a comment she once made comparing marriage to slavery, she was denounced as a threat to the existence of the traditional family in America. In the 1990s, however, such assaults also won her adherents. After the Republican Convention, Mrs Clinton began to attract female supporters in her crowds who shared her goals of careerism and independence.[4]

In actuality this female defender of the nation was not the radical feminist that many thought she was. Her activities suggested, rather, that she embodied a modified form of feminism that was deemed more palatable for public consumption. She called for selflessness and led the movement for the reform of health care as a progressive who wanted to show concern for the national community and alter the ideology of privatism of the Republicans. And she was frequently portrayed as a mother who was concerned over the welfare of her daughter. But she was every bit the image of a competent professional when she testified on health reform before Congress. And her spouse never tired of telling anyone who would listen how much he sought and respected her advice on weighty matters. When he was accused of marital infidelity, she chose to 'stand by her man' instead of asserting her independence. John Wayne's masculinity was unequivocal. He was the strong male warrior who died for his nation and protected its families. Hillary Clinton feminism was a mediation. She had to reconcile the radical quest for independence from men that characterized the women's movement of the 1960s and traditional notions of mothering and marriage.

Male flight

In the 1990s Hillary Clinton fashioned a new definition of womanhood that appealed to the widest possible audience. Rejecting categorical definitions of gender roles, she attempted to construct a model that reigned in the extremes not only of feminism and motherhood but also of a rising impulse of male separatism. In seizing a public role she not only attempted to save the nation but to save and redefine the institution of marriage and the family that had long been seen as the heart of national society.

The logical explanation for the emergence of Hillary Clinton would be that she was a product of the feminist movement. But she was reacting to much more than feminism. In her alliance with her spouse she represented an attack on the idea that men could flourish without females. By the late 1980s, in fact, American men displayed an expanding interest in abandoning their traditional ties to women and even the nation. The strongest expression of this movement was to be found in the scores of films and books in the 1980s that reflected upon America's experience in Vietnam.

In a penetrating study of these cultural texts Susan Jeffords demonstrated how a male point of view dominated the public memory of the war. Decoding books and films produced largely by men who were part of the war effort, Jeffords discovered that these authors esteemed the comradeship of warriors and articulated a longing for a restoration of masculine power in society. Jeffords called this pattern an attempt at 'remasculinization'. In the aftermath of World War II there was a hope that Americans could re-establish traditional family roles and resume their life in the heterosexual family. But in the 1980s the dream of many combatants evoked a world in which men no longer needed women at all. Thus, in William Broyles' 1986 book, *Brothers in Arms*, the true meaning of the war was to be found in the 'enduring memory' of comradeship among the warriors. Broyles saw this idea as a form of patriotism because individuals were willing to die for something beyond their own life. Like Hillary Clinton, Broyles venerated selflessness over egoism. Unlike the First Lady, however, he felt that such sentiments now resided mainly with men who had been to war rather than with self-seeking women active in the economy and in politics.[5]

This world of male comradeship was not only a world without a significant role for women but one in which male citizens were estranged from the American government, if not the idea of the nation. As depicted by the movie character John Rambo, men who had fought in Vietnam felt betrayed by their government for not giving them the full compliment of resources and support to actually win the war. In *First Blood*, a highly popular movie, John Rambo is a Vietnam veteran who returns from southeast Asia troubled and angry. He was a masculine fighting machine in Vietnam but back in the United States he could not get a decent job. In the film a confused Rambo finally vents his frustration by destroying property in a small town before he is arrested and breaks down and cries for his dead comrades.[6]

Rambo is rejuvenated, however, in a second film, *First Blood, Part Two*. Now strong and self-reliant again, he leads a mythical rescue of American prisoners of war left behind in Asia. Fighting off scores of enemy guards in a heroic manner, he accomplishes his rescue singlehandedly and restores an American sense of masculinity through violence.[7]

To a surprising extent, however, the reassertion of American masculinity is never enough in the Vietnam narratives. These stories not only reveal their desire to overcome the legacy of defeat but to marginalize women from men's lives. Jeffords actually feels that this viewpoint is largely responsible for their popularity. In other words they are texts that are implicated not only in the memory of the war but in the current crisis over masculine power and authority. The point is made clearly in John Wheeler's, *Touched By Fire*, another account of the meaning of the war by a veteran. Wheeler contends that Americans have lost their sense of commitment to the nation and to the ideal of national unity. In part he attributes this decomposition to the pursuit of careers by women, and he suggests that the women's movement and its quest for power and rights instead of national unity was furthered at the expense of the Vietnam veterans. His point is that the women's movement drew energy from the war and the manner in which it undercut faith in all institutions of traditional authority. Wheeler believed that women's rise to power was achieved 'across the backs of the American men in Vietnam'. And unlike the aftermath of World War II, they failed to relinquish the gains they had made to returning soldiers.[8]

Male independence is powerfully expressed in the award winning film *The Deer Hunter* (1979). The movie follows the lives of a group of young men from a Pennsylvania steel town to Vietnam. The central character, Michael, is the exemplar of the masculine code. He can kill deer in Pennsylvania or an enemy guard in Vietnam with one shot. Significantly, he has very little contact with women in his daily life. His friend, Stevie, however, succumbs to the love of a woman and marries before he leaves for war. Symbolically, Michael returns from Vietnam a war hero while Stevie is emasculated and returns a paraplegic. American war heroes are still ultimately masculine. The deer hunter, Michael, embodies many traits found in the traditional western hero of American film. He lives alone on the edge of town in a trailer removed from obligations to women and to community. He remains uncorrupted in the 'wilderness' rather than in relationships with women and children. Like the western hero, Michael is not only celibate but capable of resorting to violence to protect women and the community itself. Not surprisingly many scenes in the steel town are shot in male enclaves such as bars.[9] *The Deer Hunter* ends with an implication that the experience of defeat and the direct confrontation with violence in war can actually moderate the male drive toward independence and hostility itself. Michael apparently learns from the experience of captivity in the war that he is not omnipotent. Thus, in the film's ending all the surviving characters, male and female, join in a toast. Michael rejoins America when he rejoins this group of men and women he knows. The implication, of course, is that the national community's viability is contingent upon the moderation of male independence and aggression.[10]

It should not be surprising that many of the films remembering and interpreting Vietnam resorted to so many of the elements of the western genre and, what Richard Slotkin has called the 'Myth of the Frontier'. Slotkin calls it 'our oldest and most characteristic myth'. As expressed in literature, film, and novels, it has always been associated with the idea of conflict. White men pursued progress and regeneration through a clash with savages on the frontier or with Communists in Vietnam. Slotkin is not surprised to find that American troops in Vietnam referred to enemy sectors as 'Indian territory'. In the narratives of the frontier the mythical hero must discipline the savage and the 'dark side of his nature' as he did in *The Deer Hunter*. As mass culture became a key site for political and cultural discourse in the twentieth century, issues central to the construction of American nationality were frequently worked out and discussed in films. *The Deer Hunter* revealed how much such vital matters now revolved around gender.[11]

Interestingly, Slotkin suggests that the pursuit of regeneration through violence can turn out to be so violent that American masculinity itself can be destroyed or changed rather than reborn. There was a hint of this in the final scene of *The Deer Hunter*. In 1973, when the last American combat forces were brought home, the pre-eminence of the westerns among the genres of mythic discourse and movies suddenly stopped. The western's version of masculinity and nationality had been, at least for a time, crippled. In its original inception the myth had attempted to define American nationality in a way that muted racial and cultural heterogeneity.[12] When an attempt was made to revive the masculine version of the nation in the 1980s, the western genre was displaced by films about Vietnam. But such films no longer sought to marginalize blacks (who fought in Vietnam) or immigrants as they had in the past but females. Women were now seen as the most direct threat to the masculine nation.[13]

The male flight from women, however, was about more than the rising power of females. There is considerable evidence to suggest that in the 1950s American men were already beginning to disavow themselves from any form of interdependence with women. Implicitly, such action constituted an abrogation of their role as defenders of the nation and its families. Barbara Ehrenreich, who has studied the flight of males from the ideal of obligations, concluded that by the 1970s adult manhood was no longer burdened with the expectation of marriage. This might imply that men no longer considered it mandatory to become warriors either, although this point has yet to be investigated. More significantly, this action on the part of many men took place before the emergence of a modern feminist movement. Thus the first issue of *Playboy* magazine in 1953 portrayed women as money-hungry sex objects and fostered an idealized world of pleasure for men through sex and consumption outside of marriage. This appealed to males who longed for an escape from the responsibilities of suburban families and corporate regimentation. By the late 1950s several polls discovered an increased tolerance of people who rejected marriage as a way of life.[14]

Interestingly, when the image of an independent woman was widely promoted by feminists in the 1970s and 1980s to counter models of male autonomy, the reaction was more pronounced. An extensive 'backlash' took place in American politics and culture. Intent on restraining the female drive for power and self-sufficiency, this movement drew support from men in all social ranks, some women, and the media. Author Susan Faludi has argued that this retaliation was so strong that the women's movement was able to make only modest advances. She criticized reports that said American women had major gains by asking why it was that they still represented two-thirds of all poor adults and were twice as likely as men to earn less than $30,000 per year when they worked full-time.[15]

The American feminist revolt of the 1960s and 1970s was grounded in a revolt against the traditional family and its capacity for sexual violence and repression. As such it was a direct attack upon the veneration of male violence in general and the ideal of the breadwinner. The feminist vision of self-fulfillment outside the boundaries of marriage and the family in the workplace now came to resemble the one for men. Little concerned with any defense or even theory of the nation-state, the goal of this movement focused on escape from the family and success in the workplace. That is why a leading feminist thinker like Shulamith Firestone argued in 1970 that families as we know them should be abolished so that women could be as free as men to construct their identities through work and a career. Firestone called for, consequently, the diffusion of child-rearing responsibilities throughout society so that women would no longer have to carry a disproportionate share of the burden.[16] Faludi claims that feminism's quest was essentially an attempt to allow women to define themselves rather than be defined by men. But she says this agenda was undercut by the dominant politics and culture of the 1980s. The administration of Ronald Reagan, for instance, shut down the federal Office of Domestic Violence in 1981 only two years after it had been established. Additional restrictions were added to the process of getting an abortion. And conservatives who opposed female equality promoted studies like *The Divorce Revolution: The Unexpected Social and Economic Consequences for Women and Children in America*, by Lenore Weitzman, which warned women of the dire economic consequences that awaited them if they divorced. American audiences also flocked to theaters to see films like *Fatal Attraction* in which a single, career woman is killed when she threatens the marriage of a woman who has chosen to find gratification through a husband and children.[17]

Faludi argues that the resistance to feminism originated especially in the anxieties of fundamentalist male preachers, the media, and downwardly mobile, lower-middle-class white males. New Right preachers began the assault in the late 1970s when they saw declining membership in many of their rural congregations and a similar decrease in their ability to influence female followers. It was at this point that they began a concerted effort to blame the feminist movement for the 'dismantling of the traditional familial support system'. New Right leaders like Jerry Falwell and organizations like the Heritage Foundation called for a law that would require marriage and motherhood to be taught as proper careers for girls, and for repeal of all federal laws protecting battered wives from their husbands. In 1980 these Christian conservatives forced the Republican party to draft a platform opposed to the Equal Right Amendment for women, the first time in forty years that the party failed to endorse the measure.[18]

Lower-middle-class males were receptive to attacks on feminism because they had encountered uncertain economic circumstances in the 1980s. Confronted with declining openings in industrial and union jobs as the American economy deindustrialized, they suddenly realized that their ability to fill the traditional roles of fatherhood and breadwinner was problematic. Faludi cites surveys that indicate that American men have largely defined masculinity as the assumption of the role of 'good provider' for a family. This view inferred a dependent role for women and children. Young men in the 1980s were increasingly likely to find only lower paying jobs in the service sector of the American economy, however, that made it difficult for them to become 'good providers' as many of their fathers and older brothers. Pollster Lou Harris observed that the increasing economic polarization of American society and the relegation of many workers to low wage jobs led to an increase in the proportion of Americans who describe themselves as 'powerless'.[19]

Although Faludi is correct in asserting that there were widespread repercussions to feminism in the 1980s, however, she fails to make a distinction between the call for a return to traditional relationships between men and women and the more extreme desire for male independence that was central to much of the discourse surrounding Vietnam. Preacher Jerry Falwell and soldier John Rambo were not identical. Rambo was willing to abandon fatherhood and the family. The fact that the more prevalent form of backlash was encoded in a general call for a return to 'family values' suggests that the extreme of 'remasculinization' was rejected by even much of the New Right. The quintessential statement of this point was made by Vice President Dan Quayle in 1992, when he criticized a television program for suggesting that a single parent could raise a child better than the team of a man and a woman. Clearly family values were frequently a symbolic weapon in the effort to reaffirm male domination and the traditional role of provider. They could frustrate the drive for female independence and power. But two points have to be made. First, male dominance and female submission were not the only realities of family life. Evidence that women were entering the workforce and negotiating more equitable arrangements at home were found in studies as early as the 1950s.[20] And secondly, family values implied not only a moderation of the notion of female independence but of male independence as well. It rejected the male radicalism that had been articulated by some of the men who returned from Vietnam. In the celebration of family values both sexes were encouraged to return to notions of obligation to others and, by implication, to the idea of serving the collective interests of society and the nation. Men could not only be warriors; they also had to be fathers. Family values, for all its conservative dimensions, rejected the idea that males could remain violent and separate from women. And as Hillary Clinton's role suggested, such a symbol left room for a new compromise that stood in the way of a complete return to domesticity.

The movement to restore the family was grounded in an attempt to re-establish the saliency of motherhood and fatherhood as ideal roles for adults. This movement came not only at a time when the nation was filled with assertions of male and female independence but when economic change rendered the traditional division of work and domestic roles nearly unattainable. Women entered the workforce in record numbers not only to achieve careers but more frequently to help their families. Since the 1970s male breadwinners have been increasingly unable to support their families alone. Over the past twenty years men's average weekly earning (adjusted for inflation) declined 14.3 per cent. Increases in income fathers formerly took for granted are less certain. According to Robert Griswold, a thirty-year old man in 1949 would see his real earnings increase by 63 per cent by the time he turned forty, but the same man in 1973 would experience a 1 per cent decline in his real average earnings over the same ten year period. Median family income grew in the 1970s and 1980s mainly in households where women entered the workplace.[21] Without the work of wives, 60 per cent of the American population would have experienced a decline in real income between 1979 and 1986.[22] Certainly some men, besides the younger ones cited by Faludi, had difficulties assuming the traditional role of breadwinner, or resented the extent to which they were dependent upon their wives' income if they did marry. And many divorced fathers have tended to conclude that they are no longer important to their children and have stopped making payments to support them.[23] But dramatic economic change threatened to disrupt not so much the old notion of fatherhood, for that was in decline before the 1970s, but the idea of a 'new fatherhood'.

During the 1950s, with the rise of the middle class, autocratic notions of the breadwinner gave way to a new image of 'father' as more considerate of his spouse and children. Authoritarian commands were replaced by family discussions or reliance on outside counselors and experts. It was true that this version of fatherhood still held little room for an extensive female role in the workplace or male participation in housework, but it could be considered a step in that direction. Not all males in the 1950s were buying *Playboy*, as the popularity of television shows like *Father Knows Best* testified.[24] Even as Americans divorced more and feminists attacked the very premise of marriage, millions of Americans attempted to redefine the institution of marriage and make it work.

In the 1980s an attempt to continue the reconstruction of gender relations within marriage, outside the agenda of the New Right, radical feminism and extreme masculinity, was revived. This undertaking represented both a continuation of the ideal of a companionate marriage that emerged in the 1950s and recognition of the subordination of women in the past. Reports on numerous studies show that American fathers recognized that older attitudes toward women and their work were now obsolete. Witnesses testified in June 1991 before the House Select Committee on Children, Youth, and Families that fathers now found their working and parenting lives in sharp conflict, an indication that men were feeling the pull of greater domestic responsibilities. Other surveys indicated that about one-half of the fathers surveyed in Washington DC reduced their working hours to spend more time with their children and 23 per cent reported that they had passed up a promotion for the same reason. In 1990 one poll said that 39 per cent of fathers claimed they would quit their jobs if they could in order to spend more time with their children. *Time* magazine reported that 48 per cent of men between the ages of eighteen and twenty-four expressed an interest in staying home with their children. Another 74 per cent of the men said they would rather have a 'daddy track' job than a 'fast track job'.[25]

The rise of a new conception of fatherhood, more willing to share housework, child care and income responsibilities while expanding, is far from dominant. Sociologist Kathleen Gerson reports that models of masculinity in American culture are now simply more diverse than before. Some men cling to the traditional 'breadwinner' role which expects women to remain at home; males also continue to seek autonomy or what Gerson calls 'the ideal of the unfettered loner' with no meaningful relationships with women or children. But she also finds the new 'involved' male who rejects the view that masculinity is the opposite of womanhood and that men must dominate women. Studies of this involved group have suggested, moreover, that the pursuit of gender equality by men involves a rejection of the single-minded focus on careerism. These studies do acknowledge that these men have accepted child care tasks more easily than housework; but they also show that many men have moderated the attachment to work and career that marked the breadwinner ethic of the 1950s. This has come about both voluntarily and involuntarily. Some men have deliberately chosen to expend less energy at work for the sake of helping at home and sharing the task of earning income with women. Others have simply lost the ability to be a sole breadwinner because of deindustrialization and corporate layoffs. Thus Faludi's point that economic decline has led only to male backlash is doubtful, for there is another trend: a growing number of men have decided to become more like their mothers than their fathers, a decision that is clearly based in some cases on negative images of fathers and a rejection of their ways. When the rise of the women's movement is factored into the changing economic circumstances of men, and the inevitable reactions of sons against fathers, the choice for some males was to see if the whole thing could work.[26]

The complement to the movement to create a more malleable and cooperative fatherhood was a new attempt to create a version of motherhood that would allow for both work and parental opportunities. Clearly such a model could place an inordinate amount of responsibility upon women, but many appeared ready to give it a try. Economic realities and personal aspirations continued to propel women into this expanded ideal of mothering. By 1993 58 per cent of mothers in the United States worked. By the late 1980s many female organizations advocated a national child care policy over a simple quest for women's rights. As feminist reformers of the 1920s moderated their support for an Equal Rights Amendment in order to gain support for minimum wages and maximum hours to protect motherhood, the goals of female activists now became increasingly child centered. With an increase in the rate of divorce and the number of working women, child care now became an issue that stood at the heart of the attempt to reconcile motherhood and work. Even Betty Friedan, whose writing inspired the feminist revolt of the 1960s, now called upon women in the 1980s to address family concerns and the 'maternal call'.[27]

A determined effort to get greater federal support for child care was launched by the Alliance for Better Child Care. The group, under the leadership of Marian Wright Edelman, introduced legislation in Congress in 1987 because they did not share the conservative view that working women were a serious threat to the future of the traditional family. The alliance of 122 religious, educational, and business groups acknowledged the growing need and desire for female labor and argued that quality child care was critical for the children and for the parents. They hoped that the government would contribute money and higher standards to the child care industry in the country. In congressional hearings government leaders heard stories of injuries to children not properly cared for by unlicensed day care providers. Public opinion polls showed that there was division in the population over the idea of government support for child care, because many citizens still felt it was primarily a mother's responsibility. Still, a Gallup poll in May, 1988 showed that 52 per cent of likely voters in the fall presidential election would vote for a candidate who favored more day care services.[28]

Edelman, in particular, had long advocated government action on behalf of needy children and mothers as both a humane and patriotic gesture. Drawing upon her memories of communal sharing in a black congregation in South Carolina, and her involvement in the Civil Rights Movement of the 1960s, Edelman established the Children's Defense Fund. As a tireless activist she promoted her vision of a nation that granted more justice to young and female citizens who required greater health and educational opportunities. She attacked 'men in power' who opposed more government support for child care, and claimed they were insensitive to the needs of poor women who had to juggle work and family. And she continuously expressed her fear and concern for the future of the nation. For her, paid maternity leaves were crucial to 'America's future' and 'our national security'. Such supports, she argued, would deter the greatest threat she saw to America: a decline in family stability and the ideal of moral responsibility for others. She argued that the fate of 'our nation … is inextricably intertwined with its poor and nonwhite children as with its white and privileged ones'.[29]

The Republican administration of George Bush was reluctant to give Edelman and the alliance all that it wanted. The right wing of Bush's party defended traditional motherhood; but the movement to reconstruct gender relationships was able to force Bush to at least offer tax credits to help working parents pay for child care. Bush had already acknowledged in his 1990 State of the Union message that the government had to expand child care alternatives for working parents. In the end he signed a bill that provided only about 20 per cent of what the alliance originally sought; and much of that money would go to families of four making less than $30,000, a restriction that would not help most of the middle class. The power of the backlash was real but not unlimited.[30]

Family and nation

There was an implied attempt to defend the nation in the call to save motherhood and fatherhood. Like all cultural ideals and symbolic expressions, family values attempted both to reconcile discordant attitudes and contest opposing points of view. Although it was often portrayed simply as a conservative backlash, it also represented an effort to reduce the growing separation between the sexes and the revolt against marriage by both men and women. But it also had to mediate several versions of the family ideal it tried to save. Thus, while some of those who adhered to family values saw motherhood as submission, others were willing to strike a compromise between family and work. Both the conservative and liberal versions of family values, however, were concerned that the continued existence of the nation was contingent upon saving the family form. This was matter that did not trouble radical women or men in the decades after World War II; but it clearly concerned those who wanted to moderate the ideals of extreme individualism.

Gender roles were central to the construction of the idea of nationalism and patriotism since the nineteenth century. Usually the idea of the nation venerated symbols of strong masculinity, and for this reason nationalism frequently reached its strongest point of cultural appeal and attraction in periods of war. During these moments nations celebrated male warriors and masculine bonds. Unfortunately, those who were unable to meet the standards of virility were marginalized. Women were relegated to a service role in which they served strong men in the nation, and socialized children in the ways of patriotism and civic responsibility. In Germany in the 1930s an effort was made to restrain excessive female influence on young boys in order to protect their manlike qualities. In fact both fascist dictatorships in Germany and Italy sought to push women back into domestic and motherly roles that would serve the state. Fears of excessive female attention toward boys was expressed in the United States during World War II when so many males were away at war. In most versions of nationalism males have been charged with the responsibility for protecting not only the nation but the nation's females. It is for this reason that an enemy has frequently decided to dishonor a captive nation by a mass rape of female citizens.[31]

The link between manhood and nationalism, of course, did not mean that women had no role in sustaining and defending the nation. Women were envisioned not only as dependents within a nationalist sphere but also as servants of the nation itself. Fascist Italy called upon its female citizens to produce more children for the state economy, a policy that met wide resistance. In the United States during World War II females were encouraged to perform public duty, and help men, by toiling in war plants. Thus modern nations did find ways to define types of female citizenship. What was antithetical to the historic idea of nationalism was any position that argued for the separation of men and women and for the abandonment of their interdependency. Calls for equality and rights were not nearly as threatening to the project of nationhood as the idea that men and women simply did not need each other.[32] For that reason the American government felt that it could not mobilize its citizens during the war if it did not appeal to the ties that people had to family members. Simple calls of duty to the nation would not work. But when soldiers were told that they were protecting their families back home, or women were informed that their labor would hasten the return of husbands and fathers, patriotism flourished. In an intriguing essay historian Robert Westbrook has described how patriotism and the notion of political obligation was engendered during World War II by the celebration of what Franklin Roosevelt called the 'Four Freedoms'. It was difficult for the liberal state, as Westbrook argued, to evoke a sense of obligation if its ultimate role was to protect private and group interests not destroy them. But when the enemy was portrayed in posters as a threat to the interest of the American family, the perception of what the nation stood for was altered. Private and public interests were conflated. As Westbrook shows, when artist Norman Rockwell illustrated the idea of 'Freedom from Want' with a portrait of a large, extended family sitting down to a bountiful turkey dinner, he was able to clinch the case that the destiny of families was interconnected to the fate of the nation. Similarly, in the 1943 movie *Guadalcanal Diary*, a marine lying fatally wounded on the beach reaches in death for his helmet and photograph of his family.[33]

The public expression of the intimate link between the family, gender roles and the welfare of the nation was not only strong during wartime. The 'gendering of national imagery' inevitably depended upon the family trope because it sustained an impression of male dominance. Nations were known as motherlands or fatherlands and compared to families in terms of their unity and visions of reciprocity. But, as Anne McClintock has argued, these representations depended upon the social reality of female subordination within the family. Comparing nations to families inferred that relations of power between men and women within the nations were unequal, but we can supplement McClintock's point by suggesting that they also inferred a place and a voice for women in the national experiment.[34]

In both the decades before the war and the one that followed it specific viewpoints were voiced on female roles for the nation. Women's concerns were submerged during the Great Depression to public preoccupation with the unemployed male. Gains in the effort to stem female and child abuse were arrested, and a massive labor movement worried mostly about men and their position in the workplace. Working-class females were relegated to roles as auxiliaries during strikes. Liberal reforms won by labor from the New Deal state were based on the idea of the 'family wage', which assumed that a male breadwinner had to earn enough to be able to keep his spouse in a domestic role and earn enough to be a proper breadwinner. Elizabeth Faue argued that this concept could be seen in the way the New Deal treated relief recipients. The focus of state programs were relief projects for unemployed men. Almost no attempt was made to meet the needs of women workers. Ultimately both the state and the new unions that came into power favored masculine interests and were insensitive, in Faue's view, to 'reproductive labor and the importance of women's work to a family economy'. In her case study of Minneapolis, unions did not get around to proclaiming that women could stand on an equal footing with men until women were suddenly numerous in war plants and, thus, vital to unionization drives. It was at this time that union leaders used the language of patriotism and equality in an effort to attract female support and membership.[35]

In the decade after World War II patriotic appeals were made again to women. This time they were expected to be mothers who held traditional families together as part of a larger effort to retain a presumed sense of American moral superiority and inner unity in the face of two challenges to the nation. From inside the nation came a rising tide of materialism and youth rebellion that threatened existing structures of authority. From outside the nation came the threat of world communism. Thus in the 1950s Americans reversed the rising divorce rates of earlier decades. Men and women who had experienced the disruptions of depression and war saw the family not as a site of repression but as a place where could be found fulfillment and stability. The culture of the 1950s was more 'family-centered' than at any other time in this century.[36]

In the 1970s and 1980s a new combination of working-class families and conservatives mounted a strong challenge to the idea that the nation-state could abandon its traditional role of protecting families. In the eyes of these groups it was liberals, not Communists, who sought to increase opportunities for independence on the part of women and racial minorities, and who were seen as threatening and destructive of national values. In working-class neighborhoods men and women sought to protect their traditional lifestyles and housing values by mounting an effort to block school integration, busing, and eventually womens' right to abortion. Unlike the Great Depression the threat here was cultural as well as economic, and they did not hesitate to tie the defense of their familial world to a defense of the nation. Thus, in a famous photograph of the 1970s, anti busing protestors from the working-class wards of Boston attacked a black man during a demonstration with the staff of a large American flag and sang patriotic songs like 'America the beautiful'.[37] In part this is why many working-class sons made Vietnam a 'working-class war'; they saw military service and patriotism as a natural extension of the their roles as men fulfilled through work – in this case in the military – and through protecting family and nation.[38]

The 'New Christian Right' began to mount their defense of the nation by the late 1970s. Rural Protestants and the Catholic working-class did not always overcome their distrust of each other, but they frequently shared the desire to protect the nation by protecting traditional gender roles. This meant they were unequivocal in their support for patriotic rhetoric, a strong military, the defeat of the ERA, and pro-life campaigns. The abortion issue especially evoked an emotional defense of motherhood as the primary means of realizing female identity. For both Protestants and Catholics, America as a society was great when it obeyed the law of God and the call of motherhood and fatherhood. They now believed that as the ideal of the traditional family declined so did the power of the nation.[39]

However the inability of conservatives to sustain their attack on Hillary Clinton after the Republican convention in 1992 demonstrated that the American political culture was now truly multivocal. Family values and marriage were symbols that could no longer be defined in one way, but they still remained connected to a larger concern for the survival of the national social fabric in the present and in the future. Their potential to become simply symbols of repression was muted by determined attempts to make them symbols of cooperation. To the extent that they restrained impulses toward separateness and male violence, they promised to serve as a basis for rethinking just who were the real Americans.[40]

Notes

1. R. Nelson, *The Hillary Factor* (Gallen, New York: 1993), p. 32.
2. J. Basinger, *The World War II Combat Film: A History of a Genre* (Columbia University Press, New York: 1986), pp. 163–70.
3. D. Wattenburg, 'The Lady Macbeth of Little Rock', *The American Spectator* 25 (1992), pp. 25–32.
4. *New York Times*, 24 September 1992, pp. 1, 23; ibid., 28 November 1992, p. 19.
5. S. Jeffords, *The Remasculinization of America: Gender and the Vietnam War* (Indiana University Press, Bloomington, Ind.: 1989), pp. 57, 168–9.

6. Ibid., pp. 5, 127–35.
7. Ibid., pp. 127–35.
8. J. Wheeler, *Touched By Fire* (Franklin-Watts, New York: 1989), pp. 140–4; Jeffords, *The Remasculinization of America*, pp. 73, 116.
9. J. Hellman, 'Vietnam and the Hollywood genre film: inversions of American mythology in *The Deer Hunter* and *Apocalypse Now*', in M. Anderegg (ed.), *Inventing Vietnam: The War in Film and Television* (Temple University Press, Philadelphia: 1991), pp. 56–80.
10. Ibid., pp. 65–8.
11. R. Slotkin, *Gunfighter Nation: The Myth of the Frontier in Twentieth Century America* (Harper Perennial, New York: 1992), pp. 10–13.
12. Ibid., pp. 627–55.
13. B. Ehrenreich, *The Hearts of Men: American Dreams and the Flight from Commitment* (Anchor-Doubleday, Garden City, NY: 1983).
14. Ibid., p. 13.
15. S. Faludi, *Backlash: The Undeclared War Against American Women* (Doubleday, New York: 1991), p. ix.
16. S. Firestone, *The Dialectic of Sex: The Case for a Feminist Revolution* (William Morrow, New York: 1970). The point that feminism had 'no theory of the state' is made by C. A. MacKinnon, *Toward a Feminist Theory of the State* (Harvard University Press, Cambridge, Mass.: 1989), pp. 157– 60. MacKinnon does say that feminism had a theory of power in which society and the liberal state were seen as sites of male domination. She attempts in her work to develop a theory that compels a state to go to special lengths on behalf of women and feels that male domination is so complete that to simply pass laws that will protect all citizens equally, including women, will be insufficient to help feminism. If Benedict Anderson's view that the basis of national loyalty has largely been grounded in a perception that the state is an entity that is fair and above the control of any one interest or group, then we might infer that feminism's disinterest in the state was grounded in its perception that it was unable to render justice to females. See B. Anderson, *Imagined Communities: Reflections on the Origins and Spread of Nationalism* (Verso, London: 1983), pp. 141–54.
17. Faludi, *Backlash*, p. xix.
18. Ibid., pp. 235–6.
19. Ibid.; L. Harris, *Inside America* (Vintage, New York: 1987), pp. 33–7; 129–32.
20. M. Komarovsky, *Blue-Collar Marriage* (Random House, New York: 1962).
21. R. L. Griswold, *Fatherhood in America: A History* (Basic Books, New York: 1993), pp. 222–3.
22. S. Coontz, *The Way We Never Were: American Families and the Nostalgia Trap* (Basic Books, New York: 1992), p. 260.
23. Griswold, *Fatherhood in America*, pp. 220–4.
24. Ibid., pp. 183–7.
25. Ibid., pp. 223–7.
26. See K. Gerson, *No Man's Land: Men's Changing Commitments to Family and Work* (Basic Books, New York: 1993), pp. 109–30; 141–50; A. Hochschild, *The Second Shift* (Avon Books, New York: 1989), pp. 216–38.
27. M. F. Berry, *The Politics of Parenthood: Child Care, Women's Rights, and the*

Myth of the Good Mother (Viking, New York: 1993), p. 171; Faludi, *Backlash*, p. 318.

28. Berry, *The Politics of Parenthood*, pp. 180–1.
29. M. W. Edelman, *The Measure of Our Success: A Letter to My Children and Yours* (HarperPerennial, New York: 1993), pp. 19, 43, 54–55; see also N. Atkins, 'Marian Wright Edelman: on the front lines of the battle to save America's children', *Rolling Stone*, 10 December 1992, pp. 126–37. Atkins called Edelman, 'America's Mom'.
30. Berry, *The Politics of Parenthood*, pp. 180–92.
31. G. Mosse, *Confronting the Nation: Jewish and Christian Nationalism* (Brandeis University Press, Hanover NH: 1981), pp. 15, 46, 77, 140–2.
32. V. De Grazia, *How Fascism Ruled Women: Italy, 1922–1945* (University of California Press, Berkeley: 1992), pp. 5, 14; V. Sapiro, 'Engendering cultural differences', in C. Young (ed.), *The Rising Tide of Cultural Pluralism: Concepts and Reality* (University of Wisconsin Press, Madison: 1993), pp. 36–52.
33. R. Westbrook, 'Fighting for the American family: private interests and political obligations in World War II', in R. W. Fox and T. J. J. Lears (eds), *The Power of Culture: Critical Essays in American History* (University of Chicago Press, Chicago: 1993), pp. 195–221.
34. A. McClintock, 'Family feuds: gender, nationalism, and the family', *Feminist Review* no. 44 (1993), pp. 61–80.
35. E. Faue, *Community of Suffering and Struggle: Women, Men, and the Labor Movement in Minneapolis, 1915–1945* (University of North Carolina Press, Chapel Hill: 1991), pp. 153–83.
36. Coontz, *The Way We Never Were*, pp. 37–38; E. Tyler May, 'Cold War – warm hearth: politics and the family in postwar America', in S. Fraser and G. Gerstle (eds), *The Rise and Fall of the New Deal Order, 1930–1980* (Princeton University Press, Princeton, NJ: 1989), pp. 153–80.
37. R. Formisano, *Boston Against Busing: Race, Class, and Ethnicity in the 1960s* and 1970s (University of North Carolina Press, Chapel Hill: 1991), pp. 15–51.
38. C. G. Appy, *Working-Class War: American Combat Soldiers and Vietnam* (University of North Carolina Press, Chapel Hill: 1993), p. 53.
39. S. Bruce, *The Rise and Fall of the New Christian Right: Conservative Protestant Politics in America, 1978–1988* (Oxford University Press, Oxford: 1988), pp. 81–3.
40. A. Apadurai, 'Patriotism and its future', *Public Culture* 5 (1993), pp. 411–14, 421, suggests that we are now in a postnational period where the nation–state has become obsolete and other formations for allegiance and identity have taken its place.

9

Women and the Political Sphere: The Contemporary Debate in the United States

Raffaella Baritono

The object of this essay is to analyse the American debate about the relationship between women and the political sphere. This is a debate which, especially in recent years, is raising fundamental issues such as women's secular exclusion from the political sphere and the very question of legitimacy and of changing processes in western democracies.

The relevance of the meditations and theoretical proposals offered by women philosophers and political scientists is witnessed, not only by the growing weight of courses in women's studies within academic curricula, but also by the visibility of a research that is finding space in mainstream academic journals such as *The Annals of the American Academy of Political and Social Sciences*, *The American Political Science Review*, and *Political Theory*. Until recently these had given scarce or no attention to the subject. In 1991 *The Annals* devoted a special issue, edited by Janet K. Boles, to the perspectives of American feminism that contained essays by several well-known scholars, from Janet Boles herself to Virginia Shapiro, Jean B. Elshtain and Carol Mueller.[1]

If the scientific contribution of women is beginning to go beyond the limits of historical reviews such as *Signs*, *Feminist Studies* and *Women and Politics*, reception of results peculiar to women's research in the fields of both theory and political processes is still very sparse. Barbara Nelson has, for instance, pointed out how in handbooks still in use in the late 1980s only one, Lipsitz's, devotes some attention to the question of women's suffrage, and none of them evidences the fundamental role played by allowing women the right to vote within the ambit of a new concept of the meaning of politics.

The same lack of attention towards women, as well as Afro-Americans, is found also in the analyses of those who have reflected on the methodological and epistemological criteria of political science, such as David Ricci, Raymond Seidelman and Edward J. Harpham.[2] Also, while Seidelman's and Harpham's work is, as Nelson points out, 'more silent than wilfully blind to the central question of where women belong in politics and its study', Ricci's starts from an assumption that women philosophers and political scientists have proved to be conceptually wrong: that is, that the Western humanistic tradition has been both 'womanistic' and 'manistic' at the same time, thus backing a universalistic interpretation which is, as Joan Kelly has objected, substantially andro-centric.[3]

On the other hand, the literature that, especially in the last ten years, feminist scholars and theorists have produced on the relationship between women and the political sphere has not only revealed theoretical foundations for the exclusion of women from politics but has also disclosed, through a debunking of the concepts that are at the basis of democratic societies, the crucial problems that must be solved in order to overcome the present crisis of legitimacy.

It will not be possible to discuss all the contributions that have been made in recent years. The subject will therefore be dealt with in a limited fashion with regard to the complexity and richness of the reflections, theories and contributions that women have made. Two different, although interrelated aspects will be examined: on one hand, a re-reading of the classical texts of political thought by some women political philosophers; on the other, the need to re-think politics as a whole, both as a process and as a place where decisions are produced, concerning both men and women, in today's society. As to this last point, two scholars, Iris Marion Young and Seyla Benhabib, will be focused upon, since their analyses appear to be meaningful in a debate concerning contemporary American society.

II

Contradictions existing in the theory of the social contract were revealed at the time of the American and French revolutions. In Europe, Olympe de Gouges and Mary Wollstonecraft, respectively the authors of *La Declaration des droits de la femme et de la citoyenne* (1791) and the *Vindication of the Rights of Women* (1792), both asserted the rights of equality and demanded citizenship to be extended to women, even though, at the same time, the universalism of the French Declaration of 1789 was criticized.[4]

In the United States the question of including women in the political sphere had been posed very clearly in 1776 by Abigail Adams, the wife of the future president John Adams. Abigail, in her letters to her husband, pleaded the cause of citizenship for women, appealing to the same reasons that were driving the American colonists to separate from their English mother country and to declare their independence.[5]

John Adams' negative answer was extremely indicative, not only of the reasons given for the refusal of citizenship to women, but also of the barriers that were already being set up against extension of the newly born American democracy. Women were excluded from the political sphere because they were put on the same level as people who, for several reasons, needed wardship: children, restless youths, native Americans and black slaves.[6]

This was a list that referred to Aristotle's typologies which formed the basis of the distinction between the political sphere, the place of the adult free man, and the sphere of the home, the place of women, slaves and adolescents; but it was also indicative of the process of inclusion/exclusion on which American democracy was based; that is to say of the general choice between discrimination and homologation which Western culture posed for all misfits from the Enlightenment onwards, as Anna Rossi-Doria, among others, has pointed out. However, to women who are neither a minority nor outcasts this choice was presented in a special way.[7]

Tension between the claim for universal rights and defence of the specific differences of women permeated the theoretical and political course of the suffragist movement. It had to face the contradiction underlying, on the one hand, the request for access to the public sphere and complaint against oppression in the private sphere and, on the other, acknowledgement of maternity as a collective value that had to be transferred from the domestic to the social and political environment.[8]

In contemporary debate the works of Carole Pateman, Susan Okin, Arlene Saxonhouse, Jean Bethke Elshtain and Christine Di Stefano have analysed and pointed out the contradictions existing in both political theory and in the way in which the dichotomy between the public and the private sphere has been taking shape.[9]

In one of her first studies on the relationship between women and political theory Susan Moller Okin examined the arguments of Plato, Aristotle, Rousseau and John Stuart Mill about the social and political role of woman. She pointed out that two different interrelated themes emerged from this analysis. On one hand was the conception of the family as a natural and necessary institution in which the woman's role was defined on the basis of her biological difference, her reproductive capacity and her child-rearing function;[10] hence the ascription to women of a moral code and a conception of rights fundamentally different from the ones ascribed to men. On the other hand, Okin noted that the biological difference redefining the sexual diversification of roles within the family underlay the limited and limiting role assigned to women, corresponding to what was thought to be 'their real nature'. Women were given a role that was separate and often opposed to that of men; a hypostasized role within a concept of nature blocked in the reproductive and sexual function. Unlike man, woman was not considered as a subject who, apart from the reproductive function, could interact with other social and environmental factors. Consequently, women's nature could be considered as dependent on the will of a specific social and economic structure. The question that political theory has set itself throughout the centuries has, according to Okin, always been about the function that women should carry out and never about what a woman was or about her potential for action.

Complaint against the public–private dichotomy, and the confinement of woman to the latter on the basis of an inferred biological difference, is evident also in Arlene Saxonhouse's analysis of the role of women in the history of political thought, from ancient Greece to Machiavelli, and in the work of Jean Bethke Elshtain, and Carole Pateman. In *The Disorder of Women: Democracy, Feminism and Political Theory* (1989), Pateman maintains that feminist theory is strictly linked to questions of democracy and citizenship, to the concept of power and legitimacy. She further points out how these concepts take completely different meanings from those of orthodox political theory, because feminist theory bases its analysis on a problem removed from modern political reflection: that is, the problem of patriarchal power. The idea of patriarchal power has, for the American scholar, a double meaning: on the one hand, it points to the father's power over his son; on the other, to the husband's over his wife. The hierarchical father/son relationship comes to be replaced by a pact among 'brothers' that excludes women from the public realm and subjects them to the will of men within the family. The separation of civil society from the family sphere is above all a division between the reason of men and the bodies of women.[11]

One of the recurring themes in the several essays that make up Pateman's book is this division between what is public and what is private, represented by women, women's bodies, womanhood. According to Pateman, the patriarchal construction of the male/female difference in social contract theory makes woman a subject lacking the necessary abilities for political life. Unlike men, who are considered as rational beings capable of sublimating passions and of developing the sense of justice that is peculiar to an abstract moral and juridical order, women can not transcend their body and sexual passions and are therefore incapable of developing any moral order. For social contract theorists women enter civil society as subjects of a private sphere, separated as such from the public world of freedom, equality, rights, contract, interests and citizenship. This does not mean that women have been entirely separated from the political sphere, but their inclusion has taken place in a different way; as subjects that – owing to their sexual being – could not enjoy the same political status as men. Hence the paradoxes, the dilemmas and the contradictions that the acquisition of political citizenship has involved for women. Hence, however, also the paradox of democratic theories which, never facing the patriarchal implications, solve the question of citizenship on the one hand by homologation to the masculine model and, on the other, disregard the requests of women to make the qualities and duties that are specific to them, or that they have traditionally been assigned (motherhood, child-rearing, assistance), an integral part of citizenship. Adriana Cavarero has phrased the problem as follows:

> In political doctrine this means that men, neutral individuals at first, then citizens, just because of their universal/neutral acceptation potentially include also women, so that when women decide to take hold of

their rights and their citizenship the doctrine can but enact this including/homologating power already owned by the male subject. Modern right has, in fact, finally included women as equal to men, or as if women, *in spite of the female sexual difference*, were men.[12]

The process of inclusion of women in the political sphere and re-conceptualization of the basic categories of a liberal democracy, has been and still is more controversial. There are, among American women scholars, profound differences on this matter which recall divisions within the American feminist movement which, in their turn, can be traced back to the problematic relationship with liberalism, Marxism, Lacanian psychoanalytical theories and post-structuralism. The question over which these fractures have occurred concerns above all overcoming the public/private dichotomy, motherhood and values connected with the family in general, the question of difference/s (gender, class, religion, etc.).

There is general agreement about the mystification of liberal universalism that has produced a sort of 'unequal equality', and in claims that the making of the liberal democratic state has taken place on the basis of a sexual difference, socially and historically established, which has seen the survival of a patriarchal structure of subordination of women (in the private sphere) and of exclusion (in the public one). The question of how to reconstruct the relationship of women with the political sphere, starting from the acknowledgement of difference, is seen as more controversial. If some scholars start from Carol Gilligan's[13] and Adrienne Rich's[14] works, and propose a reconceptualization of the public/private relationship founded on the 'ethics of caring', that is to say on a moral approach based on the meaning of bonds deriving responsibilities, others are extremely critical of a definition of difference that could possibly wrap women back in the family sphere. Still others, resorting to Lacan's psychoanalytical critics and to Luce Irigaray, believe that the heart of the matter is not so much the building of a concept of female difference but rather the 'deconstruction' of the gender structure lying inside political and philosophical discourse.[15]

Jean Bethke Elshtain, examining the masculine/feminine question in political theory, takes caring as a differentiating element of the feminine, and has suggested overcoming the public/private dichotomy through a reassertion of the importance of family bonds in child-rearing as a foundation for social development. Elshtain starts from the assumption that the individual cannot be considered apart from his/her family bonds, considered not so much as the outcome of a long socio-historical experience but rather as a trans-historical datum present at all times and all over the world.[16] This is an acknowledgement of the importance of the family and of what Sara Ruddick has defined as 'maternal thinking', leading not so much to the inclusion of one sphere within the other but to a reconstruction of social structures on the basis of equal dignity and importance in the private as well as in the social sphere. Elshtain suggests the legitimating of the family and private sphere as a way of setting up an 'ethical polity', in which 'the active citizen would be one who had affirmed as part of what it meant to be fully human, a devotion to public, moral responsibilities and ends'.[17]

Elshtain's position has been strongly attacked by Mary G. Dietz, who considers the assertion of family values to have been taken as an attempt at holding back, in the 1980s, the defence of the family led by the New Right. Dietz contests the one-dimensional characterization of woman emerging from Elshtain's analysis and believes that, as it has been defined, 'ethical polity only corroborates and strengthens the separation between the public and the private sphere'.[18]

The difference between Elshtain's and Dietz's positions can be measured also by the different interpretations that the two scholars give of Sophocles' Antigone. If, for the former, the figure of the Greek heroine is actually the maternal one, the bearer of family values opposed to rationality and politics, for the latter the clash between Antigone and Creon is the clash between two 'political' positions: that of Creon, representing the will of the State, and Antigone's, expressing the values of civil society.[19] As Linda Zerilli has pointed out, on one hand Antigone is seen as a mother, on the other she rebels as a citizen.[20]

What most matters for Mary Dietz is that in Elshtain's analysis there is no trace of a theoretical connection linking motherly to democratic virtues. Being a mother, or better still being a good mother, does not necessarily mean being a good citizen and the language of change will not have to be the one-dimensional one of the identity of potential mothers, but that of freedom, equality, justice and citizenship.

Between Elshtain's position and Dietz's there are those of scholars such as Nancy Holmstrom, Christine Sypnowich and, at least in a first phase, Catherine MacKinnon, who have deemed it right to use Marxist anthropological analysis.[21] There are also scholars who have experienced the fascination of psychoanalysis and of post-structuralism. Of these, only Linda Zerilli's analysis of political language can be cited, along with Nancy Hirschmann's concept of political obligation, Diane Coole's concept of freedom and Cristina Di Stefano's study of the male figure.[22] According to them, psychoanalytical object relations theory helps in understanding how the concepts of political obligation, freedom, and the very category of the masculine have been produced and defined within a process of separation/alterity of the male/female; in particular as a result of the acquisition of freedom by the male individual through a separation from his mother.[23]

This kind of approach is particularly intriguing in Christine Di Stefano's analysis of the way in which the notion of masculine is presented in modern eurocentric political theory. Di Stefano examines, the views of Thomas Hobbes, Karl Marx and John Stuart Mill in analysing the theoretical course of the concept of male as seen in opposition to the 'other' female. In the construction of masculinity or of the male (apart from its variations), the m/other figure, as seen in its symbolical essence, plays a fundamental role in the acquisition of a male identity. She states that 'She has a "privileged" position vis-à-vis modern masculine gender identity, as the "other" against which he derives the substance and location of his counter identity.'[24]

The feminist re-reading of male political texts is, for Di Stefano, not only a way of knowing what has been and still is the dominating culture but also an attempt at 'discovering' the voices of other individuals who are different in sex, race, religion, ethnicity, and are too often oppressed or confined to silence. One sentence is particularly meaningful, when she writes that 'political theory, as we are coming to appreciate, is suffused with the muffled voices of such "others"'.[25]

The concept of difference worked out by feminist theory should, accordingly, also serve this purpose: not to let the voices of 'others' be oppressed or attributed to a neutral and abstract individuality in political theory as well as in democratic political practice. This, however, as many feminist theorists have often pointed out, challenges both theory and the democratic political model, because, as Cavarero rightly notices, 'the practical and theoretical horizon of the sexual difference is not a simple negotiation of shares, but a critical key which allows reflection ... the abstractive boulder lying at the basis of the democratic model'.[26]

If, however, feminist theorists have evidenced the specificity of gender difference, this does not mean (as Afro-American women have often pointed out since they have lived and are still living in a double exclusion, as women and as blacks) that it must be overrated in comparison to other differences, of class, ethnic or racial. Eventually it should be considered as complementary and interacting. The recognition of differences in American society raises a number of questions and causes a number of conflicts in all fields of social and political life, concerning the possibility and the capability of founding a multi-ethnic and multicultural society.

Anne Phillips, in an article published in a special issue of *Political Studies* (1992) about the future of democracy, has wondered whether the active involvement of women in decision-making processes and the acknowledgement of gender difference meant an attack on liberal democratic principles or if, on the contrary, they are but a step towards the widening of spaces for participation within liberal democracies.[27] The claim to political legitimacy for gender difference leads to the similar claim for political acknowledgement of all other differences. This has led to requests for new ways of political legitimation and a widening of participation in democracy. However, at the same time, these requests pose a very strong question about the ways of according voice and political access to differences without falling into the chasm of political fragmentation and disintegration. This is, for example, the sense of the worries voiced by scholars, albeit liberal, like Arthur Schlesinger Jr. in *The Disuniting of America* (1992) and Charles Taylor in *Multiculturalism and the Politics of Recognition* (1992). The problem that political theory must face is, therefore, in being able to put forward a political model of social relation that can take in and give voice to different social groups, as well as understanding whether or not this model can be compatible with the upholding of principles peculiar to a liberal democracy. This has become the crucial point of the debate among American women philosophers and political scientists, which also accounts for the change in quality that has taken place.

III

Recognition of the importance of groups and differences is not new in history or in American political science. According to Sheldon Wolin, social, gender, class, ethnic or racial differences have disappeared or been reduced to the status of interests and as such have been connected, in praxis as well as in theory, to the existing political-constitutional system.[28] This question can not be dealt with specifically here. It should however be borne in mind that, above all as concerns social scientists at the beginning of the century, especially Arthur Bentley and Mary Parker Follett, acceptance of the reality of social groups and associations, far from being a model of hypostasization of interests and groups, was instead the datum on which a political model of democracy could be founded. This was based on criticism of the atomistic individual in favor of the search for a 'new individualism', an individualism deriving from the social processes of interaction.[29]

The case of theories based on 'interest-group pluralism', which have dominated the American political scene at least up to the 1980s, is different. They have in fact shown their inadequacy in representing the plurality of interests present in society and have favoured a sort of privileged access to the strongest interest groups, especially from an economic point of view.[30]

In the debate among American feminists about the possibility of advancing a solution to the crisis of contemporary society, starting from the recognition of difference, at least two positions must be singled out. First, the position of women scholars like Susan Moller Okin and Mary Dietz, who seek a sort of reconciliation with liberal democratic theories. Second, there are women scholars such as Iris Marion Young, Anne Phillips, Martha Minow, Elizabeth Spelman, who maintain the need for a political and institutional acknowledgement of difference. Between these two poles is Seyla Benhabib's analysis aimed at finding a possible point of mediation between respect for the liberal democratic principles of protection of the individual and the right of differences to have access to a substantive democracy.[31]

The analyses move within a scheme of reference of which the fundamental lines have been drawn by John Rawls' contractualism and by the communitarian theories of Alasdair McIntyre, Michael Sandel and Michael Walzer.

Susan Okin believes that Rawls' theory of justice can somehow potentially be made use of from a feminist point of view. Rawls believes family bonds to be important for the moral education of children, but he does not consider them to be subjected to those principles of justice that are vital to society. On the other hand, in his theory the natural state is translated into what he describes as an 'original position', that is to say a sort of zero setting process of particular contingencies necessary to reach an agreement between the parts on general principles of justice.[32]

As, according to Okin's analysis, Rawls does not mention gender condition among the conditions that individuals must ignore ('the veil of ignorance'), then it is possible to foreshadow, at least potentially, really genderless social relations and institutions.[33] Okin's attempt is thus to overcome the distinction between the ethics of justice that would fulfil the criteria of rationality, and to overcome the particular without failing to respect individualities and differences.[34]

A completely opposite position is the one maintained by Iris Marion Young. She does not aim to find a point of mediation between liberal universalism and the acknowledgement of differences, but to foreshadow the ways in which a process of legitimation and representation of differences (of race, class, religion, etc.) will start.

At the base of her analysis is recognition on the one hand of the importance of subjectivity and of political experiences in the feminist movement, and on the other of the influence of Marxist methodology and post-modern and post-structuralist theories. Hers is, above all, a reflection on the oppression and subordination of groups and minorities, the roots of which go back, both to the proliferation of groups and opposition movements born in the 1960s and 1970s, and to the fact that discussions on gender have given rise to the need to take into account, also among women, of all the other differences (not only in class or race, but in culture, etc.). Acknowledgement of the reality of groups and difference does not have, in Young's analysis, any reference to the theory of 'interest-group pluralism', towards which she is rather critical.[35] On the other hand, if she is obviously critical of liberal individualism, she is also critical of communitarian theories, which conceive of the individual only within a system of interaction with the community in which he/she lives.[36] For Young this process of interaction between individuals is based on a logic of identity among subjects belonging to the community itself.[37] In her analysis the only way to bring about both full access of minorities and recognition of differences is to redefine the processes of political representation. For Young, a truly participatory democracy must foresee institutional mechanisms of representation for social groups: from the activation of instruments favouring self-organization to a veto procedure for social groups over policies in which they have a specific interest.[38] Not all groups will have admittance to the mechanism of representation; these will be granted only to socially, culturally or economically disadvantaged groups, to oppressed groups or groups representing 'major identities'. Iris Young insists on the mobile and flexible quality of groups, and on the fact that what characterizes them is not so much their aggregation of interests or ideologies as their shared values, points of view and cultural affinities. Her views are controversial.

Young's ideas of a multicultural society, her ideal of urban life as an alternative to the concept of community, allowing space for confrontation and interaction between groups without aiming at assimilation or flattening of differences, are stimulating but risk being seen as utopian. It is difficult to understand what prescribing rules could acknowledge differences without running the risk of fragmentation and social separation on one hand, and a social and institutional hypostasization of groups on the other.[39]

The attempt to reconcile what is left of universalistic individualism after the attacks delivered by communitarians and by feminism and post-modernism, is at the core of Seyla Benhabib's work.[40] In *Situating the Self* she analyses in detail three general themes that have emerged from the rethinking of Enlightenment universalism: skepticism towards a 'legislating reason'; rejection of an abstract, nostalgic ideal of the autonomous male ego of the universalistic tradition; and finally the demystification of this universalistic tradition and of its ability to deal with the multiplicity and complexity of contexts and situations in social life. If Benhabib believes these three crucial issues to be legitimate she is at least convinced that there is still space for a 'post-Enlightenment' defence of universalism: a non-legislative universalism, however, therefore a bearer of abstract normative requests; but also an interactive one, aware of gender differences and sensitive to the diversity of situations and conditions.

Benhabib aims therefore at a softening of the boundaries between universalistic theories and feminist, communitarian and post-modern positions. Hence her reflection on the fundamental concepts of universalistic theory (the abstract concept of reason, the idea of a subjectivity not linked to the body) and the re-reading of Hannah Arendt and her concept of 'public space'. Hence also the analysis of communitarian theories, rejection of an integrative conception of community and recognition that the public sphere, after 'ignoring' women, cannot simply make up for this mistake by including them because the exclusion of women was not an omission but an epistemological negation.

For Benhabib it is a matter of reformulating universalistic principles according to a procedural interactive criterion, of working at the construction of ethics according to which the scope of moral conversation should not necessarily be the attainment of consent or unanimity. It involves understanding the concept of 'general interest' more as an ideal of regulation than as the object of substantial consent. The possibility of taking collective decisions through the activation of procedural mechanisms, open and accessible to everybody, becomes fundamental. Hence a much more open and rich interpretation of public space: 'I plead for a radically procedural model of the public sphere, neither the scope nor the agenda of which can be limited a priori, and whose lines can be redrawn by the participants in the conversation.'[41]

Benhabib's theoretical proposal is therefore defined as participatory democracy of a procedural type, adapting the liberal ideal of respect for individual and constitutional rights to the need to open access to decisional mechanisms and to the different clashing voices in the social context without favouring the rise or strengthening of 'tribalism';[42] a procedural democracy, open, tolerant, and respectful of he and she individuals and of differences.

The idea of a democracy based on procedural rules, on flexible processes of interaction between politics and society, made of fluid and dynamic social aggregations, is not completely unknown in the American political tradition. This was the spirit of Arthur Bentley's and Mary Parker Follett's work, but it was also the spirit of the debate on pluralism in the early years of this century. Raymond Seidelman has rightly noticed that, according to Bentley, for example, the group was neither refined in terms of structures, nor of functions, nor of common interests, but as activities, as 'mental construct',[43] within a frame of reference where the basic datum was the governing 'process' regarding both society and political institutions.

A passage by Mary Parker Follett may be quoted. She was a scholar whose work was, in her day, appreciated by such intellectuals as Herbert Croly, Roscoe Pound, Louis Brandeis, Harold Laski etc., but who has been almost entirely ignored by later scholars; so much so that her reputation is more based on her studies in administration and management than on her theoretical writing. She stated in 1918 in *The New State: Group Organization, the Solution of Popular Government*:

> Thus group organization releases us from the domination of mere numbers. Thus democracy transcends time and space, it can never be understood except as a spiritual force ... The group organization movement means the substitution of intention for accident, of organized purpose for scattered desire. It rests on the solid assumption that this is a man-made not a machine-made world, that men and women are capable of constructing their own life, and that not upon socialism

> or any rule or any order or any plan or any utopia can we rest our hearts, but only on the force of a united and creative citizenship.[44]

A reading of American progressive political theorists, who have been ignored by Rawls, McIntyre, Young and Benhabib, probably because they were too preoccupied with 'interest group pluralism', would open interesting speculations about the possible future development of the American political system.

Notes

1. J. K. Boles (ed.), 'American feminism: new issues for a mature movement', *The Annals of the American Academy of Political and Social Sciences* 515 (1991). See also V. Sapiro, *The Political Integration of Women: Roles, Socialization, and Politics* (University of Illinois Press, Chicago: 1983), p. 3; B. J. Nelson, 'Women and knowledge in political science: texts, histories, and epistemologies', *Women and Politics* 9, 2 (1989), pp. 1–25.
2. Nelson, 'Women and knowledge', pp. 11–12; D. Ricci, *The Tragedy of Political Science: Politics, Scholarship, and Democracy* (Yale University Press, New Haven: 1984); R. J. Seidelmann and E. J. Harpham, *Disenchanted Realists: Political Science and the American Crisis 1884–1984* (SUNY Press, Albany, NY: 1985).
3. Nelson, 'Women and knowledge', p. 16; J. Kelly, 'Did women have a Renaissance?', in J. Kelly (ed.), *Women History and Theory* (University of Chicago Press, Chicago, Ill.: 1984), pp. 19–50.
4. See A. Groppi, 'Le radici di un problema', in G. Bonacchi and A. Groppi (eds), *Il dilemma della cittadinanza* (Laterza, Rome and Bari: 1993), pp. 4–5; U. Gerhard, 'Sulla libertà, uguaglianza e dignità delle donne: il "differente" diritto di Olympe de Gouges', ibid., pp. 37–58.
5. Abigail Adams to John Adams, 31 March 1776 in L. H. Butterfield, W. D. Garrett, and M. E. Sprague (eds), *The Adams Papers, Series II, Adams Family Correspondence*, I, December 1761– May 1776 (Harvard University Press, Cambridge, Mass.: 1963), p. 370, cited in A. Rossi-Doria (ed.), *La libertà delle donne: Voci della tradizione politica suffragista* (Rosenberg & Sellier, Turin: 1990), p. 47. See also Sapiro, *The Political Integration of Women*, pp. 15–16.
6. John Adams to Abigail Adams, 14 April 1776 in Butterfield, Garrett, and Sprague (eds), *The Adams Papers*, p. 382, cited in Rossi-Doria (ed.), *La libertà delle donne*, p. 48.
7. A. Rossi-Doria, 'Le idee del suffragismo', in Idem (ed.), *La libertà delle donne*, pp. 266–7. See also Idem, 'Rappresentare un corpo: individualità e "anima collettiva" nelle lotte per il suffragio', in Bonacchi and Groppi (eds), *Il dilemma della cittadinanza*, pp. 95–9. On equality and difference in the American political tradition, see R. M. Smith, 'Beyond Tocqueville, Myrdal and Hartz: the multiple traditions in America', *American Political Science Review* 87 (1993), pp. 549–66.

8. Rossi-Doria, 'Rappresentare un corpo', p. 96. On the suffragist movement and the role of women in nineteenth-century America see, among others, A. S. Kranditor, *The Ideas of Women Suffrage Movement 1890–1920* (Anchor Books, Garden City: 1971); E. Condliffe Langemann, *A Generation of Women: Education in the Lives of Progressive Reformers* (Harvard University Press, Cambridge, Mass.: 1979); E. C. DuBois, 'Outgrowing the compact of the Fathers: equal rights, woman suffrage, and the United States Constitution, 1820–1878', in D. Thelen (ed.), *The Constitution and American Life* (Cornell University Press, Ithaca and London: 1988), pp. 176–202; S. M. Buechler, *Women's Movements in the United States: Women Suffrage, Equal Rights, and Beyond* (Rutgers University Press, New Brunswick and London: 1990); E. Fitzpatrick, *Endless Crusade: Women Social Scientists and Progressive Reform* (Oxford University Press, New York: 1990); L. D. Ginzberg, *Women and the Work of Benevolence: Morality, Politics, and Class in the Nineteenth-Century United States* (Yale University Press, New Haven and London: 1990); J. Kleinberg, *Women in American Society 1820–1920* (British Association for American Studies, Brighton: 1990); M. Ryan, *Women in Public: Between Banners and Ballots 1825–1880* (The Johns Hopkins University Press, Baltimore: 1990); M. L. Kornbluh, 'Men, women, and politics in the nineteenth and twentieth centuries', *Reviews in American History* 20 (1992), pp. 72–7; E. S. Clemens, 'Organizational repertoires and institutional change: women's groups and the transformation of US politics, 1890–1920', *American Journal of Sociology* 98 (1993), pp. 753–98.
9. S. Moller Okin, *Women in Western Political Thought* (Princeton University Press, Princeton, NJ: 1979); A. Saxonhouse, *Women in the History of Political Thought: Ancient Greece to Machiavelli* (Praeger, New York: 1985); J. Bethke Elshtain, *Meditations on Modern Political Thought: Masculine/Feminine Themes from Luther to Arendt* (Praeger, New York: 1986); C. Pateman, *The Disorder of Women: Democracy, Feminism and Political Theory* (Stanford University Press, Stanford: 1989).
10. Moller Okin, *Women in Western Political Thought*, pp. 9–12.
11. Pateman, *The Disorder of Women*, p. 2.
12. A. Cavarero, 'Il modello democratico nell'orizzonte della differenza sessuale', *Democrazia e Diritto* 30 (1990), pp. 230–1. On the relationship between law and gender in the Italian debate, see the issue 'Diritto sessuato?', *Democrazia e Diritto* 33 (1993).
13. C. Gilligan, *In a Different Voice: Psychological Theory and Women's Development* (Harvard University Press, Cambridge, Mass.: 1982).
14. A. Rich, *Of Woman Born* (W.W. Norton, New York: 1976).
15. The debate among American feminists is also discussed in A. E. Galeotti, 'Cittadinanza e differenza di genere: il problema della doppia lealtà', in Bonacchi and Groppi (eds), *Il dilemma della cittadinanza*, pp. 190–213.
16. J. Bethke Elshtain, *Public Man, Private Woman: Women in Social and Political Thought* (Princeton University Press, Princeton, NJ: 1981), pp. 326–7.
17. Ibid., p. 351. See S. Ruddick, 'Maternal Thinking' and 'Preservative Love', both published in J. Trebilcot (ed.), *Mothering: Essays in Feminist Theory* (Rowman and Allanheld, Totowa: 1983), pp. 213–62.

18. M. G. Dietz, 'Citizenship with a feminist face: the problem with maternal thinking', *Political Theory* 13 (1985), pp. 19–37. The risk of a new encapsulation of women in the family sphere is also denounced by G. Zincone, *Da sudditi a cittadini: Le vie dello stato e le vie della società civile* (Il Mulino, Bologna: 1992), p. 196. On the women of the New Right see R. E. Klatch, *Women of the New Right* (Temple University Press, Philadelphia: 1987).
19. Ibid., p. 29. See also P. Boling, 'The democratic potential of mothering', *Political Theory* 19 (1991), pp. 606–25.
20. L. M. G. Zerilli, 'Machiavelli's sisters: women and "the conversation" of political theory', *Political Theory* 19 (1991), pp. 252–76.
21. C. A. MacKinnon, 'Feminism, Marxism, method, and the state: an agenda for theory', *Signs: Journal of Women in Culture and Society* 7 (1982), pp. 515–44; Idem, 'Feminism, Marxism, method, and the state: toward a feminist jurisprudence', ibid. 8 (1983), pp. 635–58; N. Holmstrom, 'A Marxist theory of women's nature', in C. R. Sunstein (ed.), *Feminism and Political Theory* (The University of Chicago Press, Chicago and London: 1990), pp. 69–86; C. Sypnowich, 'Justice, community, and the antinomies of feminist theory', *Political Theory* 21 (1993), pp. 484–506.
22. N. J. Hirschmann, 'Freedom, recognition, and obligation: a feminist approach to political theory', *American Political Science Review* 83 (1989), pp. 1227–44; C. Di Stefano, *Configurations of Masculinity: A Feminist Perspective on Modern Political Theory* (Cornell University Press, Ithaca and London: 1991); D. Coole, 'Constructing and deconstructing liberty: a feminist and poststructuralist analysis', *Political Studies* 41 (1993), pp. 83–95.
23. Hirschmann, 'Freedom, recognition, and obligation', pp. 236–8; Coole, 'Constructing and deconstructing liberty', pp. 92–5.
24. Di Stefano, *Configurations of Masculinity*, p. 13.
25. Ibid., p. 28.
26. Cavarero, 'Il modello democratico nell'orizzonte della differenza sessuale', p. 241. See also K. B. Jones, 'Citizenship in a woman-friendly polity', *Signs. Journal of Women in Culture and Society* 15 (1990), pp. 781–812.
27. A. Phillips, 'Must feminists give up on liberal democracy?', *Political Studies* 40 (special issue 1992), pp. 68–82.
28. S. S. Wolin, Democracy, difference, and recognition', *Political Theory* 21 (1993), pp. 464–83.
29. A. Bentley, *The Process of Government* (The University of Chicago Press, Chicago: 1908); M. P. Follett, *The New State: Group Organization the Solution of Popular Government* (Longmans, Green and Co., New York: 1918); H. Croly, *Progressive Democracy* (Macmillan, New York: 1914); J. Dewey, *Individualism Old and New* (Macmillan, New York: 1930).
30. A very critical approach to 'interest-group pluralism' is T. Lowi, *The End of Liberalism* (Norton, New York: 1973) and Idem, 'I gruppi e lo stato: un aggiornamento sull'esperienza americana', *Teoria politica* 7 (1991), pp. 3–30. Exponents of the so-called 'return to the state' are also critical. See, e.g., the debate published in *American Political Science Review* 82, No. 3 (1991) with articles by T. Lowi, G. Almond, E. A. Nordlinger, S. Fabbrini. See also T. Mitchell, 'The limits of the state: beyond statist approaches and

their critics', *American Political Science Review* 85 (1991), pp. 77–96; R. J. Ellis, 'Pluralist political science and "the State": distinguishing between autonomy and coherence', *Polity* 24 (1992), pp. 569–89. On the literature on the relationship between welfare state and women see, among others, T. Skocpol, *Protecting Soldiers and Mothers: The Politics of Social Provision in the United States, 1870s–1920s* (Harvard University Press, Cambridge, Mass.: 1992); A. S. Orloff, 'Gender and the social rights of citizenship: the comparative analysis of gender relations and welfare state', *American Sociological Review* 58 (1993), pp. 303–28; E. Vezzosi, 'From Roosevelt to Roosevelt: women's welfare and maternity policies in the United States, 1909–1935', *Storia Nordamericana* 5 (1988), pp. 95–114.

31. I. M. Young, *Justice and the Politics of Difference* (Princeton University Press, Princeton, NJ: 1990); Idem, 'Polity and group difference: a critique of the ideal of universal citizenship', in Sunstein (ed.), *Feminism and Political Thought*, pp. 117–41; S. Moller Okin, *Justice, Gender, and the Family* (Basic Books, New York: 1989); Idem, 'John Rawls: justice as fairness – for whom?', in M. Shanley and C. Pateman (eds), *Feminist Interpretation and Political Theory* (The Pennsylvania State University Press, Baskerville: 1991), pp. 181–98; E. V. Spelman, 'Simone de Beauvoir and women: just who does she think "we" is?', in Shanley and Pateman (eds), *Feminist Interpretation*, pp. 199–216; M. Dietz, 'Hannah Arendt and feminist politics', ibid., pp. 232–52; S. Benhabib, *Situating the Self: Gender, Community and Postmodernism in Contemporary Ethics* (Polity Press, Cambridge: 1992). See also V. Sapiro, 'Feminism: a generation later', *The Annals of the American Academy of Political and Social Sciences* 514 (1991), pp. 10–22.
32. J. Rawls, *A Theory of Justice* (Oxford University Press, London-Oxford-New York: 1971) pp. 118–19.
33. Moller Okin, 'John Rawls', pp. 195–6. See also Idem, *Justice, Gender, and the Family*, p. 22.
34. C. R. Sunstein, 'Introduction' to Idem, *Feminism and Political Theory*, p. 4.
35. Young, *Justice and the Politics of Difference*, p. 75; Idem, 'Polity and group difference', p. 124.
36. On the problematic relationship between feminists and communitarians, see M. Friedman, 'Feminism and modern friendship: dislocating the community', in Sunstein (ed.), *Feminism and Political Theory*, pp. 143–58.
37. Young, *The Politics of Difference*, p. 229.
38. Ibid., p. 184.
39. See M. S. Williams, 'Justice toward groups: political not juridical', p. 23, paper delivered at the Fulbright Colloquium 1993, 'Citizenship and Rights in Multicultural Societies', Bologna, 15–17 April 1993; Phillips, 'Must feminists give up on liberal democracy?', p. 79; Wolin, 'Democracy, difference, and re-cognition', p. 480; Galeotti, 'Cittadinanza e differenza di genere', p. 199. See also G. Zincone, 'Donne, cittadinanza, differenza', *Il Mulino* 50 (1991), pp. 778–87 and Idem, *Da sudditi a cittadini*, p. 228–31.
40. Benhabib, *Situating the Self*.
41. Ibid., p. 12.
42. On the ability of liberalism to face the risk of a new tribalism, see A. Besussi, 'To share or not to share? A defence of citizenship against tribalism',

paper delivered at the Fulbright Colloquium 1993, 'Citizenship and Rights in Multicultural Societies'.

43. Seidelman and Harpham, *Disenchanted Realists*, p. 72; Bentley, *The Process of Government*.

44. Follett, *The New State*, p. 144.

10

Psychoanalysis and Ethnic Identity in the Multiculturalism Debate

Daria Frezza

Multiculturalism and psychoanalytic discourse

The debate on multiculturalism, which has been one of the more controversial public issues in the last few years, has affected all the main fields of social science, including psychology and psychoanalysis. Where these two disciplines have been concerned, however, the discussion has been bounded within sectorial limits, without making an effective impact on the more general debate. Leaving aside the possible reasons for this phenomenon, it is worthwhile shedding light on the main issues that have been discussed by psychologists and psychoanalysts as they intersect the general problems involved in the question of multiculturalism as a whole.

The main issues I want to focus on are: (1) the radical turn in analysis of ethnic groups' mental disorders as far as the so-called 'social adjustment' process is concerned, and the analysis of the emotional significance of ethnic community in the self-identity process at the individual and at the group level; (2) the new attention paid within the psychoanalytic community to specific subjective aspects, including race, of the psychotherapist or psychoanalyst and the general implications which can be drawn from this new perspective.

The first important remark concerning point (1) is how memory is built up, be it individual or collective memory, the memory of a particular ethnic group or that of the entire nation. This aspect, which is one of the focal points of the debate among historians, has always raised a special interest on the part of psychoanalysts who have studied the emotional mechanisms contributing to the building of memory.

From this point of view, as emphasis has been displaced from an assimilationist approach to a more careful analysis of reciprocal interaction between ethnic groups, the problem of immigration has gained new attention as a historical and symbolic event deeply rooted in the memory of different ethnic groups. According to the historian James P. Shenton, 'what historians have understood is that immigration is a two-way street'.[1] From this point of view there has been a new evaluation of ethnic heritage in immigration studies. On the psychoanalytic level this has led to special interest in the psychological dimension of migration, in the emotional vicissitudes that take place in the passage from the community of origin to the new one.[2] The emotional complexity of the whole experience has been carefully analysed, focusing on how the immigrant draws from the world of his cultural traditions in the impact with the new situation with which he has to cope, how he uses and reconstructs a historical memory of his own and of his group. In lexical terminology, the turn has been from a definition of 'social adjustment' to one of 'acculturation', to a 'cross-cultural passage' or 'cultural transformation', more cautious about a revaluation of ethnic cultural identity, and finally to a more problematic 'two-way identity' which is able to revaluate ethnic cultural values as opposed to those of the larger society.

The warning against a process which might give way to 'the disuniting of America'[3] has been challenged on many sides by a new cultural approach aimed at discarding the traditional idea of assimilation to an Anglo-American model. The common heritage of collective memory has been questioned on behalf of a redefinition and renegotiation of cultural values from different ethnic and social groups confronting the larger American society. Criticizing the 'universalistic' theories of the generation after World War II based on general concepts like 'human nature', David A. Hollinger referred to the 'Kinsey reports on sexual behavior in human male and in human female' as an example of this frame of ideas, where the implication of an 'inquiry species-wide in scope' was in reality supported by extremely sectional interviews with a particular sample of men and women in a particular location in time and space.[4] A new ethnocentrism has been claimed to be the only possible perspective. The importance of a more strict contextual analysis of different conceptions has been reaffirmed together with a critical definition of the process of inclusion-exclusion in the circle of the 'we', taking care not to exchange sectional parts with the whole.[5] Freudian theory, based on universalistic assumptions about 'human nature' also has been analysed critically. Scientific coherence has been questioned on the basis of clinical results, and an attempt has been made to circumscribe Freudian theory within the historical context in which it was conceived. What is contended is its soundness in different cultural contexts. The idea has been advanced that 'early psychoanalytic theory was the self-analysis of Victorian Europe'.[6]

With regard to the second point of my analysis I want to highlight some of the problems concerning the psychoanalytic community. In recent years different schools and groups with diverse theoretical and clinical approaches have become increasingly numerous. Many of them, with a psychodynamic orientation (Jungians, Adlerians, Reichians), together with behaviourist and cognitive groups have questioned Freudian hegemony. On the other hand, within Freudian psychoanalytic discourse the theoretical frame of metapsychology has been critically analysed in relation to the scientific level of clinical technique.[7] The spreading of 'pluralistic criteria for psychotherapy', for instance, has meant to some psychotherapists not so much to give way to a form of eclecticism or absolute relativism, as to keep as a point of reference Thomas Kuhn's concept of epistemic communities based on coherence of scientific paradigms accepted within the community itself.[8] My analysis deals only with the Freudian and neo-Freudian Jungian and cognitivist approaches. In order to have a better understanding of the relevance of the present questions it is, in my opinion, important to place them in a historical perspective.

Mental health and social adjustment

Freudian psychoanalysis in the United States developed in a closer relationship with the social sciences than in Europe. In the American frame the emphasis had always been on analysis of cultural aspects of personality interacting with the environment. In the debate underway in the first decades of the century in the social sciences, beginning with anthropology, between 'nature' and 'nurture', psychoanalysis was oriented toward highlighting the importance of cultural and mental factors in the development of individual personality, in contrast with those geneticists, anthropologists, psychiatrists who based the theories of human behaviour on genetically predetermined, organic data.

The neo-Freudian school of Karen Horney, Abraham Kardiner, and Harry S. Sullivan, has stressed the relevance of cultural and interpersonal factors on the character development of the individual and in the construction of psychological defense mechanisms, in the process of dynamic interaction with the environment.[9]

In the 1930s and 1940s the soundness of a process of assimilation to the mainstream American model was never questioned in the psychoanalytic and, more generally, in the social psychology discourse. In other words, what was beyond dispute was the problem of a 'social adjustment' as a healthy process and, vice versa, of a 'maladjustment' as a psychopathological symptom. It is remarkable that a French scholar, George Devereux, a refugee during World War II whose interdisciplinary field of study included psychoanalysis and ethnology, questioned this approach. Precisely because of his particular cultural position he could critically highlight this problem, comparing primitive communities and highly industrialized countries. Considering first the usual confusion between the two terms, individual neurosis and maladjustment, Devereux analysed through examples taken from primitive societies (such as a Native American Apache tribe) how neurotic individuals set out on the way to recovery, in relation to the degree of symptom acceptance on the part of the community itself. The therapist, then, must 'free the patient of his personal neurosis without converting it into the prevailing social neurosis'.[10] Having made a clear distinction between the two aspects, Devereux is, on the other hand, conscious of the relevance of the customs and cultural traditions of a society as a protective element of the society in relationship with the individual and vice-versa.

In the distinction between the two aspects, individual and social, as far as the mechanisms of assimilation and conformism are concerned, the scholar refers as a major example to the paradoxical case of Germany under Nazism. He wonders about the opportuneness of the non-conformist individual to adopt measures of apparent adjustment to the majority rules, quoting on this subject La Rochefoucauld's saying: '*Il est bien fol de vouloir être sage tout seul.*'[11]

The power of attraction exerted by different cultures on the single individual cannot overshadow the relativity of the value systems of these cultures. He notices, in fact, that '... by looking upon our own culture with the eyes of other tribes, we shall find it as neurotic as we may have assumed theirs to be when we looked upon it with the eyes of our own cultural standards ... '.[12] The same can be said for individuals, whose neuroses are no longer called so, once they have been transplanted in different cultures.

During the years of the war against Nazism Devereux concluded his analysis with the following question: 'Society can always defend itself against a number of unorganized neurotics each afflicted with different symptoms evaluating reality differently, but who is to protect mankind against the organized neurosis of society?'[13]

The contrast between a society at the same time protective and authoritarian and a hazardous position of psychological loneliness as the inevitable heritage of contemporary human condition is the basic interpretative line of Eric Fromm's famous *Escape from Freedom*.[14] Using interdisciplinary tools, Fromm reconstructs the historical process and the psychological mechanisms of social consensus to the Nazi regime. In Fromm's view, too, Freud's dynamic psychology must cope with the problem of social adjustment. He stresses the importance of the protective role of the community and the great effort to overcome it. The psychological development of the individual is, in his analysis, a difficult evolution toward self-identity in a so-called process of 'individuation' in which the major problems are those of separation from the maternal figure. The resulting psychological problems give way to escape mechanisms against the increasing feeling of psychic loneliness.

The strain between this evolutionary process and the need of emotional belonging to a community whose cultural and symbolic values constitute the connective tissue for individual evolution, are, according to Fromm, the two guide lines along which the process of civilization has developed.[15] I would like to make a few more remarks on psychological aspects of the concept of community, considering its crucial role in this debate.

Community and ethnicity

The concept of community, one of the most fundamental unit-ideas in sociological theory, has had different meanings in different times. Since the colonial community based on a shared territory, according to Thomas Bender, it has become more 'a network of social relations marked by mutually emotional bonds'.[16] The meaning of these bonds is mainly an ideal sharing of common values, emotions and symbols. In this sense it can be extended to the whole nation. From the psychological point of view the sense of connectedness which comes from belonging to the community is expressed by the term 'we'. The inclusion in the 'we-ness' of the community and the boundary around it, marks off an inside from an outside, as many scholars have pointed out, and therefore the presence of a 'they-ness'. The two notions, 'they' and 'we', are dynamically related and the result of this interaction is given by power relations and constant negotiations of one group with the others. The particular kind of relationship set up in the community had already been described at the beginning of the century by Charles H. Cooley as an 'intimate face to face association and cooperation' that is typical of the 'primary group'.[17]

In the social sciences starting from Ferdinand Tönnies's famous theory of 'Gemeinschaft' and 'Gesellschaft', the concept of a uni-linear progress – from the rural pre-industrial community, connected by territorial biological and cultural bonds, toward a highly technological and industrial urban society – was proposed by Louis Wirth and Talcott Parsons. This concept is today challenged by scholars who see a more complex interconnection between the two typologies and a coexistence and reinforcement of a community-type relationship within the industrial society. In the early decades of the century such scholars as Charles Cooley, Elton Mayo and John Dewey already developed this kind of scientific perspective that has been revaluated as more in accordance with the present debate.[18] From this point of view, the assimilation of minority groups, where community ties are persistently strong to the larger society is perceived as a far more complex and eventful process.

Only recently psychoanalysis has dealt with this subject, which traditionally belonged to the cultural area of sociologists, social psychologists and anthropologists. Until the 1960s scholars were mainly concerned with the analysis of 'stereotypes' and 'social prejudice' as defense mechanisms that strengthened the group's ties and helped to keep a social distance between the community and the rest of society, with a psychological projection, at the same time, outside the community circle, of their own repressed negative aspects.[19] The removal of these obstacles, together with the improvement of social and economic conditions, would thus help the assimilation process.

Since the 1960s a radical change of perspective has been under way challenging the legitimacy of this assimilative point of view. Following the struggles for civil rights and the unprecedented increase in immigration from Asia and Central America, there has been a profound reorientation of America's self image. The whole process has gone through a new debate, which has increasingly focused on the ethnic aspect of community. Following the quest for an affirmative black identity on the part of the Afro-American population, an attempt for a revaluation of all different ethnic traditions on the part of the older immigrant groups of European descent, as well as of the more recent ones coming from Latin American and Asian countries, has given rise in the last decades to the flourishing of a new wave of ethnic studies.[20]

The general debate about ethnicity has included a wide spectrum of positions, from Clifford Geertz's 'primordial character' to Herbert Gans's 'symbolic aspect, doomed to fade away before the irresistible sources of assimilation'.[21] The main focus has been recently on the concept of 'the invention of ethnicity' as developed by Werner Sollors.[22] According to this perspective, a group of historians including Rudolph Vecoli and George Pozzetta has stated that ethnicity must be understood neither as primordial nor as purely instrumental:

> Rather ethnicity itself is understood as a cultural construction accomplished over historical time. Ethnic groups in modern settings are constantly recreating themselves and ethnicity is continuously being reinvented in response to changing realities both within the group and the host society. By historicizing the phenomenon, the concept of invention allows for appearance, metamorphosis, disappearance, and reappearance of ethnicities.[23]

Within psychoanalytic discourse, ethnicity has been increasingly used to highlight the cultural aspect of different groups' identity; but it has also been linked to deeper irrational feelings.

The psychoanalyst Mario Rendon remarks on this subject:

> The word 'ethnicity' itself has an interesting history. It is relatively new in its present connotations, or at least is being used more and more to denote something that at times we used to refer to as culture or race ... it is a sort of compromise between culture, a human-made system of symbolism, and race, a natural given.[24]

In order to specify the sectional character of this concept, as opposed to the universalistic meaning of culture, Rendon further states: 'Ethnicity is the history of our identification ... It is thus the shape of our psyche ... Ethnicity denotes the personal peculiarity of what we call culture as opposed to the universality of particular cultures or of civilization.'[25] As ethnicity is 'the shape of our psyche', it acquires its emotional significance in the intersection between the development process of the individual and that of the group; it provides 'the logical and emotional frame of reference within which we understand the domain of the so-called reality'.[26] The cultural aspects of ethnicity, that can be historically created or recreated, find its roots in the irrational aspects of the personality. These are not to be understood in anthropological terms, like Geertz's primordial aspect, but in psychoanalytical terms, as the emotional process of self-identity formation of the individual within the group. The ethnic community is perceived as one of the 'concentric circles that start with ourselves expand progressively to our families ... and communities ... with their religious, educational ... and other institutions.'[27]

Ethnic culture as maternal holding

The reorientation of cultural perspective in recent studies about ethnic immigration can be followed by an analysis of the great change that has taken place in the use of lexical terms.

The psychoanalyst Ivana Antokoletz proposes changing 'acculturation' to 'cultural transformation' which, in her opinion, 'suggests a synthesis, a discarding of aspects of both cultures to create a new way of being that includes aspects of both'.[28] Her focus is mainly on the new immigration from Latin America and Asia but her analysis has more general implications. Antokoletz's essay is based on the assumption that community group life functions as an emotional holding for the individual. She establishes, in this way, a psychological analogy between cultural experience within the community and the first emotional experience of the new-born baby with the mother. Drawing on the theories of an English psychoanalyst Donald Winnicott, Antokoletz defines the cultural experience of the community as a psychologically potential space between the individual and the external environment similar to that one which initially joins or separates the baby and the mother: 'Metaphorically the meaning of the holding environment extends beyond the infantile period to the broader caretaking functions of the parent in relation to the older child ... to cultural and religious experience.'[29] Community, then, is like a psychological environment that helps emotional development as it gives the individual ways of gaining recognition and approval from the members of the group. If, on the other hand, the environment fails in helping in the fulfillment of the individual's psychological needs, his evolution would be along the lines of what has been called a 'pseudo-self' who adjusts himself to meet external demands, but at the same time hides or distorts his true nature. Many deviant or pathological behaviors can be seen as proof of this psychological conflict. The very concept of 'social desirability', according to the definition of some social psychologists, or, in other words, the roots of social conformism, find a possible psychological explanation. The concept of ethnic culture as an emotional holding, thus becomes a way of shedding light on the eventful journey from the country of origin to a new one. One of the most important problems, in this passage, concerns the so-called 'invention of ethnicity' that I have formerly analyzed. From a psychoanalytical point of view the 'invention' process corresponds to a profound need of self-identity development. After the painful experience of migration, having to cope with the loss of the native cultural holding, the new immigrant yearns for the recreation of ethnic tradition perceived as a first emotional source of social identity.

One of the more relevant problems in this passage is the over-evaluation or idealization of cultural symbols of the community of origin. It can be interpreted as a defense mechanism against the feeling of loss and mourning. This could be the case of more recent Latin American or Asian immigration. But it could also be seen as a response to the psychological need for building a stronger group identity, weaving an ideal continuity with the past by building new historical myths with a positive value as a way of tightening community bonds. The recent debate on Martin Bernal's *Black Athena* is, in this sense, a good example.[30] The idealization of the community of origin acquires, in psychological terms, a defensive purpose.

The new immigrant experiences a lack of social cohesiveness as a breakdown of his own self-image. According to Heinz Kohut's theory, to which Antololetz refers, the environment is experienced as:

> [a] contextual system between the person … and those aspects of others, or the ambience or symbols that are … part of the self and enhance and nourish the self … Cultural groups continue to serve mirroring and idealizing functions throughout a person's life, by supplying culturally accepted ways of recognition and approval from other group members.[31]

When this experience is lacking the individual is deprived of the emotional soundness that comes from belonging to the community as a 'cohesive harmonious unit' given by coordinates of time (the historical continuity with the past) and space. The cutting of these ties places the immigrant in the psychological condition of the traveller, in a quest for the cultural readjustment of both heritages.

A two way identity

On the peculiarity of this condition Anna Freud wrote to Ernest Jones at the beginning of her own migration experience before leaving Wien: 'We are no longer completely here, and yet nor are we completely there with you.'[32]

Marc Kaminsky, arguing against Antokoletz, has placed more emphasis on this particular psychological condition. He has defined it as a boundary area between the two different worlds, where the passage from the community of origin to the new one is far more complex and less foregone in its final results, once ethnic cultural values have undergone a positive revaluation. The author attempts to shed light on a creative process through which:

> ethnic and minority people can work through the binary opposition between imprisonment in the 'family ideology' of the ethnic enclave, on the one side, and on the other the white-out of ethnically inflected or 'colored' ways of being (speaking acting, feeling, relating, valuing) demanded by assimilationist norms.[33]

This new point of view thus opposes the concept of community as emotional holding and aims, at the same time, stressing the condition of uprooting and exile as one harboring a great potential creativity. The man who weaves his life at the border of the two cultures but is not quite at home in either is, in this sense, a symbolic figure with a hyphenated or hybrid identity.

One of the most fascinating and complex questions within this subject concerns language. As the psychoanalyst Jacqueline Amati has remarked, very little attention has been given till now to this subject despite its great relevance in Freud's 'talking cure'. According to Amati: 'Analysis of multilingual patients raises many questions and reflections about the links between memory, language, splitting and repression and why some things can be remembered in one language but are forgotten in another.'[34] The sociologist George H. Mead had already stated, in the 1930s, that one 'who learns a new language, gets a new soul'.[35] The tracing of memory and emotional feelings, bound together, give way to cognitive maps in which memories of the past are afterward reinscribed or translated. The learning of languages is inscribed in those maps, starting from the 'mother tongue', that in which the relationship between things and their symbolic verbal representations has been set up for the first time within the close maternal bond.[36]

Studies about bilingualism have analysed 'the experience of a sense of "dual self" in patients, depending on whether they spoke the native or the acquired language'.[37] The 'dual self' experienced by the bilingual patient sheds light on one of the more complex psychological problems of the two way identity process.

Cultural variations in emotions

A new scale has been introduced in a more thorough analysis of pathological disorders, trying to avoid, as George Devereux had already suggested in the 1940s, an overlaying of personal psychic diseases with an unsuccessful assimilation process. In the cognitivist approach, discarding a universalistic conception of emotional psychic structures, different reactions from ethnic groups to emotional events are analysed according to the different perceptions of these events, based on individual biological and psychic factors, but also on cultural behavioral reactions to each particular experience.[38] The examples mentioned by the authors, from love to jealousy to shame or mourning, shed light in a more direct way on concepts that are well known in anthropological research, but not yet familiar to social psychologists or psychoanalysts.

The need for a redefinition of the very concept of mental health has been claimed from many different points of view.[39] The intense feeling of connectedness with one's own ethnic group and the significance of a positive self-perception of one's own cultural identity give way to a critical re-examination of the whole concept.

Cultural differentiations can lead to behaviors that cannot be judged as deviant if they are related to their original ethnic community. On the psychiatric side, at odds with this scientific perspective, great emphasis has been laid on biological-organic factors as an essential base for mental disorders. Thus the same scientific approach challenged in the first decades of the century by psychologists, psychoanalysts and anthropologists has returned in a more sophisticated form.[40]

A comparative analysis of different ethnic and racial groups has been undertaken in epidemiological studies attempting to shed light on the self perception of the specific condition of being a minority group as far as mental health is concerned, and on particular mental disorders of every group.[41] An interesting analysis of Afro-American mental disorders has shown a prevalence of the anxious kind of pathologies, like agoraphobia,[42] pointing out a useful source for historical research.

The color of the patient-therapist dyad

On the second point of my analysis I would like to make some very brief remarks concerning the scientific community of psychoanalysts.

An interesting aspect that emerges from statistical inquiries is the nearly complete absence of psychoanalysts and therapists of ethnic and racial minority groups. In the increasing attention to transference dynamics, therapist identity has become more and more a crucial factor. The therapist, like the social worker, is no longer perceived as an objective neutral expert, but is viewed as a figure who concentrates in himself power relationships between the ethnic community and the larger society.

The values that the therapist consciously or unconsciously transmits to the patient through transference are now more thoroughly analysed. These may carry an indirect devaluation of the experience of origin and, at the same time, a support for the new country of arrival.[43] Freudian and Jungian analysts have stressed the relevance of ethnic and racial factors which involve cultural and more deeply emotional and irrational aspects of personality.

In the past, according to the psychoanalyst Dorothy E. Holmes, race problems had been in general undervalued, in an attempt to overcome obstacles due to racial prejudice, in sight of a 'politically correct' psychoanalytic setting.[44] On the contrary Holmes claims the potential usefulness of the race problem as capable of raising, in the relationship between patient and psychoanalyst, the more repressed aspects like rage, anxiety, guilt sense, and masochism. Race is then viewed as the focal point around which defense mechanisms are organized. From this point of view the white patient-white therapist dyad can show a collusive aspect avoiding deeper unconscious feelings.

This new field of research has striking similarities with work done in oral history and particularly with interviewing methodologies. Great emphasis has recently been laid on the non-neutrality of the interviewer and on his subjective influence over the way the interview has been constructed. The analysis of the impact of race and ethnicity on the interview's setting is an important facet of the whole question.[45]

The Jungian psychoanalyst Polly Young-Eisendrath believes that the absence of black analysts in the scientific community is a symptom of unresolved problems in the Jungian discourse.[46] She is concerned about 'psychological effects of racism, a "de facto" racism that necessarily influences our theory making and the treatment we offer in a racially and culturally diverse society'.[47] In the symbolic opposition between the two colors, black and white, starting from James Hillman's work on symbolic values of color and on white supremacy over black, Eisendrath assumes as a theoretical paradigm the primitive unconscious split mechanism studied by Melanie Klein between the good aspects of the self experienced as positive, and negative ones, projected on an external group, the blacks. She wonders about 'the meaning of blackness imagined, created, constructed within mainstream European culture'.[48] White people endow blacks with a sensuality and an instinctiveness that they lack, with an unconscious mechanism of splitting and projection. She remarks that 'when we project darkness, confusion, even the evil of our own motives on to images of black women and men, we aggressively destroy the possibility for true difference in dialogue with such people'.[49] Whites cannot have a real dialogue with a real external group if blacks are perceived only as a mirror of the negative aspects of the self. Eisendrath quotes Jung's remarks about America:

> ... It would be difficult not to see that the coloured man, with his primitive mobility, his expressive emotionality, his childlike directness ... has infected American 'behaviour'. ... Apparently he (the American)

> can assimilate the primitive influence with little risk to himself. What would happen if there were a considerable increase in the coloured population is another matter.[50]

The Jungian analyst wonders about the influence of these stereotypes[51] on the Jungian scientific community, where there is only one color and one race: the white one, with the consequence that, in Clifford Geertz's words: 'the sovereignty of the familiar impoverishes every one'.[52]

Conclusions

The multiculturalism debate, in conclusion, has deeply affected psychoanalytic discourse; on one hand discarding the whole stand point of the scientific community on a subject like racism, raising problems about how to deal with it, and on the other hand analyzing in a new perspective immigration and psychological mechanisms that bring individuals to identify with ethnic communities.

From a view of the immigration process as a 'social adjustment' where ethnic and racial differences should be 'whited out' in sight of one hegemonic Anglo-Protestant identity, the new point of arrival is now the building of a more complex two way identity. In order not to be the simple summing up of different experiences, or just the reversal of the preceding condition from uniqueness to extreme heterogeneity, this new vision about possible processes of integration of far away experiences raises new issues for which there are no simplistic solutions.

Notes

1. J. P. Shenton, *Ethnicity and Immigration*, in E. Foner (ed.), *The New American History* (Temple University Press, Philadelphia: 1990), p. 252.
2. L. Grinberg and R. Grinberg, *Psychoanalytic Perspectives on Migration and Exile* (Yale University Press, New Haven: 1989). See also what Ernest Wolf, a refugee himself, writes on this subject: 'Emigrants to a new country are familiar with the discontinuity of their sense of self which disconcertingly is accompanied by symptoms of depression, hypochondria, even paranoia': *Advances in Self Psychology* (International University Press, New York: 1980), quoted by R. Gruenthal, 'Discussions of some problems of cross-cultural psychotherapy with refugees seeking therapy by C. I. Dahl', *American Journal of Psychoanalysis* 49 (1989), p. 41.
3. A. M. Schlesinger Jr., *The Disuniting of America: Reflections on a Multicultural Society* (Whittle Direct Books, Knoxville, Tn.: 1991).
4. D. A. Hollinger, 'How wide the circle of the we? American intellectuals and the problem of ethnos since World War II', *American Historical Review* 98 (1993), p. 317.

5. R. N. Bellah et al., *Habits of the Heart: Individualism and Commitment in American Life* (University of California Press, Berkeley, Cal.: 1985); R. Rorty, *Contingency, Irony and Solidarity* (Cambridge University Press, New York: 1989). For a critical discussion of the whole question, see C. Taylor, 'Cross-purposes: the liberal communitarian debate', in N. Rosemblum (ed.), *Liberalism and The Moral Life* (Harvard University Press, Cambridge, Mass.: 1989); Hollinger, 'How wide the circle of the we?'.
6. M. Rendon, 'Discussions of some problems of cross-cultural psychotherapy with refugees seeking therapy by C. I. Dahl', *American Journal of Psychoanalysis* 49 (1989), p. 47. For an analysis of Freud's theories linked with his gender and racial traits, see S. Gilman, *Freud, Race and Gender* (Princeton University Press, Princeton: 1993).
7. G. S. Klein, *Psychoanalytic Theory: An Exploration of Essentials* (International University Press, New York: 1976); A. Grünbaum, *The Foundations of Psychoanalysis: A Philosophical Critique* (University of California Press, Berkeley: 1984). See also R. Schafer, *The Analytic Attitude* (Basic Books, New York: 1982); D. P. Spence, *Narrative Truth and Historical Truth: Meaning and Interpretation in Psychoanalysis* (W. W. Norton, New York: 1982). An interesting debate has been raised on this subject by F. Crews, 'The unknown Freud', *New York Review of Books*, 18 November 1993, pp. 55–66; 'War over psychoanalysis: F. Crews vs. the Freudians', *New York Review of Books*, 3 February 1994, pp. 34–43.
8. T. S. Kuhn, *The Structure of Scientific Revolutions*, (University of Chicago Press, Chicago: 1970); see also D. A. Hollinger, 'T. S. Kuhn's theory of science and its implications for history', *American Historical Review* 78 (1973), pp. 370–93; C. Strenger and H. Omer, 'Pluralistic criteria for psychotherapy: an alternative to sectarianism, anarchy, and utopian integration', *American Journal of Psychotherapy* 46 (1992), pp. 111–30.
9. K. Horney, *The Neurotic Personality of Our Time* (W. W. Norton, New York: 1937); H. S. Sullivan, 'The modified psychoanalytic treatment of schizophrenia' (1931), in *Schizophrenia as Human Process* (W. W. Norton, New York: 1962), pp. 261–84; A. Kardiner et al., *The Individual and His Society* (Columbia University Press, New York: 1939).
10. G. Devereux, 'Maladjustment and social neurosis', *American Sociological Review* 46 (1940), p. 846.
11. Ibid.
12. Ibid.
13. Ibid. p. 851.
14. E. Fromm, *Escape from Freedom* (Holt, Rinehart Winston, New York: 1941).
15. Ibid., pp. 11–43.
16. T. Bender, *Community and Social Change in America* (Rutgers University Press, New Brunswick, NJ: 1978), p. 7.
17. C. H. Cooley, *Social Organization* (Scribner's Sons, New York: 1909), p. 23.
18. See for the whole question Bender, *Community and Social Change in America*.
19. For one of the first work on social prejudice see E. Bogardus, 'A social distance scale', *Sociological and Social Research* 17 (1933), pp. 265–71. Among the many works on this subject after World War II through the 1950s, see T. W. Adorno et al., *The Authoritarian Personality* (Harper and

Row, New York: 1950); N. W. Hackermann and M. Jahoda, *Antisemitism and Emotional Disorder*, (Harper and Row, New York: 1950); B. Bettelheim and M. Janovitz, *Dynamics of Prejudice* (Harper and Row, New York: 1950); M. Sherif and C. W. Sherif, *Groups in Harmony and Tension: An Integration of Studies on Intergroup Relations* (Harper and Row, New York: 1953); G. W. Allport, *The Nature of Prejudice* (Doubleday, Garden City, NY: 1954).

20. For an extensive critical review of the literature on this subject, see, besides Shenton, *Ethnicity and Immigration*, A. M. Martellone, 'Trent'anni di studi su etnia e politica', in E. Fano (ed.), *Una e divisibile: Tendenze attuali della storiografia statunitense* (Ponte alle Grazie, Florence: 1991), pp. 161–95.
21. K. N. Conzen, D. A. Gerber, E. Morawska, G. E. Pozzetta and R. J. Vecoli, 'The invention of ethnicity: a perspective from the USA', *AltreItalie* 3 (1990), p. 38.
22. W. Sollors (ed.), *The Invention of Ethnicity* (Oxford University Press, New York: 1989); see also Idem, *Beyond Ethnicity: Consent and Descent in American History* (Oxford University Press, New York: 1986).
23. Conzen et al., 'The invention of ethnicity', p. 38. On the same subject see also the 'Forum on Italo-American ethnic identity', *AltreItalie* 3 (1991), pp. 105–23.
24. M. Rendon, 'The psychoanalysis of ethnicity and the ethnicity of psychoanalysis', *American Journal of Psychoanalysis* 53 (1993), pp.117–18. For the use of ethnicity and race in clinical practice see E. Pinder Hughes, *Understanding Race Ethnicity and Power: The Key of efficacy in clinical practice* (The Free Press, New York: 1989).
25. Rendon,'The psychoanalysis of ethnicity', pp. 111–12.
26. Ibid., p. 112.
27. Ibid., p. 111.
28. I. C. Antokoletz, 'A psychoanalytic view of cross-cultural passages', *American Journal of Psychoanalysis* 53 (1993), pp. 35–6.
29. Ibid., p. 38.
30. M. Bernal, *Black Athena: The Afro-Asiatic Roots of Classical Civilization* (2 vols.; Rutgers University Press, New Brunswick, NJ: 1987 and 1991). For the debate about Bernal's work, see M. M. Levine, 'The Use and abuse of *Black Athena* vol. 1', *American Historical Review* 97 (1992), pp. 440–60; R. L. Pounder, '*Black Athena* 2: history without rules', ibid., pp. 461–4.
31. Antokoletz, 'A psychoanalytic view', p. 43.
32. Anna Freud to Ernest Jones, 25 May 1938, quoted by R. Steiner, 'It is a new kind of diaspora', *International Review of Psychoanalysis* 16 (1989), pp. 57–8. In the present psychoanalytic discourse, owing to the great attention to the multiculturalism debate, new light has been shed on psychoanalysts' own migration experiences. On this subject see A. Limentani, 'The psychoanalytic movement during the years of the war (1930–45) according to the Archives of the IPA', *International Review of Psychoanalysis* 16 (1989), pp. 3–13. For an analysis of the psychoanalytic group within the more general intellectual migration process in the 1930s, see H. Stuart Hughes, *The Sea Change: The Migration of Social Thought 1930–1965* (Harper and Row, New York: 1975); L. A. Coser, *Refugee Scholars in America: Their Impact and Their Experience* (Yale University Press, New Haven: 1984); but

see also N. G. Hale, 'From Bergasse 19 to Central Park West: the Americanization of psychoanalysis', *Journal of the History of Behavioral Sciences* 14 (1978), pp. 299–315.

33. M. Kaminsky, 'On the site of loss: a response to Antokoletz's paper on cross-cultural transformation', *American Journal of Psychoanalysis*, 53 (1993), p. 106.

34. J. Amati Mehler, 'On multilingualism', *International Psychoanalytic Newsletter* (1993), p. 18. The same subject has been developed in a volume: J. A. Mehler, S. Argentieri, and J. Canestri, *La Babele dell'inconscio: Lingua materna e lingue straniere in una dimensione psicoanalitica* (Cortina, Milan: 1991). Among the most recent works, see also L. R. Marcos, 'Understanding ethnicity in psychotherapy with Hispanic patients', *American Journal of Psychoanalysis*, 48 (1988), pp. 35–42.

35. G. H. Mead, 'The community and the institution', in A. Strauss (ed.), *On Social Psychology* (University of Chicago Press, Chicago: 1956), p. 258. This essay had already been published in C. W. Morris (ed.), *Mind, Self and Society* (University of Chicago Press, Chicago: 1934), pp. 260–328.

36. For an example of this process, see E. Canetti, *La lingua salvata: Storia di una giovinezza* (Adelphi, Milan: 1985), pp. 13–52.

37. Antokoletz, 'A psychoanalytic view', p. 38; see also L. R. Marcos and L. D. Urunjo, 'Dynamic psychotherapy with the bilingual patient', *American Journal of Psychotherapy* 33 (1979), pp. 331–8.

38. B. Mesquita and N. H. Frijda, 'Culture variations in emotions: a review', *Psychological Bulletin* 112 (1992), pp. 179–204.

39. W. A. Vega and R. G. Rumbaut, 'Ethnic minorities and mental health', *Annual Review of Sociology* 17 (1991), pp. 351–83.

40. For the debate on this subject, see L. F. Di Lalla and I. I. Gottesman, 'Biological and genetic contributors to violence: Widom's untold tale', *Psychological Bulletin* 109 (1991), pp. 125–9; C. S. Widom, 'A tail on untold tale: response to "Biological and Genetic Contributors to Violence Widom's Untold Tale"', ibid., pp. 130–2.

41. Vega and Rumbaut, 'Ethnic minorities and mental health'.

42 A. M. Neal and S. M. Turner, 'Anxiety disorders research with African Americans: current status', *Psychological Bulletin* 109 (1991), pp. 400–10. For another interesting example of research on a minority group's mental health, see also L. French: 'Social problems among Cherokee females: ambivalence and role identity', *American Journal of Psychoanalysis* 36 (1976), pp. 163–9.

43. For this kind of approach, see Pinder Hughes, *Understanding Race Ethnicity and Power*.

44. D. E. Holmes, 'Race and transference in psychoanalysis and psychotherapy', *International Journal of Psychoanalysis* 1 (1992), pp. 1–11.

45. R. Grele, 'The Development of cultural peculiarities and the state of oral history in the United States', *Bios. Zeitschrift für Biographie Forschung und Oral History*, Special Issue (1990), pp. 3–15; G. Contini and A. Martini, *Verba manent: L'uso delle fonti orali nella storia contemporanea* (La Nuova Italia, Florence: 1993).

46. P. Young-Eisendrath, 'The absence of Black Americans as Jungian analysts', *Quadrant* 20 (1987), pp. 42–53. I wish to thank Professor Michael V. Adams,

of the New School for Social Research, New York, for his valuable suggestions on this subject. See also J. Hillman, 'Notes on White supremacy, essaying an archetypal account of historical events', *Spring* (1986), pp. 29–58; M. V. Adams, 'Racial identity dreams: colorism and multicultural psychoanalysis', unpublished typescript, pp. 1–14.

47. Young-Eisendrath, 'The absence of Black Americans', p. 41.
48. Ibid., p. 44.
49. Ibid., p. 45.
50. C. G. Jung, *Collected Works* (Routledge and Kegan – Pantheon Books, London and New York: 1957), X, pp. 508–9, quoted by Young-Eisendrath, 'The absence of Black Americans', p. 48.
51. Stereotypes about America were very common in Europe at the beginning of the century among intellectuals and scholars. See, for instance, for Freud's attitude: S. Freud, *On the History of Psycho-analytic Movement*, J. Strachey (ed.), *The Standard Edition of the Complete Psychological Works of Sigmund Freud* (Hogarth Press, London: 1957), XIV, p. 32; P. Gay, *Freud, a Life for Our Time* (W. W. Norton, New York: 1988), pp. 188–93, 450–4, 512–18. But see also N. G. Hale, *Freud and the Americans: The Beginning of Psychoanalysis in the United States 1876–1917* (Harvard University Press, Cambridge: 1971); J. M. Quen and T. E. Carlson (eds), *American Psychoanalysis: Origins and Development* (Brunner Mazel, New York: 1978).
52. Young-Eisendrath, 'The absence of Black Americans', p. 45.

11

The Geography of Historical Memory and the Remaking of Public Culture

Thomas Bender

In April 1990 *Time* magazine, in a cover story, introduced its readers to what has since become known as the 'multiculturalism' debate.[1] Arthur Schlesinger had not yet fashioned the phrase 'the disuniting of America', but that notion was very much on the minds of the editors.[2] Still, the article was measured, not panicky, like so much of the popular discussion of the issue.

At the heart of the magazine's account was a question central to the geography of historical memory. Was it necessary, in order to be a proper American, to have a common history and a common culture, that everyone study and care about the history of the Pilgrims? A *Time* researcher queried several notable intellectuals and public figures, including the sociologist Nathan Glazer and Donna Shalala, the current Secretary of Health and Social Welfare in the Clinton administration. Telling these notables that a historian had recently claimed that no such study was necessary, the journalists sought reactions. The responses were an odd mixture of puzzlement and moderation.

If the answers were not very interesting, the question, perhaps rephrased, deserves to be asked. Why the Pilgrims? Why not Captain John Smith, or Phillip de Nueve, the Spanish Viceroy who established Los Angeles? Or the pueblo Indians who have been living at Acoma in New Mexico for 800 years, the oldest continuously inhabited American settlement? Why is our geographical understanding of American origins so restricted?

The historical memory of educated Americans represents our history as New England writ large. Sometimes the South is included, but even then the origin myth of America is British. We are, in David Hackett Fischer's phrase, 'Albion's Seed'. Even more typically, we are understood to be the product of a North–South counterpoint, a contest between alternative British models, what Michael Zuckerman calls the 'Puritan and Cavalier'. Even Fischer's effort to establish four British-derived 'folklore' regions and traditions is reduced into a dyadic North-South contrast by 1860.[3]

Several generations of historians have collaborated in the making of this story. And it continues. Even with all the recent imperialism-sensitive changes in accounts of the founding, beginning as far back as Gary Nash's

Red, White, and Black (1983), contact and origins are, at their best, about Europeans, especially those from Britain, Africans, and Indians.[4] It is not only framed in terms of an Atlantic world, it is confined to its geographical boundaries. Even when regard is paid to the moment of contact as a process of interaction, the story is soon anglicized, more often than not by the second chapter.

The Atlantic perspective on colonial history, surely an important and worthwhile historiographical development, has had the effect of reenforcing this perspective. Everything is Atlantic derived, and the interactional understanding of American history and geography does not get beyond the seaboard, does not become continental. The coast is indeed a seedbed awaiting a British planting. Fischer assumes that the British constitute a 'charter group' (to borrow a phrase from Donald Meinig), and he argues that these British-derived 'folkways' remain determinative, even today, although no more than 20 per cent of the population has any British ancestors.[5] Even if one multiplies the micro-units of society (as Donald Meinig has done in the first volume of his geographical history of the United States[6]), this notion of a 'charter group' and the Atlantic-focused approach has the effect, whatever the intention, of summoning again the old genetic (or germ theory) approach to American history.[7]

No American historian has thought more about the geography of American history and historiography than Frederick Jackson Turner, and I will draw upon him here and in my conclusion. A hundred years ago Turner challenged both the Atlantic focus and the germ theory of American development. 'The true point of view in the history of this nation – he insisted – is not the Atlantic coast, it is the Great West.' 'The germ theory of politics – he added – has been sufficiently emphasized.'[8] Of course, as the *Time* story reveals, the genetic understanding of American history, based usually on a New England charter, persists.

I will address the New England problem in a moment, but first, I want to join Turner and argue a bit more broadly than he did that the true focus must be on the *continent* and the complexity of geographical/cultural constructions that play themselves out in relation to each other over time on the continental expanse that became the United States.[9]

This idea of multiplying and reframing the narratives of American history originates, I think, with Walt Whitman. In 1883, having been asked to write a poem for a celebration marking the 333rd anniversary of the founding of Santa Fe, Whitman responded, apologetically, with only a brief letter. But it sought to expand the historical memory of America's founding so as to provide a place for Santa Fe, founded almost a century before the arrival of the Puritans in New England:

> We Americans have yet to really learn our own antecedents, and sort them, to unify them. They will be found ampler than has been supposed,

> and in widely different sources. Thus far, impress'd by New England writers and school masters, we tacitly abandon ourselves to the notion that our United States have been fashion'd from the British Islands only ... which is a very great mistake. Many leading traits for our future national personality, and some of the best ones, will certainly prove to have originated from other than British stock.[10]

Whitman's reflections bring to mind Jane Tompkins's famous chapter on the canonization of Nathaniel Hawthorne. She is often both careless and extreme, but she is surely correct to emphasize the importance of 'local customs' and 'temporary opinions' in the making of canonical authors.[11] Site specific factors always play into the making of literature. So, too, with the making of historical memory and formal narratives. Our geography of historical memory is itself historical.

Several historians, including Patricia Bonomi, Michael Zuckerman, Jack P. Greene, and myself, among others, have sought to displace the centrality of New England in our national memory, proposing instead the social and political precociousness of the middle colonies.[12] These writers have emphasized the Americanness of the pluralism and toleration of the middle colonies, compared to the homogeneity and intolerance of New England. Both New England and Virginia, according to Zuckerman, with their homogeneous, clear, and contrasting images of Puritan and Cavalier supply the catch phrases out of which historical memory is made.[13] This projection of homogeneity fits well with the nineteenth century rejection of polyethnic unity in the name of pure nationalities.[14]

But there is more to the making of American nationalism than linguistic convenience and the dream of purity. There are biographies and institutional histories that must be attended to, the histories of local particulars proposed by Jane Tompkins, focused in this instance on regions.

In exploring the dominance of New England we are drawn into a southern counterpoint, as William R. Taylor demonstrated in his fascinating *Cavalier and Yankee* (1961).[15] Indeed, it is this North–South counterpoint, as we shall see, that enfranchises the myths of Massachusetts and Virginia at the expense of other regional historical memories.

Why the initial – and persisting – dominance of New England? Partly, as Perry Miller, Sacvan Bercovitch, and others have shown, Puritanism offered a powerful language for the discussion of national meaning, and that availability no doubt drew historians. The Puritan tradition gave a moral meaning to America, and it established a role of moral commentator for New England writers and historians.[16]

The culture of New England was not firmly bounded by the western and southern borders of Massachusetts and Connecticut; it expanded across the northern states in the early nineteenth century. The declining economy of New England encouraged the migration of New Englanders, many of whom were educated (especially ministers). They brought New England's moral and cultural commitments, gradually identified as the culture of Whiggism, to New York and the old northwest, thus furthering the New England cast of the national culture.[17]

The idea of New England origins sustained a 'New England clerisy', in the phrase of Lewis Simpson. This group, heavily Unitarian in the early years of American national self-consciousness, became a national class that devoted itself to discussion of the moral meaning and condition of the new nation.[18] Many of these moralists were historians, using history as a form of moral exhortation, teaching virtue and illustrating God's work in the very particular history of America.[19] New England's historians, in other words, were prepared to do the work that Herder and Schiller had put on the agenda of romantic nationalism. Jediah Morse, J. G. Palfrey, Jared Sparks, and George Bancroft, among others, were inclined to see God's work in history, and they assimilated God's work into the making of the American nation. The history they wrote was as much rooted in the religious history of New England as in trans-Atlantic historicism. Bancroft, for example, claimed that his history was most influenced by his reading of Jonathan Edwards.[20]

Whitman was correct in naming New England historians and schoolmasters. They institutionalized historical memory in the new nation. After the revolution, there were no historical societies to collect and preserve the nation's history. The Massachusetts Historical Society, founded in 1791, by Jeremy Belknap, was the first. Even though there were state historical societies in all regions by the Civil War, the Massachusetts Society remained by far the most prominent till the end of the century.[21]

In 1789 there was as yet no place for history in the school curriculum, but by 1860 elementary and secondary schools gave a prominent place to history. This development, too, was the work of New Englanders. Massachusetts and Connecticut had led the way, being the first states to require history in the schools. Noah Webster, another New Englander, did 'more than any other' educator to make history a subject in American schools, according to George Callcott, the closest student of the writing and teaching of history in the first half of the nineteenth century.[22]

It was New Englanders who wrote the history read in schools and elsewhere. Of the 145 historians listed in the *Dictionary of American Biography* who were active in the period 1800–1860, half were from New England, and half of the New Englanders were from Massachusetts. Let me put this into demographic perspective. In 1860, 10 per cent of the American population lived in New England, but 48 per cent of the historians were New Englanders.[23] George Bancroft, of course, was the most notable of these historians of America, and his history was not only infused with the moral and religious perspectives of New England, but his American nationalism was, in the words of David Van Tassell, generalized 'from the history of the New England states and rode roughshod over the past of other regions'.[24]

More than regional geography is at work here, however. Americans were keenly interested in the question of national character in the early nineteenth century. Eric Hobsbawm and Terence Ranger have recently focused attention on the 'invention' of national traditions, but this invention was distinctive for Americans: they had also invented their nation in a way that no other nation at that time had.[25] They were defining American nationality at a time, moreover, when national character easily took on a racial cast, and this incorporation was manifest by 1830. Anglo-Saxon racial qualities were thought to undergird American nationality. English, Dutch, and German racial types 'represented vigor and a striving for liberty'.[26] Bancroft and others absorbed this Anglo-Saxonism over the course of the first half of the century.

It was this ideology – sharpened and deepened in a series of particular historical events – that excluded Indians and African Americans from the meaning of America. It also excluded those Europeans Whitman had in mind, those who preceded the English to America. The language that excluded Spanish and Mexican experiences from American historical memory emerged from the confluence of Anglo-Saxon racism and expansionist greed in the interpretation of the battle for Texas. Texas and the Alamo played a crucial role in the shaping of American nationalism and American historical narratives.

The language of American expansion had the effect of denying the value of the European-derived cultures that were encountered in the trans-Mississippi West or the Southeast, where Spanish and French settlement had long preceded English settlement, as well as the Asian cultures that later confronted Anglo culture in the West. New England virtue and energy triumphed in 1836 and 1846 in Texas, containing and restricting the meaning of America.

The Anglos were described as a 'superior race of men'. Henry Stuart Foote, in his *Texas and the Texans* (1846), for example, wrote that before the arrival of the Anglos, 'ignorance and despotism have hung like a dark cloud' over the 'noble forests and luxuriant prairies' of Texas. It was a moral and racial contest of epic proportions, or, in Foote's language, a 'sublime collision of moral influences'.[27]

The meaning of this collision was transmuted into a myth of Anglo-American superiority with the story of the Alamo, where the brave John Travis stood against the barbarian Mexicans and died. This framing, this language is, of course, reminiscent of the seventeenth century European language of conquest and possession that was directed against Native Americans. It allowed Europeans to see a vacant continent; similarly, it allowed them to overlook hispanic heritages in a landscape dotted with Spanish place names.[28]

This act of taking and forgetting was further obscured by the sectional crisis it precipitated and by the resulting Civil War. In 1860, even before the war broke out, most Americans looked upon their society as divided into two sections, North and South.[29] The Civil War, a defining event in so many ways, solidified the North/South, or bipolar, understanding of American nationality. After about 1880, as Richard Hofstadter has observed, the War had become the 'climactic experience of American life', and national history came to be told 'in terms dictated by Civil War controversies'.[30] The great historians of the United States in the second half of the nineteenth century, the period when the discipline began to be professionalized, wrote their most important works on the Civil War: Herman von Holst, James Schouler, James Ford Rhodes, John W. Burgess, and William A. Dunning, for example. The North/South dialogue was so central, so important, that other voices had no place in the making of American public culture after the war.

Reading Eric Foner's moving history of Reconstruction, one is impressed by the historiographical centrality of the war. In his account, as in those of W. E. B. DuBois and Frederick Douglass, the memory of the war puts racial justice and, to some extent, class justice on the agenda of American public life.[31] There is a moral force and elegance to this narrative of America. Yet I am coming to believe that we are in danger of unduly enlarging the story of North and South, even black and white. These dyadic representations of the past may re-enforce binaries that we do not want re-enforced and occlude what Sacvan Bercovitch calls the 'experiential pluralism' of American life.[32]

Recent scholarship on race and culture,[33] influenced by pragmatism and both modernist and poststructuralist ideas, seeks to emphasize the constructed character of race, the contingency and multiplicity of identities, even along the seemingly fixed color line that has been the site of so much injustice in American life. Another body of writing, literary scholarship identified with the hispanic southwest and emphasizing the notion of 'borderlands', re-enforces the effort by African-American intellectuals to weaken the category of race. Ramón Saldívar and José Saldívar describe this literature in terms of hybridity and betweenness.[34]

Might a historical narrative of America incorporating multiple origins constitute a strategy of representation that would sustain and enrich such modernist identities – and allow, as well, for the making of a public culture, however contingent? A revised geography of American historical memory, I want to argue, provides not only a fuller moral endorsement of pluralism, tolerance, and the recognition of multiple identities, but also some clue into the way in which a common public culture and history is formed out of such fragmented and contingent historical materials.[35]

The recognition of multiple origins helps, but that only begins the task. One must also understand how the narratives of multiple origins might become a national narrative. We must also ask for a fuller notion of the patterns of contest for visibility and recognition in a pluralistic setting that is usually marked by unequal resources.

Neither New England nor Virginia are useful as laboratories for such an inquiry into the dynamics of the making of public culture in a pluralized society.[36] Both have such clearly established dominant cultures that a dyadic relationship is unavoidable, as is a simple assimilationist/resistance model of group relations. Neither colonial Massachussetts nor Virginia, moreover, established a public sphere, though for opposite reasons. In New England, the quest for homogeneity, combined with the intensity and egalitarianism of local life, diminished the possibility and the necessity of a public realm, while in the South a combination of social distention and hierarchy produced the same result.

It is important to be clear about what is meant by the public, especially when speaking about its absence in the South, where, as Charles Sydnor long ago argued, colonial Virginia's culture nurtured leaders.[37] What is the relation of leadership, at least as practiced in eighteenth century Virginia, to public culture? The leadership offered by the Virginia elite was more a form of aristocratic service (framed within the restrictive context of Anglo-American republicanism) than an expression of public life. It certainly did not invite a diversity of voices in public, nor was it an exploration of difference in the interest of constructing an identity in which all could share – as agents.

In New England, where Republicanism and Protestant Christianity were effectively assimilated to each other, most powerfully in the mind of Samuel Adams, who dreamed of a Christian Sparta, there was an important egalitarian impulse, but this equality was premised upon cultural sameness.

The invention of a pluralized public culture in colonial America was the result of a very different experience, and it was first theorized in New York. As early as 1733, one finds a bold defense of particularistic interests as the foundation of a public life.[38] A writer in the *New York Gazette* said that one need not worry about competing 'parties, cabals, and intrigues'. They strengthen rather than weaken civic life. 'I may venture to say that some opposition, though it proceed not entirely from a public spirit, is not only necessary in free governments but of great service to the public.'[39] William Livingston, speaking of the contests among various religious groups in New York made much the same point in the 1750s, in a series of brilliant essays in *The Independent Reflector*.[40]

This post-Republican form of public culture was constituted by open struggle; public life was not, as in Renaissance Venice, a mere affirmation of existing hierarchies of power.[41] Entry into the public realm was often in the spirit of a challenge or of a response to a challenge. This practice produced a modern and contentious political culture quite early. As Gary Nash has written, the 'ethnic based, issue-oriented politics in New York cracked the traditional order'. Nash has made much the same point about Philadelphia, British America's largest city. Exclusions remained – and still remain – in our cities, of course, but the construction of a public sphere produced a logic of inclusion and a strategy for it.[42]

The making of a public terrain where difference might find temporary and contingent unity was not unique to the middle colonies, nor was it a strictly urban phenomenon. Richard White's recent book, *The Middle Ground: Indians, Empires, and Republics in the Great Lakes Region, 1650–1815* provides an exceptionally rich account of the construction of a public culture by French, English, and Algonquians.[43]

White's history is cognizant of the Atlantic world, but the association does not represent represent lineage. It is not genetic. Rather the Atlantic linkage is played out (with others) in a place that defines a social field.[44] The stories he tells are located on a common terrain, what he calls the *pays d'en haut*, and he observes with great insight the ways distinct peoples and cultures formed a shared (but not uniform) culture, one that worked without either full comprehension or the overcoming of difference.

The 'middle ground', as he describes it, was a place 'in between: in between cultures, people, and in between empires and the nonstate world of villages'. Because each of these peoples had reasons to make the middle ground safe, they learned to 'adjust their differences through what amounts to a process of creative, and often expedient, misunderstandings'. The participants sought to understand the other on the other's terms, but that effort fell short (necessarily) of complete mutual comprehension. Yet it established new meanings, constructed, in other words, a platform, that might be shared and that could be the basis for further collaborations. Participants made culture work for them on the common ground, all the while insisting upon their particularistic or separate identities and their common humanity.

Our sense of the geography of historical memory needs to be expanded to incorporate this achievement, for it reveals an important and encouraging possibility: the construction of a public culture out of unlikely and very different social elements. But the talk, sympathy, and, even, the interest that were central to this experiential pluralism are not enough. Talk in public is transformative only under certain circumstances.[45] It cannot alone transform society. Rather a pre-existing rough equality makes such achievements possible. Absolute equality is not necessary, but all participants must have enough power to affect the definition of collective meaning and the character of material exchanges. Whether on the middle ground of the Upper Midwest or in the public spaces of cities, the capacity of public discourse to overcome material inequality is both real and limited. When inequality reaches a certain degree (as we see in so many of our cities today), the stimulus of interest and the bridging capacity of communication are inadequate to the making of a public culture.

The development of serious inequality, in fact, undermined the 'middle ground' in the Great Lakes Region in the eighteenth century. When the power of the Indians declined in relation to the power of the empires, when the whites achieved the power to dictate the terms of accommodation, the middle ground dissolved. This case emphasizes how historically contingent the making of public culture is. It is the product of interest and historical circumstance; its creation is neither inevitable nor impossible. The importance of an interest in accommodation and of a 'reasonable' degree of equality (a phrase whose meaning is contextual but no less fundamental for that) are equally evident in the emergence of a public culture in the middle colony cities.

A moral impulse in me wants to make this case, along with that of New York, exemplary. Here is a 'usable past' that speaks to contemporary concerns about sameness, difference, and commonality. Here – in a shift in the geography of historical memory from Massachusetts and Virginia to New York and Turner's Great West – is a history that speaks to our present. Surprisingly, it is this geography of historical memory that informs Randolph Bourne's essay, 'Trans-national America' (1916), where he offers metropolitan life and life in the immigrant communities of the Upper Midwest as paradigmatic of the cosmopolitanism he envisioned.

It is hard to resist invoking this particular geography of origins and cultural diversity as a usable past.[46] But moral exhortation, useful, even necessary, at times, does not advance our understanding of how a pluralized public culture is made and works. We need to look more closely at the way many memories, many stories, impinge upon each other and become a common resource of the public culture. New England, Virginia, the Great Lakes, and the middle colonies all offer but partial stories of America; none is paradigmatic. Who would wish to impose one of these particular stories on the whole, as the whole? That would be in principle quite like Bancroft's New England imperialism. Rather than choosing a part for the whole, we need to understand the ways in which the parts make a whole.

The emphasis in current historiography is on various forms of what Clifford Geertz has denoted 'local knowledge'.[47] As I have observed elsewhere, there is a tendency toward self-enclosure in much of this scholarship, making synthesis difficult.[48] Although I have sought to persuade historians to look again at the great synthesis of Charles and Mary Beard, *The Rise of American Civilization* (1927), in comparison to current practice that synthesis is rather 'thin description'.[49]

It is to Frederick Jackson Turner, not to the Beards, to whom we might turn for illumination on the problem of bringing thickly described local cultures into a synthesis. I do not refer to his much cited and influential prose poem, 'The significance of the frontier in American history' (1893), but rather to the work for which he should be remembered by historians,[50] his unfinished masterpiece, *The United States 1830–1850* (1935), which anticipates so much of the work of Fernand Braudel on the Mediterranean and the so-called Annales school. It explores geographical regions and sections, culture and politics.[51] After finely delineating the geography and cultural making of six sections and many regions within and transcending these sections, Turner narrates the ways in which a national political culture is made. He is particularly eager to explain the ways in which political leaders must establish multiple identities that allow them to construct at once sectional, regional, and national constituencies.

Here is history grounded in geography and differences, a history that refuses to privilege either the Atlantic seaboard or the English heritage.[52] It is continental, analytical, dynamic. The drama of his history is the play between local cultures and an always changing American national one. The genius of American politics and culture, as he presents it, is the negotiation between and among those elements of American nationality, recognizing the contingent (or historical) construction of each, and the possibility of variability. History for him is a process of making, not the playing out of a genetic code. We would, of course, expand the story today, giving more attention to non-spatial local cultures, but with his framework we could still control the richly complex array of narratives that constitute the American past.

Notes

1. The article was prompted in part by a proposed revision of the New York State Schools' curriculum that condemned Western Civilization in the interest of raising the esteem of students of color.
2. See A. M. Schlesinger, Jr., *The Disuniting of America* (Whittle Direct Books, Knoxville, Tenn.: 1991). His interest in the issue was prompted by the same curriculum proposal.
3. M. Zuckerman, 'Puritans, cavalier, and the motley middle', in Idem (ed.), *Friends and Neighbors: Group Life in America's First Plural Society* (Temple University Press, Philadelphia: 1982), pp. 3 –25; D. Hackett Fischer, *Albion's Seed: Four British Folkways in America* (Oxford University Press, New York: 1989).
4. I have in mind, beyond G. Nash, *Red, White, and Black: The Peoples of Early America* (Prentice-Hall, Englewood Cliffs: 1983), the path-breaking scholarship of J. Axtell, *The European and the Indian: Essays in the Ethnohistory of Colonial North America* (Oxford University Press, New York: 1983) and his *The Invasion Within* (Oxford University Press, New York: 1985); M. Merrell, *The Indians' New World: Catawabs and Their Neighbors from European Contact through the Era of Removal* (University of North Carolina Press, Chapel Hill: 1989); W. Cronon, *Changes in the Land: Indians, Colonists, and the Ecology of New England* (Hill and Wang, New York: 1983).
5. Fischer, *Albion's Seed*, p. 6.

6. D. W. Meinig, *The Shaping of America: A Geographical Perspective on 500 Years of History*, I, *Atlantic America 1492–1800* (Yale University Press, New Haven: 1986).
7. Two recent books, both worried by the narrow Anglo-centrism and New England focus of historiography, in fact re-enforce both the genetic and the Atlantic coast parochialism. See P. Morgan (ed.), *Diversity and Unity in Early North America* (Routledge, London: 1993); Zuckerman (ed.), *Friends and Neighbors*.
8. F. J. Turner, *Frontier and Section: Selected Essays of Frederick Jackson Turner*, ed. R. Billington (Prentice-Hall, Englewood Cliffs, NJ: 1961), p. 38.
9. I am not going to develop a second point but I should acknowledge it here: this process of constructing a nation over time is not isolated in space; extra-territorial linkages extending at their fullest extent to the global are a part of the story. National boundaries, whether political and cultural, are permeable and fuzzy at the edges.
10. M. Cowley (ed.), *Complete Prose and Poetry of Walt Whitman* (2 vols., Pellegrini and Cudahy, New York: 1948), II, p. 402.
11. J. Tompkins, *Sensational Designs* (Oxford University Press, New York: 1985), chap. 1.
12. See P. Bonomi, 'The middle colonies: embryo of the new political order', in A. Vaughn and G. A. Billias (eds), *Perspectives on Early American History* (Harper, New York: 1973), pp. 63–92; M. Zuckerman, 'Puritans, cavaliers, and the motley middle'; J. P. Greene, *Pursuits of Happiness: The Social Development of Early Modern British Colonies and the Formation of American Culture* (University of North Carolina Press, Chapel Hill: 1988); T. Bender, 'New York in theory', in L. Berlowitz, D. Donohogue, and L. Menand (eds), *America in Theory* (Oxford University Press, New York: 1988), pp. 53–65.
13. Zuckerman, 'Puritans, cavaliers, and the motley middle', p. 7.
14. See W. H. McNeill, *Polyethnicity and National Unity in World History* (University of Toronto Press, Toronto: 1986).
15. W. R. Taylor, *Cavalier and Yankee* (Brazillers, New York: 1961).
16. See especially P. Miller, *An Errand into the Wilderness* (Harvard University Press, Cambridge, Mass.: 1956); S. Bercovitch, *The Puritan Origins of the American Self* (Yale University Press, New Haven: 1975) and his *The American Jeremiad* (University of Wisconsin, Madison: 1978).
17. See F. J. Turner, *The United States 1830–1850* (1935; Norton, New York: 1965), pp. 47–54. The best study of the culture of Whiggism is D. Walker Howe, *The Political Culture of the American Whigs* (University of Chicago Press, Chicago: 1979).
18. See L. P. Simpson, *The Man of Letters in New England and the South* (Louisiana State University Press, Baton Rouge: 1973).
19. See G. H. Callcott, *History in the United States 1800–1860* (Johns Hopkins University Press, Baltimore: 1970), pp. 180–9.
20. Ibid., pp. 8, 16.
21. Ibid., p. 35.
22. Ibid., p. 57.
23. Ibid., pp. 55–68.

24. D. Van Tassell, *Recording America's Past: An Interpretation of the Development of Historical Studies in America 1607–1884* (University of Chicago Press, Chicago: 1960), p. 154.
25. See E. Hobsbawm and T. Ranger (eds), *The Invention of Tradition* (Oxford University Press, New York: 1983).
26. Callcott, *History*, pp. 166, 170–1.
27. Quotes from D. J. Weber, *The Spanish Frontier in North America* (Yale University Press, New Haven: 1992), p. 339. See also R. Gutiérrez, *When Jesus Came, The Corn Mother Went Away* (Stanford University Press, Stanford: 1991), pp. 338–9.
28. There was less conflict in Arizona and California; hence less need for a language of justification. Texas was the focus. See Weber, *The Spanish Frontier*, chap. 12.
29. See Taylor, *Cavalier and Yankee*.
30. R. Hofstadter, *The Progressive Historians* (A. Knopf, New York: 1969), p. 26.
31. See E. Foner, *Reconstruction: America's Unfinished Revolution, 1863–1877* (Harper and Row, New York: 1988).
32. See S. Bercovitch, *The Rites of Ascent: Transformations in the Symbolic Construction of America* (Routledge, New York: 1993), p. 14, though he uses it in a different connection.
33. I refer specifically to K. A. Appiah, *In My Father's House: Africa in the Philosophy of Culture* (Oxford University Press, New York: 1992), but other writers could be cited, including the historian Barbara Fields, the sociologist Mary Waters, and the literary critic Werner Sollors, and any number of poststructuralist anthropologists. These others are less directly concerned in their formulations with exploring the meaning of modernism, but the implications of the work points in the same direction.
34. See R. Saldívar, 'The borderlands of culture: Américo Paredes's *George Washington Gómez* and Chicano literature at the end of the twentieth century', *American Literary History* 5 (1993), pp. 272– 93; J. D. Saldívar, *The Dialectics of Our America: Genealogy, Cultural Critique, and Literary History* (Duke University Press, Durham, NC: 1991).
35. I should note here that the earlier writing, referred to in note 12 and including my own cited there, has the common flaw of being more of a moral brief than an approach to a theory of pluralistic nationality.
36. This paragraph – and the four that follow – are based upon a fuller analysis in my 'New York in theory.'
37. C. Sydnor, *Gentlemen Freeholders: Political Practices in Washington's Virginia* (University of North Carolina Press, Chapel Hill: 1952).
38. There is no easy and short definition of the public, but in general I am following the guiding points specified by the early sociologist Robert Park (University of Chicago) whose Heidelberg dissertation in 1904 was the first theoretical inquiry into the nature of the public. He understood the public as a modern circumstance, and he made two points about it. First, the public is made up of different cultures and points of view, and, second, it is dialogic and inclusive. Or put differently, the public is marked by a diversity that finds unity in a larger discussion of its composition and purposes. The public in this formulation is a conversation; it is not represented

by sameness. Indeed, sameness stops that conversation that is the public. One should note, however, that Park, like Jürgen Habermas in our own day, has in mind a vision of reasoned debate that may exclude forms of political expression that ought not be excluded. Park's dissertation is the title essay in R. Park, *The Crowd and the Public and Other Essays* (University of Chicago Press, Chicago: 1972).

39. Quoted in B. Bailyn, *The Origins of American Politics* (A. Knopf, New York: 1968), p. 128.
40. W. Livingston, *The Independent Reflector: or Weekly Essays on Sundry Important Subjects More Particularly Adapted to the Province of New York*, ed. M. M. Klein (Harvard University Press, Cambridge, Mass.: 1963), esp. pp. 178–97.
41. E. Muir, *Civic Ritual in Renaissance Venice* (Princeton University Press, Princeton, NJ: 1981).
42. G. Nash, 'The transformation of urban politics, 1700–1765', *Journal of American History* 60 (1974), pp. 605–32. And this logic is revealed in Nash's recent book on African Americans in Philadelphia. He shows that they became a recognized community in Philadelphia and as such participated in the city's public culture, advocating their own interests. See G. Nash, *Forging Freedom: The Formation of Philadelphia's Black Community 1720–1840* (Harvard University Press, Cambridge, Mass.: 1988).
43. R. White, *The Middle Ground: Indians, Empires, and Republics in the Great Lakes Region 1650–1815* (Cambridge University Press, New York: 1991).
44. On the usefulness of the idea of a 'field' in historical analysis, see my comments in my *Intellect and Public Life* (Johns Hopkins University Press, Baltimore: 1993), p. xiv. K. Lewin, *Field Theory in Social Science* (Harper, New York: 1951) is very suggestive. Of course, a similar notion has recently been formulated by Pierre Bourdieu. See, for example, his recent collection of essays, *The Field of Cultural Production* (Columbia University Press, New York: 1993).
45. Jürgen Habermas grasped this in his first book, *The Structural Transformation of the Public Sphere* (1962; MIT Press, Cambridge, Mass.: 1989). His later work is less sensitive to this historical and sociological issue, nor is much of the commentary on his work by political theorists. Historians are in general quicker to see that one must incorporate into any theory of the public not only the ideal of plural and equal access but also some notion of how such a social circumstance might be created through democratic politics. Put most bluntly: can talk in public bring about a democratic society, or does a democratic society bring about a representational public sphere?
46. I recently did this in 'The experience of community and the making of public culture', Stans Lecture, Minnesota Historical Society, St Paul, Minn., 4 November 1994.
47. See C. Geertz, *Local Knowledge* (Basic Books, New York: 1983).
48. See especially T. Bender, 'Wholes and parts: the need for synthesis in American history', *Journal of American History* 73 (1986), pp. 120–36.
49. See T. Bender, 'The new history – then and now', *Reviews in American History* 12 (1984), pp. 612–22.

50. It is striking how little attention is given to *The United States 1830–1850* by the 'new Western historians', who have been so critical of Turner. They spend much time on an essay he completed in his hotel room the morning he presented it, but largely ignore a masterwork that occupied him for more than twenty years. Patricia Limerick, one of the leaders of this movement, recently acknowledged (at a session on regions and national synthesis at the OAH, 1993) that she had no opinion on the book; she had not looked at it since her qualifying examinations in graduate school.
51. See R. M. Andrews, 'Some implications of the Annales school and its methods for a revision of historical writing about the United States', *Review* 1 (1978), pp. 165–80, and for the specific comparison with Braudel, p. 173.
52. Given my emphasis here on Texas and the Spanish heritage, I should say something about his treatment of these key issues. He does not adequately develop the Spanish side in the chapter on Texas and the West, but he conceptualizes the story in a way that provides a space for a proper development. He writes, for example, that 'a special form of society developed from the meeting of the Spanish and American frontiers and the different habits, institutions, and purposes of the two peoples' (Turner, *The United States*, p. 354).

12

Culture, Politics and the Making of a Collective Past in Contemporary America: The View from Italy

Ferdinando Fasce

The ongoing American debate on multiculturalism and the need for an inclusive vision of the national past seems to be particularly worthy of attention in today's Europe, given the disruptive challenges of resurgent ethno-racial strife, as well as the cultural and social problems posed by the ever-expanding migratory processes brought about by Eastern Europe's and Northern Africa's economic collapse. Indeed even a cursory glance at the most recent additions to the European bookshelf bears witness to the increasing concern for such issues as nationalism, ethnicity, and racism in the Old World. After the sudden demise of the hopes for a glowing future nurtured in the wake of the revolutions of 1989, one is faced 'with a bizarre resurrection of the ghosts of particularism'.[1]

The American scene should be especially important for a country like Italy which for the first time in its history has to deal with huge immigration waves in the midst of a serious economic crisis and a dramatic transition of its national political system. The heated (and unprecedented) discussion of Italy's national identity, which is presently engaging historians and sociologists, shows the urgency with which the 'political theatre', as one British observer defined the peninsula's troubled current situation, calls for a fresh and unbiased assessment of her past.[2]

Yet, with very few and laudable exceptions,[3] the American debate has found echoes in Italy mainly through impressionistic and hasty accounts. These accounts are largely dominated by such catch phrases as 'cultural wars' or 'politically correct'. Missing is any attempt to relate in a systematic way the most recent historiographical and cultural American developments to earlier phases of the discussion. The ultimate result of this is to replicate, on a much larger scale, what an American scholar poignantly indicated as 'a glaring problem ... in the culture wars' which are presently being fought on the other side of the Atlantic, that is 'the lack of historical perspective'.[4]

It is my conviction that in order to gain a less superficial understanding of the current American debate it is necessary to cast it against a broader background. To this end this essay sketches some major developments of the discussion in the United States over the last decade and a half on how to reach a new and more balanced relationship between academic research, history for a mass audience, and the use of the past as part of the present political and civic debate.

In writing this article I had in mind, as an ideal reader to whom address my arguments, an Italian Rip Van Winkle who had fallen asleep some twenty years ago on a page of one of the very few examples of recent American social history translated into Italian. The book in question is Herbert Gutman's highly influential *Work, Culture, and Society in Industrializing America*. The paragraph on which my Rip would fall asleep is the oft-mentioned one in which Gutman warned practitioners and general readers against the dangers of the 'balkanizing thrust in the new social history'. What would happen, I argue, should Rip awaken twenty years later and find that very same word, 'balkanization', as a key issue in such a different book as Arthur Schlesinger's no less influential *The Disuniting of America* (currently under translation into Italian)?[5]

What I am offering in this paper is simply an attempt to update that ideal reader and connect at least some of the numerous threads running through that complex web suspended between academic and cultural institutions, society, and the public which we call history.

The perspective assumed here runs the risk of recounting an all too familiar story, while suffering from a certain degree of parochialism. I hope instead that the 'de-centering' virtues inherent in an outsider's point of view may counteract that risk and contribute to further develop a much-needed, truly transatlantic exchange on how to make sense out of an undeniably different yet similar past in the light of an increasingly shared (and yet dramatically divisive) present.

As is well known, the late 1970s and early 1980s witnessed the emergence of a new need within American history: to grapple, from a broad and comprehensive perspective, with the many threads of historical knowledge which had radically changed the shape of the discipline since the beginning of the 1960s. For all the differences among the voices which took part in what only gradually (and for a short time) became a dialogue, three main common features characterized the articulation of this need. First, there was a widespread appreciation for the enrichment that the emerging trends had brought to the conventional wisdom both in the range of available information and in the methodological awareness shown by scholars. With various and contrasting tones, this appreciation encompassed not only the leading exponents of the new tendencies, but also major figures of the historical establishment such as the presidents of the two main professional associations and other well-established scholars. For example, the Organization of American Historians' president Carl Degler welcomed the beneficial effects that the ensuing attention to the 'diversity' and 'complexity' of the American past would yield for both the profession and the wider public. The doyen of Southern historiographical liberalism C. Vann Woodward remarked that 'The New History undoubtedly started a rejuvenation of professional scholarship'. Not without qualifications and never dismissing his deep sense of irony, Bernard Bailyn, at that time president of the American Historical Association, called for a serious engagement with the challenges brought by cliometricians and community studies to the historical conventional wisdom.[6]

To be sure, for some of these scholars a second feature of this widening concern for the overall future of American history was more prominent. This was the concern that the enormous amount of knowledge that had been accumulating in recent years would disperse within the many newly emerging or quickly reshaping sub-disciplines, increasingly so narrowly defined as to make communication among them all the more difficult to develop. Furthermore, it was feared that such knowledge might end up being confined within the enclosed garden of the academic world.[7]

Against this threat the third and decisive element of the discussion came to the fore: the urge to develop some form of synthesis. This latter was to provide the otherwise scattered fragments of what someone called 'systematic revisionism' with a broad unifying framework, while furnishing the larger audience with as comprehensive and understandable a narrative as previous generations had been able to do.[8]

For all their enthusiasm, none of the participants in this discussion could deny the difficulties that the effort would entail. Herbert Gutman, one of the leading advocates of the cause from within the ranks of the 'new history', questioned what 'if any', were the 'new understandings of black history, working-class history, or women's history ... [that] alter our understanding of American history'.[9]

Indeed such difficulties were hard to miss, if only one drew his attention to the structural and scientific conditions surrounding historical departments in the early 1980s. Demographic decline and chronic stagflation exacted a high toll on the prospects offered to the newer generations just entering the academic labor market. With intended history majors among college freshmen reaching an all-time low of 0.4 per cent in 1981, more than one-third of history Ph.D.'s were still looking for a job at the time they received their degree, as against fewer than 10 per cent only fifteen years earlier.[10]

The changing political and social climate also seemed to call into question several interpretive categories forged in the heat of the so-called 'turbulent environment' of the 1960s. Raised in that atmosphere of mass demonstrations and widespread hope in the liberating potential of collective human agency, the young scholars coming of age in the mid-and late 1970s were now called to set their investigations on such long-neglected topics as class formation or popular politics against the uncomfortable backdrop of deindustrialization, the apparently irreversible break up of the New Deal coalition, and the return of poverty.[11]

Moreover, such factors as the still pending division between 'quantifiers' and their opponents and the ever-deepening specialization of the craft further complicated matters. To give but one example taken from one of the most vital and innovative sub-fields, namely labor history, the actual workings of a major conference held in 1984 are highly revealing of the rapidly changing scholarly environment of the Reagan years. Designed as the most ambitious call for a synthesis within the field, it turned into 'Sixty characters in search of an authority', as one sympathetic observer defined it.[12]

Yet, when looking at that period in retrospect, in spite of the numerous signs of divisions and centrifugal forces dividing the profession, one is left with the impression of an extremely lively workshop. Within this workshop some of the most ingenious exponents of the two academic cohorts which had come of age in the 1960s and 1970s were trying to make sense of the wider and more complex notions of 'culture' and 'politics' which were emerging out of the work done on blacks, women, labor, and other previously neglected or misrepresented significant segments of the national experience.

Two examples immediately come to mind, examples which epitomize both the difficulties and the fertile contradictions of this phase. The first one is Gutman and his school. During the Reagan era the author of *Black Family* spent his remaining years trying to deal more explicitly than he had previously done with the elusive relationship between the controversial notion of 'culture', around which he had erected most of his pathbreaking work, and the sphere of power, in its strongest and most traditional sense.[13]

For all his undeniable eclecticism,[14] unquestionably Gutman had been able to make most out of the category of 'culture', by using it as a prism through which to cast new light on a social complexity that otherwise was doomed to get lost within the comfortable, but reductive framework of consensual history. To fully appreciate his contribution one has to bear in mind the sharp distinction drawn by historians and social scientists of the 1950s between core and periphery of scientific discourse and scholarship. At the centre stood the public sphere of institutional politics largely dominated by Cold War liberalism; in the backyard of the cultural scene lay the 'private' sphere in which such allegedly marginal components of the national experience as ethnicity, material culture, and social conflicts were allowed at best second-class citizenship. Following the lead of the British historian E. P. Thompson and such unorthodox anthropologists and sociologists as Sidney Mintz and Zygmunt Bauman, the notion of 'culture' as 'a kind of resource', distinct from 'society', as 'a kind of arena', enabled Gutman to disclose a largely unexplored space for tension and conflict, a space hardly reducible within the narrow boundaries provided by the prevailing paradigm of interest-group theory and economic pluralism. At the same time new dignity and some place within the classroom was afforded to a rich legacy of popular resistance and opposition which until then had been either removed altogether or at most confined among the shallow interstices accorded by the proponents of the modernization process to the 'victims' of that same process.[15]

However, as some critics did not fail to notice, Gutman's broad and sweeping perspective was not devoid of limitations. Belatedly reinstated at the centre of the historical stage, working-class and popular behavior and culture, if not adequately connected with the larger society and the institutional mechanisms of power, ran the risk of becoming self-enclosed. There was also the need for a less generic use than the one made by Gutman of such heuristically powerful, but also extremely ambiguous and multifarious, notions as 'community'. Others called for a more articulate examination of the ruptures and contradictions plaguing the workers' world and jeopardizing the potential for continuity and cultural transmission over time.[16]

Such limitations would impact all the more forcefully when one moved from the nineteenth century, the core of Gutman's ground-breaking work, to contemporary America, 'the twentieth century, a very different world from the one I studied', as Gutman himself poignantly recognized.[17]

How could one redefine the creative categories elaborated in *Work, Culture and Society* in order to deal with the much more functionally complex contemporary world? In that world new unifying forces have been at work, along with more powerful private and public national institutions whose impact was deeply felt by a popular universe undergoing the dramatic transition entailed by the emergence of mass culture. Was it possible in the process, it was further argued, to rescue the 'culturalist' approach from the pitfalls of self-referentiality or overspecialization and establish a dynamic relationship between the new, wider definitions of power emerging from black and women's studies and more traditional ones? Furthermore, how could one attend, on the basis of the ever-growing evidence furnished by the burgeoning field of social history, to 'rewriting the *national* experience'? These were the bold and demanding tasks that Gutman set himself and his students in the years immediately preceding his untimely death, trying at the same time to expand the scope of the inquiry and to amend his perspective along the lines suggested by such scholars as David Montgomery and Eric Foner who had most successfully committed themselves to the analysis of class and institutional power relations.[18]

As is well known, the empirical inquiry, based on a close scrutiny of census records, that Gutman pursued, and that was meant to counter the charges of 'romanticism' and 'sentimentalism' in the treatment of the lower classes brought by critics against his previous work, dealt with a reappraisal of the issues of class formation and the making and unmaking of the American working population in the nineteenth century.[19] In the meantime to root further this attempt at a realistic and plausible, and yet thoroughly engaged, vision of the past some of his students had embarked on a set of case studies of working-class and popular political history. These studies combined the vantage point of the local community with the wider background of such major national turning points as the Civil War or the Gilded Age, while at the same time engaging in a fruitful dialogue with the 'new' political and intellectual history.[20]

Some of these scholars joined Gutman in his most ambitious project, that is the above mentioned synthesis of American history from colonial times to the present from the perspective of its ever-changing working majority. The product of a truly collective endeavor, the multimedia American Social History Project (ASHP), as this initiative came to be known, would pay special attention to the evolution going on in the ways of both producing and consuming history beyond the academic sphere.[21]

Yet, when Gutman died, in 1985, the ASHP was still in the making and still pending was the problem of fully relating and comparing the most recent substantive and methodological findings to the highest points of the previous generations' scholarship. At this juncture Gutman's quest for a new meaningful narrative of the national past was picked up and further elaborated along new lines by Thomas Bender. An intellectual historian with a strong interest in social formations and institutions, Bender built upon the work of Foner, Sean Wilentz, and other scholars who had tried to compound power and society, meaning and structure. He came up with a proposal which called for a critical re-examination of the whole American saga around the pivotal category of what he termed 'public culture'. Already present in Bender's previous pioneering analysis of the evolution of the concept of 'community', the phrase 'public culture' was now more explicitly defined as the 'forum where power in its various forms, including meaning and aesthetics, is elaborated and made authoritative'.[22]

Bender engaged not only, as Gutman had suggested, with the Progressive paradigm, but also with the much more controversial, and yet hardly escapable, scholarship of the 1950s. Bender seemed especially concerned with rethinking the meandering ways through which that historiography, in its most creative and anticipatory expressions, that is in Hoftstadter's work, had tried to chart the interaction (and the tensions) between the system of values, that supposedly composed the national shared culture, and the diverse social kaleidoscope underlying it. Even though it probably overstated the continuity between Beard and Hofstadter, Bender's proposal unquestionably offered a way to rescue from the sometimes too generic category of 'consensus' an historian whose legacy looked particularly suggestive in an age of increasing disenchantment with the idea of progress. No less important was Bender's emphasis on the need to combine the concern shown by the 'old new history' for the 'public as both subject and audience' with new 'diffuse' notions of power and domination wrought by recent scholarship.[23]

The problem of the audience, as a key precondition to be taken into account by any attempt at 'making history whole again', provided a major theme of the comments elicited by this proposal. To be sure, how could one overlook the success of such books and films as *Roots*, which echoed the racial upheaval of the 1960s? Nor could the booming demand for genealogical services which Roots and the so-called ethnic revival of the 1970s had engendered be easily dismissed, nor the flourishing of nonacademic historical institutions attested by the fact that one-fourth of museums and historical societies in the US had been founded since 1970. Moreover, there was clearly discernible a process of appropriation of historical sites and symbols by the 'society of spectacle' under the guise of commercial ads, travel business, and TV. While it was hardly debatable that the main source of historical knowledge for most Americans was Disney with its permanent exhibits in Orlando which had been designed following the guideline that what mattered was, in the words of one Disney's imagineer', to 'carefully program out all the negative, unwanted elements and program in the positive elements'. On the other hand, as Roy Rosenzweig, an historian and consulting editor with the ASHP, reminded, these simultaneous tendencies towards a democratization of tradition and an expansion of the commercial use of the past outside of the usual educational avenues were accompanied by a constant levelling off of enrollments and majors in history. All this, it was argued, called for a much sharper analysis of the new configuration of the 'marketplace of memory' than the one offered by Bender.[24]

The other main critique that Bender triggered reflected the fear that, in spite of its potential comprehensiveness, the notion of 'public culture' might fall prey to the same logic of exclusion and arbitrary selection which, notwithstanding Hofstadter's personal acuteness, had by and large characterized the 'consensus' narratives.[25]

The discussion on the pros and cons of Gutman's, Bender's and such other plans for a synthesis as, for example, the 'organizational' one put forward by Louis Galambos,[26] seemed to be thriving when a short, influential, contribution, which appeared early in 1987 on the *American Historical Review* (*AHR*), signalled a sudden turn. It was the written version of the presidential address delivered by Carl Degler to the annual convention of the American Historical Association (AHA). A comparative analysis between this address and the one, which has been mentioned above, delivered by Degler in 1980 to the OAH, may be of some interest. The first remark that is in order has to do with the terminology used by the author of *Neither Black Nor White* in the two occasions. In 1980 Degler had used three key words to characterize the new historiographical tendencies: 'complexity', 'constant flux' and 'diversity'. Seven years later the first two expressions had been abandoned, while the third one remained, but with quite a different tone. Now it did not convey anymore the sense of a 'healthy mixture of races and genders' as in the early 1980s. Rather, Degler saw the emphasis on diversity as a sign of 'danger' and 'threat', something to be countered if one would rescue the sense of 'what it means to be an American'. To further substantiate this view David Potter's notion of 'national character' was called back to life. To be sure, Potter's ideas were already present in Degler's former presentation. But in that case they served a largely *indirect* double function: on the one hand, they were a kind of landmark from which to measure the long journey historians had travelled from the McCarthy era through the verge of the 1980s; on the other hand, they served as a reminder, by contrast, of the persistent need for a 'unified conception of our past'. Whereas in 1987 the idea of a 'national character' loomed like the only *positive* way out of a situation of impending chaos.[27]

True enough, Degler ingenuously emptied this category of any exceptionalist connotation, by exploiting his own conspicuous experience as a comparative historian. In his view the American distinctiveness could be captured only by engaging a thorough comparison with other countries on such key features, which American history shared with those countries, as the frontier or the slavery question. Indeed, it would be unwise to overlook the potential of this suggestion, especially in light of the all too recent acquisition of a comparative awareness among American historians. Yet, for all its merits and sophistication, this perspective leaves the impression of an attempt at moving out of the US borders a seemingly embarrassing overload of conflicts and centrifugal thrusts of a racial, ethnic, and religious nature (the class issue, which already looked like a secondary variable in 1980, seven years later had been dropped altogether from Degler's list).[28]

If not exactly a call to order, Degler's paper foreshadowed a sort of withdrawal, on the part of a significant component of the professional establishment, from the most engaging and provocative implications of the new historiography; a withdrawal that was to become all the more acute and turn at times into a direct confrontation in reply to new striking features soon to appear within and outside the academic world. Among these changes two deserve special attention. The first was the exposure of the so-called 'closing of the American mind' by Allan Bloom and other avowed conservative scholars: a strongly emotional response to the problem of history and national identity which in that same year that witnessed the appearance of Degler's *AHR* article broke into the American cultural scene. A result of the long wave of cultural conservatism sparked by the Reagan era and the 'rhetorical presidency', it shifted the emphasis to the classroom and conflated the complexity of the challenges confronting historians and the public into a one-sided battle cry against the 'amnesia epidemic' that was allegedly plaguing the nation. The only cure for such an epidemic was envisioned in strengthening patriotic indoctrination and traditional values; this indoctrination, in turn, was reductively equated to the historical consciousness in which the national community was deemed to be so badly wanting.[29]

These overheated charges flooding the media were able to overcome, at least for the moment, the more accurate evidence accumulated by such astute observers of the making and unmaking of public memory as Michael Frisch. Frisch's surveys from the classroom disclosed students who indeed contributed their full share in what seemed the efforts of the nation 'to organize amnesia'. The anecdotes on pupils asking their teachers 'who is this Malcolm the Tenth, and what was he king of, anyway?', or forgetting who had won the Vietnam war, or misspelling words such as Joseph Stallon or V. I. Lennon all militated in favor of that thesis. But this and other surveys also showed that, in Frisch's apt words, 'frantic injections of cultural symbolism are not needed and almost certainly will not be the solution to the epidemic; if anything, the lesson is that indoctrination and education need to be more effectively decoupled, not conflated'.[30]

In the heat of the campaign on the 'closing of the American mind' such words went largely unheeded. Instead, as in the unfolding of a fictional plot suited to satisfy the ever growing hunger for sensation in the 'society of spectacle', it did not take long for the conservative tendency to find its mirror-like antagonist. But in order to track it we have to move back from the media to the academic quarters. Here a new decisive element surfaced, an element which was cogently captured by a review essay appearing on the *AHR*. In it John Toews assessed the state of the art of intellectual history twenty years after the original formulation of the so-called 'linguistic turn' by philosopher Richard Rorty. The field had been undeniably enriched by the new awareness of the linguistic and textual basis of any intellectual endeavor and of the unavoidably discursive character of the rough materials, as well as the tools and the work processes, of the historian's craft. Recent developments in critical legal studies or women's studies were inescapable witness to the fruitfulness of a theory of language which would not treat it as merely reflexive. Indeed by taking into account the operations of social and cultural construction of reality and acknowledging the roles played by historical actors as producers and consumers of 'texts' one could grasp the full complexity of the social dynamics at the intersection between material conditions, ideological formations, and the making of individual and collective identities. Not to mention the fact that such an awareness could help historians in their attempts at striking a balance between their analytical and narrative tasks which often proved far from easily compatible.

Toews devoted no less attention to the damages that some extreme forms of what came to be called deconstructionism might yield when uncritically transferred from philosophy or literary criticism to history. The main damage was the breaking down of the connection between experience and meaning, the pretension to dissolve *into* a linguistic black hole the whole individual and social being, instead of working on and *within* language. This resulted in a tendency to 'free' the interpreter from any responsibility towards, first, the original context of the historical fragment on which he was working, second, the cultural and scientific community to which the interpreter claimed to belong, and last, but hardly the least, the larger public.[31]

Such a development seemed all the more disturbing in view of the simultaneous impact of the increasingly pervasive 'information society' and its 'screens of escape', the abrupt economic globalization and deindustrialization process and the resulting blurring of any fixed relations between fact and fiction, social practices and their representations. While the significance of the hermeneutic challenge cannot be exaggerated, given also the widely varied and often contradictory expressions it assumed, it is a fact that there emerged a distinct tendency to cast aside the laborious efforts at combining culture and politics, structures of meaning and power which had occupied social historians in the previous decade. Side by side with, and sometimes in place of, those efforts one could find hasty and uncritical appropriations of 'discursive' jargon as 'a provisional, nominalist version of coherence'.[32] Such was the case with some highly impressionistic and self-referential studies of popular culture,[33] or with the abstract and unqualified use of the catch word 'republicanism' that was called upon to cover any imaginable political and social episode from the Pilgrims to contemporary America.[34] Especially striking for the contrast it showed between the sophistication of the arguments and the flawed reductionism of its conclusions was the enunciation of a 'textualist' position which would definitely do away with authors and contexts in the name of 'intertextuality', that appeared in the *AHR* in 1989.[35]

Some extremely rough and trivial reverberations of these unchecked and 'therapeutic' visions of history lay behind a series of research and especially teaching experiments which were carried out under the banners of 'Afrocentrism' or the campaigns against the wrongs of the so-called 'dead white European males'. A comprehensive account of these experiments and their origins goes well beyond the limits of the present article. Probably they were the result of a sort of vicious circle set in motion by the search for symbolic compensation on the part of some representatives of minorities within the intellectual world. These intellectuals translated the deep sense of isolation felt under pressures stemming from increasing social polarization and the triumph of 'conservative equalitarianism' in the age of political deregulation.[36]

Their essentialist view of reality, as largely or solely consisting of language and culture, triggered an aggressive quest for recognition based on a rigidly prescribed ethnic (and often strictly biological) affiliation. When this tendency made some inroads into the campuses and drew an easy and disproportionate attention from the media, the field was ripe for the 'cultural wars', or the 'American *un*civil war', as different observers came to define the situation of the early 1990s.[37]

As is well known, at this point Arthur M. Schlesinger Jr., one of the most celebrated American historians of the last half century, entered the field with his influential *The Disuniting of America*. A member of a New York State's committee appointed to discuss a new curriculum for public schools, Schlesinger was urged to action by a deep and understandable concern for the consequences of Afrocentrism, which in one instance praised black people as 'sun people – warm, cooperative, and communal', as against white people as 'ice people – cold, territorial and aggressive'.[38] America's 'complexity' and 'splendid diversity' (notice the return of Degler's 1980 phrasing), he argues, must be preserved without putting at a risk the Western universalistic heritage of which the American tradition is such a large part. It is in the name of this tradition, of the American Creed and its ideal of a 'new race' ('still a good answer – still the best hope', he says) that he mounts a vehement (and in many respects convincing) attack against the intolerance and lack of intellectual honesty of those who, by practicing the 'cult of ethnicity', lay foundations for the 'balkanization' threatening at one time American knowledge and society.[39]

Yet, in spite of the intrinsic virtues of some of its arguments, one is left by Schlesinger's pamphlet with a sense of simplification, as if, along with recent contributions by other exponents of the liberal 'Old Guard', it would exemplify the substantial recoil from the 1960s and 1970s historiography on the part of the historical establishment.[40]

Where does the simplification lie? In Schlesinger's and others' elaboration one finds himself confronted with a spatial and temporal dichotomy. At one pole lay a *positive past*, made up of the *political* cohesion binding the individuals and the nation on the basis of the shared values of liberty, democracy, and human rights. At the opposite end there is a disquieting present in which the so diverse *cultural* experiences of the country, recently distorted by the 'multiculturalist' claims mentioned above, pave the way for a disintegration of America itself. Interesting enough, in Schlesinger's view, until it was held in check by the *political* consensus which is supposed to have dominated most of American history up to recent times, the *cultural* diversity made for a positive contribution to the national experience. And accordingly the proposed solution is a one-dimensional reaffirmation of the immutable political principles which have been guiding the country for over two centuries. 'The Constitution turns on individual rights, not on group rights', concludes Schlesinger, while condemning current 'multiculturalist' excesses.[41]

Although he singles out a serious question, Schlesinger leaves the impression that Afrocentrism or multiculturalism, which he correctly criticizes on purely intellectual grounds, are solely responsible for a larger process of social fragmentation that rather, as is largely known, has also a strong structural and institutional basis. Moreover, the dichotomy which he introduces between individual vs. group seems to return historical discourse to an a priori distinction between first- (that is, politics in its most traditional sense) and second-class (culture) levels of historical experience, a distinction which is clearly belied by the impressive evidence accumulated in the last decades. With seemingly good reasons Schlesinger marches against the largely self-proclaimed champions of groups who have suffered discrimination for a long period and their pretension to a sort of absolute, 'tribalistic' autonomy from an identity based interest group perspective. However, in his unqualified rejection of the 'cult of ethnicity', he risks lumping together and dismissing all the voices which over the last thirty years have enlarged our knowledge of the American past by infusing it with documented and qualified notions of class, race, ethnicity, and gender. With the result that, notwithstanding his avowed attention towards 'diversity', inadvertently Schlesinger ends up finding himself not too far from the most traditional exponents of the discipline, who reject altogether any hint at diversity and complexity. Ultimately his stand looks less as a documented argument than an attempt at reinvigorating, by an injection of ideology, the liberal 'thin man' whose public philosophy since the 1950s has rested largely on a combination of Cold War faith and interest group theory which seems hardly tenable today.[42]

In spite of the evident differences in the quality of their arguments, all three positions – the 'tribalistic', the moderate liberal, and the conservative – tend to elude the dramatic paradox presently confronting the American humanities. On the one hand, it is hardly debatable that, as Lawrence Levine and Joan Scott have pointed out, the potential of the materials and knowledge gathered by historians about different areas of the national culture and about different and large segments of its people is as wide and encompassing as never before in American history. On the other hand, this very complexity, combined with the increasing fragmentation and rearticulation of the current social scene, seems to defy any attempt at a linear and ritualistic application of received interpretive categories. While, at the third pole of the paradox, scholars are confronted with a public that looks, in the words of an historian, 'at once increasingly representative, and more fragmented, making it harder to find, to reach, and to define'.[43]

As several scholars are showing by their most recent work, to deal with this paradox on its own terms probably requires a broader and at the same time more modest effort than the ones developed by the three positions cited above. It is broader because it calls for a new and creative interaction between culture and politics through an explicit and systematic reconsideration of the tenets of American public philosophy, a reconsideration that deals for example with that 'perplexing concept of pluralism. Historically never a clear concept', as one scholar recently put it.[44]

Caught as they were by the urgent pressure of defending an all too recently acquired legitimacy within the profession for the new historiography, the students who most ardently called for a synthesis in the early 1980s could only implicitly address such questions. But now these issues need to undergo a reformulation which may at one time confront adequately the present and reflect the past in its complete articulation.

Several encouraging signs have recently emerged which show tentative, but promising ways out of the current impasse, for both American historiography and its European counterpart. One thinks immediately, for example, of David Hollinger's suggestive call for a 'post-ethnic' perspective, a perspective that may enable individuals to choose more freely their identity in the future, while at the same time helping them better appreciate the dialectics between unity and diversity punctuating the American record.[45]

At least as important are exposures of 'multiculturalist' excesses and flaws coming from both within and outside minority groups. They point the way to a full realization of the liberating potential intrinsic to the 'multicultural' approach, but one that also makes room for such topics which often both advocates and critics of multiculturalism neglect as class issues. In this latter respect particularly appropriate seems the forceful appeal made by feminist scholars like Linda Kerber to the need for an innovative use of those categories – class, race, ethnicity, and gender – which, after contributing so much to the enlargement of historical knowledge, now risk being relegated to the ritualistic atrophy of an acronym (CREG).[46]

The attention towards the larger unifying and dominating forces and powers of society cannot be decoupled, some correctly argue, from a thorough monitoring of their impact on the ways in which individual and collective memory is incessantly being made and remade over time. The resulting search for a constantly changing 'shared authority' suggested by Michael Frisch epitomizes the 'modesty' which by and large characterizes these varied attempts at a solution of the crisis in both history and public memory. The 'modesty' of this approach lies precisely in its openness and emphasis on contingency and empiricism, processes and explorations; an emphasis which, however, sustained as it is by a deep sense of individual and civic responsibility, should be able to avoid the pitfalls of sterile relativism.[47]

This is a lesson that, for the reasons stated at the outset of this paper, should be particularly welcome in Italy. Especially if, as Albert Hirschman recently argued about modern societies generally, learning how to deal with past and present divisions and conflicts without indulging in any short cut of a 'communitarian' or 'consensual' nature gains the high priority in an Italian cultural and historical agenda that the situation requires.

Comparative historians and pioneering researches on the inescapably transnational character of several past and current broad phenomena – ranging from turn-of-the-century migratory processes up to today's globalization – are paving the way for a concrete dialogue of this sort between the Old and New Worlds. Hopefully this will help us overcome the many stereotypes and myths that have accumulated in a tangled web over these past two centuries. The time may have come when we are able to deal with the simple, but far from easily acceptable, reminder recently offered us by one of the best fellow travellers whom historians can claim on both sides of the Atlantic: that ultimately 'history will decide'.[48]

Notes

I wish to thank Don Doyle, Anna Maria Martellone, and Matteo Sanfilippo for their helpful comments on earlier drafts of this article.

1. T. Judt, 'The new old nationalism', *New York Review of Books*, 26 May 1994, p. 44.
2. G. E. Rusconi, *Se cessiamo di essere una nazione* (Il Mulino, Bologna: 1993); G. De Luna (ed.), *Figli di un benessere minore: La Lega 1973–1993* (La Nuova Italia, Florence: 1994); G. Spadolini (ed.), *Nazione e nazionalità in Italia dall'alba del secolo ai nostri giorni* (Laterza, Rome and Bari: 1994); M. Sheridan, 'Political theatre', *Times Literary Supplement*, 6 January 1995, p. 27.
3. Of particular interest are the comprehensive work by T. Bonazzi and M. Dunne (eds), *Cittadinanza e diritti nelle società multiculturali* (Il Mulino, Bologna: 1994) and the brief, but insightful, discussion provided by N. Urbinati, 'Lealtà e dissenso: la democrazia pluralistica di Michael Walzer', *Teoria politica* 9 (1993), pp. 11–33. Among the Italian translations of American contributions see J. W. Scott, 'La storia negata delle minoranze americane', *L'Indice* 9 (March 1992), pp. 49–50; C. Taylor, Multiculturalismo (Anabasi: Milan, 1993); M. Waltzer, *Che cosa significa essere americani* (Marsilio, Venice: 1992), and Idem, 'Multiculturalismo e individualismo' *Micromega* 5 (November-December 1994), pp. 31–41. For an introductory, and highly impressionistic, account of the question, see R. Hughes, *La cultura del piagnisteo: La saga del politicamente corretto* (Adelphi, Milan: 1994).
4. J. Gilbert, 'Cultural skirmishes', *Reviews in American History* 21 (1993), p. 350.
5. H. G. Gutman, *Work, Culture, and Society in Industrializing America* (A. Knopf, New York: 1976), p. xiii. On Gutman and the Italian historiography, see B. Cartosio, 'Herbert Gutman in Italy: history and politics', *Labor History* 29 (1988), pp. 356–62.
6. C. N. Degler, 'Remaking American history', *Journal of American History* 67 (1980), pp. 7–25; C. Vann Woodward, 'Interpreting the past', *Dialogue* 17 (1984), pp. 49–52; B. Bailyn, 'The challenge of modern historiography', *American Historical Review* 87 (1982), pp. 1–24.
7. Vann Woodward, 'Interpreting'; Bailyn, 'The challenge'.
8. B. Bailyn, 'The central themes of the American revolution: an interpretation', in S. G. Kurtz and J. H. Hutson (eds), *Essays on the American Revolution* (North Carolina University Press, Chapel Hill: 1973), pp. 15, 23; P. Novick, *That Noble Dream: The 'Objectivity Question' and the American Historical Profession* (Cambridge University Press, New York: 1988), chapter xiii. On 'systematic revisionism' see A. Bogue, 'Systematic revisionism and a generation of ferment in American history', *Journal of*

Contemporary History 21 (1986), pp. 135–62. For an overview on the problem of synthesis, E. Fano (ed.), *Una e divisibile: Tendenze attuali della storiografia statunitense* (Ponte alle Grazie, Florence: 1991).

9. H. G. Gutman, 'Whatever happened to history?', *Nation*, 21 November 1981, p. 554.
10. Novick, *That Noble Dream*, chapter xvi; A. A. Jones, 'History majors stand apart', *OAH Newsletter* 22 (August 1994), p. 3.
11. On the economic, political, and social changes of the Reagan years see the articles by David Kennedy, Stephan Bierling and Stefano Luconi in this volume, and also P. Mattera, *Prosperity Lost* (Addison-Wesley, New York: 1990) and T. B. Edsall with M. D. Edsall, *Chain Reaction: The Impact of Race, Rights, and Taxes on American Politics* (W. W. Norton, New York and London: 1992). On immigration and ethnicity in the 1980s, see R. Daniels, *Coming to America: A History of Immigration and Ethnicity in American Life* (Harper-Collins, New York: 1990), chapter xvi.
12. M. Frisch, 'Sixty characters in search of an authority', *International Labor and Working Class History* 27 (1985), p. 102.
13. I. Berlin, 'Introduction: Herbert Gutman and the American working class', in H. G. Gutman, *Power and Culture* (Pantheon Books, New York: 1987).
14. D. Montgomery, 'Gutman's nineteenth century America', *Labor History* 19 (1978), pp. 416–29; B. Greenberg, 'What David Brody wrought: the impact of steelworkers in America the nonunion era', *Labor History* 34 (1993), p. 467.
15. Gutman, *Work, Culture, and Society*, passim. The atmosphere of the 1950s is illustrated by J. Bodnar, *Remaking America: Public Memory, Commemoration, and Patriotism in the Twentieth Century*, (Indiana University Press, Bloomington: 1992), pp. 37ff.; P. Gleason, 'Minorities (almost) all: the minority concept in American social thought', *American Quarterly* 43 (1991), pp. 392– 424 and A. Kessler-Harris, 'Social history', in E. Foner (ed.), *The New American History* (Temple University Press, Philadelphia: 1990), pp. 163–4.
16. L. T. McDonnell, 'You are too sentimental: problems and suggestions for a new labor history', *Journal of Social History* 17 (1986), pp. 629–54.
17. M. Merrill, 'Interview with Herbert Gutman', *Radical History Review* 27 (1983), p. 211.
18. D. Montgomery, *Beyond Equality. Labor, and the Radical Republicans 1862–1872* (A. Knopf, New York: 1967) and Idem, *Workers' Control in America: Studies in the History of Work, Technology, and Labor Struggles* (Cambridge University Press, New York: 1979); E. Foner, *Politics and Ideology in the Age of the Civil War* (Oxford University Press, New York: 1980), pp. 8–9.
19. Gutman, *Power and Culture*, pp. 380–95.
20. B. Levine, *The Spirit of 1848: German Immigrants, Labor Conflict, and the Coming of the Civil War* (University of Illinois Press, Urbana: 1992); L. Fink, *Workingmen's Democracy: The Knights of Labor and American Politics* (University of Illinois Press, Urbana: 1983).
21. American Social History Project, *Who Built America? Working People & the Nation's Economy, Politics, Culture & Society* (2 vols.; Pantheon Books, New

York: 1990 and 1992). The ASHP has recently produced the stunning CD-Rom *Who Built America? From the Centennial Celebration of 1876 to the Great War of 1914* (Voyager, Santa Monica: 1993). I am indebted to Stephen Brier, Joshua Brown, and Roy Rosenzweig for providing me with information and perspectives on the CD and, more in general, on the ASHP's activities.

22. T. Bender, 'Making history whole again', *New York Review of Books*, 6 October 1985, pp. 1, 42–3; and Idem, 'Wholes and parts. the need for synthesis in American history', *Journal of American History* 73 (1986), p. 131.
23. Bender, 'Wholes and parts', pp. 124ff. For a thoughtful reassessment of Hofstadter see also S. Wilentz, 'The New History and its critics', *Dissent* 36 (Spring 1989), p. 244.
24. R. Rosenzweig, 'What is the matter with history?', *Journal of American History* 74 (June 1987), pp. 117–20. On public memory, see Bodnar, *Remaking America*; M. Frisch, *A Shared Authority: Essays on the Craft and Meaning of Oral and Public History* (State University of New York Press, Albany: 1990) chapter iii; M. Kammen, *Mystic Chords of Memory: The Transformation of Tradition in American Culture* (A. Knopf, New York: 1992). On Disney, see M. Wallace, 'Mickey Mouse history: portraying the past at Disney World', *Radical History Review* 32 (1985), p. 35
25. Rosenzweig, 'What is the matter'.
26. L. Galambos, 'Technology, political economy, and professionalization: central themes of the organizational synthesis', *Business History Review* 57 (1983), pp. 471–93.
27. C. N. Degler, 'In pursuit of an American history', *American Historical Review* 92 (1987), pp. 1–12. On Potter, see the recent discussion by R. M. Collins, 'David Potter's people of plenty and the recycling of consensus history', *Reviews in American History* 16 (1988), pp. 314–20.
28. The relationship between comparative history and American historiography is brilliantly discussed by G. Frederickson, 'Comparative history', paper presented to the Conference 'La storia americana e le scienze sociali in Europa e negli Stati Uniti', Rome, 6–9 October 1993 and 'Planters, Junkers, and Pomeschikt', *Reviews in American History* 22 (1994), pp. 379–86.
29. The best available synthesis of the whole discussion can be found in Frisch, *A Shared Authority*, pp. 29–54.
30. Frisch, *A Shared Authority*, p. 54. See also C. Foster and C. Rickert-Epstein, 'College textbooks in American history: brickbats and bouquets', *History Teacher* 22 (1988), pp. 39–48 and especially B. D. Rhodes, 'Quality control in the college classroom', *OAH Newsletter* 20 (August 1992), p. 23, from which the examples of misspelling are taken.
31. J. Toews, 'Intellectual history after the linguistic turn: the autonomy of meaning and the irreducibility of experience', *American Historical Review* 92 (1987), pp. 879–905. More recent assessments of the whole question of deconstructionism, hermeneutics, and the new historicism are provided by J. and T. Kelly, 'Social history update: searching the dark alley: new historicism and social history', *Journal of Social History* 22 (1992), pp. 677–94; L. Weir, 'The wanderings of the linguistic turn in anglophone historical writing', *Journal of Historical Sociology* 6 (1993), pp. 227–45 and J. H.

Zammino, 'Are we being theoretical yet? The new historicism, the new philosophy of history', *Journal of Modern History* 65 (1993), pp. 783–814. See also D. A. Hollinger, 'Historians and the discourse of intellectuals', in J. Higham and P. Conkin (eds), *New Directions in American Intellectual History* (The Johns Hopkins University Press, Baltimore: 1979), pp. 42–63, now in D. A. Hollinger, *In the American Province: Studies in the History and Historiography of Ideas* (The Johns Hopkins University Press, Baltimore: 1989), pp. 130–51.

32. R. Wightman Fox and T. Jackson Lears (eds), *The Power of Culture: Critical Essays in American History* (University of Chicago Press, Chicago: 1993), p. 1.
33. An extensive critique of such contributions is provided by Wightman Fox and Jackson Lears (eds), *The Power of Culture* and M. Denning, 'The end of mass culture', *International Labor and Working-Class History* 37 (1990), pp. 4–18.
34. D. T. Rodgers, 'The Career of a concept', *Journal of American History* 79 (1992), pp. 11–38.
35. D. Harlan, 'Intellectual history and the return of literature', and the compelling critique provided by D. A. Hollinger, 'The return of the prodigal: the persistence of historical knowledge, *American Historical Review* 94 (1989), pp. 581–626.
36. Among the ever-expanding literature on 'Afrocentrism', 'multiculturalism' and 'politically correct' see the books and articles by Schlesinger and others, cited above, footnotes 2 and 3, and H. L. Gates, 'Black demagogues and pseudo-scholars', *New York Times*, 20 July 1992, p. 15A; S. Muwakkil, 'Dissecting Afrocentrism and its growing discontents', *In These Times*, 6–12 May 1992, p. 7; D. A. Hollinger, 'Postethnic America', *Contention* 2 (1992), pp. 79–96; P. Aufderheide (ed.), *Beyond PC: Toward a Politics of Understanding* (Graywolf Press, Saint Paul: 1992); R. Bernstein, 'Jeffries and his racial theories, return to class, to the college's Disconfiture', *New York Times*, 12 September 1993, p. 47; C. West, *Race Matters* (Vintage Books, New York: 1994); S. Dunant (ed.), *The War of the Words* (Virago, London: 1994). See also the penetrating paper by W. Sollors, '"De Pluribus Una/E Pluribus Unus", Arnold, Orwell, holocaust, and assimilation: remarks on the multiculturalism debate', John F. Kennedy Institute für Nordamerikastudien, Freie Universität Berlin, Working Paper no. 53/1992. On the question of the canon C. Davidson, 'Loose change', presidential address, American Studies Association Annual Meeting, Boston, 4 November 1993 offers a most thorough and comprehensive treatment.
37. J. Waldron, 'America's uncivil war: conservatives contra theory in United States higher education', *Times Literary Supplement*, 22 January 1993, pp. 11–12.
38. Muwakkil, 'Dissecting Afrocentrism'. A convincing critique of the 'multiculturalist' excesses is provided by T. Gitlin, 'On the virtues of a loose canon' and J. W. Scott, 'Campus communities beyond consensus', in Aufderheide (ed.), *Beyond PC*, pp. 185–90.
39. Schlesinger, *The Disuniting*, pp. 68, 72, 93, 118, 138. On the American Creed, see R. M. Smith, 'The American creed and American identity: the limits of liberal citizenship in the United States', *Western Political Quarterly*

41 (1988), pp. 225–52. It would be interesting to assess the impact of the Columbus celebrations upon the debate on multiculturalism. See for example G. Wills, 'Goodbye, Columbus', *New York Review of Books*, 22 November 1990, pp. 6–10; S. Greenblatt, 'A passing marvellous thing', *Times Literary Supplement*, 3 January 1992, pp. 14–15; F. E. Hoxie, 'Discovering America: an introduction', *Journal of American History* 79 (1992), pp. 835–40; K. Maxwell, 'Adios, Columbus!', *New York Review of Books*, 28 January 1993, pp. 38–45; I. Altman and R. D. Butler, 'The contact of cultures: perspectives on the Quincentenary', *American Historical Review* 99 (1994), pp. 478–503.

40. C. Vann Woodward, 'Freedom and the universities', in Aufderheide (ed.), *Beyond PC*; C. N. Degler, 'A challenge for multiculturalism', *Dialogue* 26 (1992), pp. 36–40. Vann Woodward's position is fittingly discussed by Scott, 'La storia negata'.

41. Schlesinger, *The Disuniting*, pp. 16, 117. For an insightful critique of Schlesinger, see E. Schrecker's review of *The Disuniting*, *Journal of American History*, 79 (1993), p. 1565.

42. On post-World War II liberalism, see D. T. Rodgers, *Contested Truths: Keywords in American Politics since Independence* (Basic Books, New York: 1987) and G. Gerstle, 'The protean character of American liberalism', *American Historical Review* 99 (1994), pp. 1043–73. The most significant example of the conservative position is G. Himmelfarb, 'Some reflections on the New History', *American Historical Review* 94 (1989), pp. 661–70.

43. T. Bender, *Intellect and Public Life: Essays on the Social History of Academic Intellectuals in the United States* (The Johns Hopkins University Press, Baltimore: 1993), p. 144.

44. Gilbert, 'Cultural skirmishes', p. 349. See also L. E. Levine, 'The unpredictable past: reflections on recent American historiography' and J. W. Scott, 'History in crisis? The others' side of the story', *American Historical Review* 94 (1989), pp. 671–92; L. E. Levine 'Clio, canons, and culture', *Journal of American History* 80 (1993), pp. 849–66.

45. D. A. Hollinger, 'How wide the circle of the "We"? American intellectuals and the problem of the ethnos since World War II', *American Historical Review* 98 (1993), pp. 317–37.

46. L. Kerber, 'Diversity and the transformation of American studies', *American Quarterly* 41 (1989), pp. 415–31. See also E. Fox-Genovese, 'Between individualism and fragmentation: American culture and the new literary studies of race and Gender', *American Quarterly* 42 (1990), pp. 7–34 and on class and ethnicity R. J. Vecoli, 'Italian Immigrants and working-class movements in the United States: a personal reflection on class and ethnicity', *Journal of the Canadian Historical Association* 4 (1993), pp. 1–13. The problem of 'CREG' is acutely addressed by G. Packer, 'Class interest, liberal style', *Dissent* 39 (Winter 1992), p. 53. On the need not to confuse class and race L. Menand 'Being an American', *Times Literary Supplement*, 30 October 1992, pp. 3–4; D. B. Davis 'The American dilemma', *New York Review of Books*, 16 July 1992, pp. 13–17 and G. Lipsitz, 'The possessive investment in whiteness: racialized social democracy and the "white" problem in American studies', paper presented to the American Studies

Association Annual Meeting, Boston, 5 November 1993 (courtesy George Lipsitz) offers particularly stimulating comments.

47. A. Hirschman, 'I conflitti come pilastri della società democratica a economia di mercato', *Stato e mercato* no. 41 (August 1994), pp. 134–52.

48. On globalization see for example L. Fink, 'Have we been here before? Prospects for a future for American unionism', unpublished paper, 1994 (courtesy Leon Fink) and J. Brecher and T. Costello, *Global Tillage or Global Village: Economic Reconstruction From the Bottom Up* (South End Press, Boston: 1994). The problem of ethnicity and transnational solidarity in the past is acutely addressed by D. Gabaccia, 'Worker internationalism and Italian labor migration, 1870–1914', *International Labor and Working-Class History* 45 (1994), pp. 63–79. On the cultural relationship between the two sides of the Atlantic see C. Chiarenza and W. L. Vance (eds), *Immaginari a confronto: I rapporti culturali tra Italia e Stati Uniti: la percezione della realtà fra stereotipo e mito* (Marsilio, Venice: 1993) and M. Vaudagna, 'The American historian in continental Europe: an Italian perspective', *Journal of American History* 79 (1992), pp. 532–42. The last quote is taken from M. Sahlins, 'Goodbye to Tristes tropes: ethnography in the context of modern world history', *Journal of Modern History* 65 (1993), p. 25.

13

'Shoot the Right Thing': African American Filmmakers and the American Public Discourse †

Saverio Giovacchini

After the extraordinary success of John Singleton's *Boyz 'N the Hood* (1991), critics started to notice changes in the Hollywood landscape. Commentators started to talk about a new wave of feature films centered on blacks, and *The New York Times Magazine* noted that for any respectable studio, black-focused projects had become 'what the car phone was to the 1980s: every studio executive has to have one'.[1] There was some truth in this observation. According to the critic Ed Guerrero practically no Hollywood film in the 1980s had dealt with African Americans.[2] In 1990, seven films directed by African Americans were released. In 1991 twelve saw some kind of commercial distribution, along with twenty other movies that featured African American actors in a prominent role. These figures vastly outnumbered the total of black-focused pictures released since the mid 1970s,[3] and, in 1991 the black actress Whoopie Goldberg won an Oscar for her performance in *Ghost*.

The new wave of the early 1990s has much in common with the 'blaxploitation' wave of the early 1970s. Like the former it comes after a period of slump in Hollywood profits and, according to the *Los Angeles Times*, it reflects the attempt of American studios to tap black audiences, starved for on-screen representation, and reportedly accounting for 30 per cent of the tickets sold, compared with blacks' 12 per cent in the population.[4] As in the former wave with its crew of Sweet Sweetbacks, Shafts, and Superflies, the new one has at its core a group of films that focus on the experience of black inner-city outcasts. Finally, as the former wave was partly a response to the revival of black activism in the 1960s, contemporary African American films reflect changes in American society and the position of African Americans within it. While African American professors have made inroads in academia, and more courses focusing on African American history were offered in American universities, blacks' marginalization in American commercial films could no longer go totally unchallenged.

Yet this new wave is also marked by a new element: this is a new alertness to the issues and loopholes concerning the celluloid making of black identity. As opposed to the blaxploitation wave of the 1970s which assumed black identity as a monolithic, 'authentic' compound largely localized in the ghetto, the films of the new generation present a variegated, diversified take on the issue of what is 'blackness' in the American 1990s.

The intent of this paper is to define the positions of some of the members of the new wave of black filmmakers concerning the issue of black identity. The picture does not pretend to be complete. Rather than a wave, in fact, this new generation of filmmakers constructs a sort of archipelago, each island of which would deserve to be mapped individually, and by a better geographer. I will therefore limit my observation to the trademark of this wave, the so-called 'homeboy' movies, and to the latest movies by Spike Lee. My choice is not completely random: among the films that have been made for commercial distribution these might well exemplify what are the two poles of the celluloid debate about 'blackness'.

I shall also argue that African American filmmakers' positions about the notion of 'blackness' may be understood using the framework provided by Tejumola Alaniyan in her essay on the debate about African American cultural identity. Alaniyan has merged the various positions into what she respectively identifies as the *sacred* and the *profane* interpretation of black cultural identity. According to Alaniyan, a sacred notion of cultural identity argues that a culture 'is a given totality, separated and separable from other cultures with the exactness of a puritanical slide rule'. The sacred version of cultural identity is marked by an internal 'organic unity', and 'monolithism or unanimism', which in turn underwrites the difference from other cultures 'a difference which is then claimed as closed, absolute and impenetrable'. As opposed to this, the profane notion of cultural identity stresses the idea of its 'historicity'. According to this notion:

> [African American] culture is perceived as a complicated, political, articulation of (often) mutually contradictory, even antagonistic elements. ... Cultural identity cannot be closed and positive, but exists as essentially fragile and vulnerable, and is constituted as transition, relation, difference, contingence, dispersion.[5]

The definition of blackness was always central to African American filmmaking. Insofar as racism is still at large in American society, and on its screens, new African American filmmakers are, partly at least, still confronted with what has been called the 'burden of representation'. In practice their participation in the public discourse as fashioned by the new media has to imply a more or less hidden agenda, according to which participation has to be beneficial to the community, and it becomes meaningful only if it is instrumental in counteracting the racist dominant discourse.

Up to here, then, nothing really is new: African Americans have traditionally been aware that the act of inscribing one's image in the new media offered potential for an assault on racist stereotypes. From Sydney Poitier to Mario Van Peebles, to the so-called Los Angeles School of black filmmakers (Charles Burnett, Haila Gerima, Larry Clark, John Reir, Ben Caldwell, Pamela Jones, Abdosh Abdulfahia, and Jama Fanaka), African Americans have tried to negotiate their presence in American cinema. So much so, in fact, that when Poitier was under fire because of his participation in *Guess Who's Coming to Dinner*, James Baldwin came to his defense, writing that the black actor 'really has no right not to appear, not only because he must work, but also for those people who need to see him. By the use of his own person, he must smuggle in a reality that he knows is not in the script'.[6]

Things, however, get more complicated if we take into account another aspect of such participation: to meet the requirements imposed by the 'burden of representation', participation in the public discourse has to be contemporaneous with an act of collective identification. For black artists, even before the birth of the movies, the act of identifying oneself with the collectivity defined by 'blackness', was pre-inscribed in participation in the public discourse. Through writing the victims of racist discourse could disclaim the authority of a racial system dehumanizing them. 'The act of writing – writes Henry Louis Gates, Jr. of the slave narratives – is for African American artists always an autobiographical act, a way to write oneself into the public space constituted by media.' Writing meant '[to] shape a public "self" in language, and [to] protest the degradation of their ethnic group by the multiple forms of American racism'.[7] Yet, in order to be an effective counter-attack against racism, the act of writing had to be contemporaneous with self-identification. ('I am black, and I write.') In similar fashion, Sydney Poitier could not participate only as Sydney Poitier: he had to participate as a member of the community defined by 'blackness'. In the process, a more or less explicit definition of 'blackness' was to become evident.

Actually, if Michael Warner is right, the necessity to identify oneself with one collective group becomes even more pressing with the evolving of a public sphere where visual media – cinema, photography and television – have come to play a large role. As opposed to the incorporeal, 'invisible', 'public' of Habermas's eighteenth century (which was explicitly genderless, classless, and colorless and implicitly white, male, and upper class), modern visual mass media imply a public whose body is again incorporated, and whose parts are separated and made more visible by the fact that it is the public body itself that is the object of visual consumption.[8]

As a result, the question of collective identity, or of 'blackness', became central whenever blacks, equipped with some measure of power, positioned themselves within the public discourse of the media. The new wave of black film, then, becomes 'new' and, for instance, different from the 'blaxploitation' wave of the 1970s, because the very notion of black identity has changed, reflecting the contemporary debate encompassing the black community about what constitutes 'blackness'.

'Homeboy' movies are the trade mark of this wave. *Juice*, *Boyz 'N the Hood*, *Menace II Society*, and *Straight out of Brooklyn* have all been tremendous box office successes, bringing enormous profits to those who have produced or distributed them. The secret of these movies' profitability lies in their limited cost due to the absence of major stars, and their capacity to appeal to a cross-over audience overlapping with that of rap music (reportedly 70 per cent white). *Juice* (Ernest Dickerson, 1992) cost $3 million and grossed $30 million. *Menace* (Hughes Brothers, 1993) cost $3.4 million and returned $28 million. *Boyz* (John Singleton, 1992) cost $6 million and grossed $60 million. Sometimes associated with this group, though more germane to the gangster genre, Mario van Peeble's *New Jack City*, focused on the rise and fall of a Harlem drug lord, was also a tremendous box office success, costing $8.5 million and grossing $45 million.

Constructed after the same fashion, all these films tend to tell the same story: the hero is a young African American male who is confronted with the harsh reality of the inner city. He and his friends have to make tough choices to survive in an environment that pushes them into crime. In the end, the hero, or some of his close associates (a close relative or a friend) will fall victim to ghetto violence.

The sense of the film is here intertwined with the construction of the film director's persona. These movies are in fact promoted as a 'true' rendition of reality in the American inner cities. 'We are not here to give people hope,' says Allen Hughes, one of the two directors of *Menace*, 'we're here to display what's going on.'[9] In the discourse surrounding these movies, the director posits himself as the *reporter*, the *trait d'union* between the ghetto and those who live outside of the inner cities. The legitimation to perform such a role is achieved by the filmmaker's positioning as an alter ego of his characters. Like them, he is a 'homeboy', sharing their social identity.

The Hughes brothers, the directors of *Menace II Society*, the story of the coming of age of a young criminal in South Central Los Angeles, are the children of a middle-class single mother, and grew up in Pomona California. They declare, however, that 50 per cent of the episodes in the film are 'from-the-heart stories of people we know'.[10] 'The kids in the movie were right on my block. Not our friends. But we knew people like that. People who fell off, who got shot, went to jail.'[11] 'This is the truth, this is what's real' was the slogan launching *Menace*.

Matty Rich, who has directed the bleak *Straight Out of Brooklyn*, was born in the neighborhood he portrays: Red Hook, Brooklyn. The film, he says, is patterned after his boyhood pal Lamont Logan, who died in jail a few years before Rich shot the film after being picked up by the police for stealing a moped: 'All of the characters in the movie were based on parts of my family, everyone in the movie played a part in my life,' says Rich who, at any rate, moved to the gentrified Park Slope section of Brooklyn when he was ten.[12]

Following the release of *Boyz 'N the Hood*, the tragic tale about coming of age in the mean streets of South Central Los Angeles, the *Los Angeles*

Times magazine *Calendar* devoted an issue to John Singleton's childhood in South Central. The director accompanied the reporter to see the spot where a friend of his was shot, and even interviewed a gang member, a Michael Winters, supposedly Singleton's childhood buddy.[13]

Ernest Dickerson, a graduate of Howard University and New York University Film School, rediscovers his origins from Newark, New Jersey, when his film *Juice* is released. 'His father died when he was eight', starts an article on *FanFare*, 'and Dickerson was raised in tough Newark housing projects by a strong nurturing mother.' 'A lot of the guys I grew up with are dead or in jail or burnt out on drugs,' adds Dickerson and – of course – he wrote *Juice*, the story of four young boys on the loose in the Harlem streets, 'adapting anecdotes told to him by adolescents and mixing his own memories of being seventeen'.[14]

In effect, these films display violence as evidence that this is not the usual, edulcorated, and censored image of the ghetto: it is 'authentic'. 'We are not here to give people hope, we're here to display what's going on' claim the Hughes brothers. In this sense, violence functions as legitimation for the authenticity of the picture, and as evidence of the inner city's problems. The ghetto and its violence, what is usually removed, has to occupy the center of the screen.

The point here is to make visible what is too often invisible. Like pornographic cinema, 'homeboy' movies exist because they 'show' something, in this case the reality of the inner city and what it does to the bodies of the people who inhabit it. In terms of narrative strategy, then, the censorial effects of a limited budget, sometimes extremely limited, do not lead the director to re-invent a language based on ellipsis and innuendoes which has been the trade mark of an aesthetically or economically censored cinema, from Lubitsch's movies of the Hays Code era to the 'poor' cinema of Jaramush's *Stranger than Paradise*.

This is clearer if we compare the ending of these films with the ending of another kind of ghetto film, *Laws of Gravity* by Nick Gomez, a 'white' homeboy film focusing on two white *Lumpenproletariats* living in a poor area of New York.

The ending of *Laws* is revelatory both for what it shares, and for what it does not share with the homeboys' films. It is the same ending: the more fragile friend is killed in the usual, meaningless, shoot-out with another desperado. Yet the *mise en scene* is in fact crucially different. Nick Gomez plays the low budget game more conventionally, though quite successfully. His film constructs its look on the censorial determinations of the low budget. It does not 'show'. We do not see the pistols exploding, the bodies collapsing, the blood running. The scene is encased in the soundtrack and left to the imagination of the spectator: the screen becomes black and we are left with a scream, a shot, the sound of steps.

On the contrary the way the same scene is repeated in the homeboys' films shows their inherent purpose. An example of a cinema obsessed with visibility, homeboys' movies cannot leave out of the picture anything that is usually removed. In *Juice*, *Boyz* and *Menace*, the endings are the same as in *Law*. The fragile friend is finally killed by another young ghetto man. Yet, as opposed to Gomez, these directors make a point of showing us everything: the stalking, the killing, the collapsing, the blood running. In *Menace*, the killing of the main character and his cousin is repeated through the use of replay. The director of *Straight* even uses the century-old rhetorical device of having the gun shooting directly into the camera to augment the theater audience's involvement, and to cancel any diaphragm that separates the audience from the ghetto in which Rich has metaphorically transported it.

But in using violence as a metonym for the entire community, and in positing themselves as the *trait d'union* between the ghetto and those who live outside of the inner cities, these filmmakers assume an ironically contradictory role. They claim to make films for their communities, and the homeboy genre certainly shows a somewhat proud image of black men yet they also objectify black bodies for the 'visual pleasure' of a non-ghetto audience on whose curiosity their films are to a large extent predicated.

In these movies, the ghetto is the place where a sacred version of blackness is localized. As Henry Louis Gates Jr. has pointed out, these films inherit the legacy of the blaxploitation movies, and reaffirm the idea 'that "authentic" African-American culture is to be found only on the streets of inner cities'.[15] Getting out of the ghettos means placing oneself outside of the community, in a sense to betray it. In *Straight*, what ultimately dooms the main character, Dennis Brown, is his eagerness to get out of Red Hook. This will lead him to steal money from a drug dealer, which will ultimately bring about the dealer's retaliation, and the death of Dennis's father.

> My movie – says Matty Rich of Straight – is about Red Hook kids that want the American dream. ... that what's the kids in the movie want. To go straight out of Brooklyn. That's what I wanted. But the movie is all about saying, 'You don't have to go over there to make it. ... Show young people self-respect and self-esteem and show them you don't have to go straight out of Brooklyn, straight out of Watts, or straight out of Chicago to make it. You don't have to live on Park Avenue to make it. You can stay home.'[16]

If you do get out, like Tre's mother in *Boyz*, you lose your identity, and are unfit to raise truly 'black' people because in fact you have nothing to communicate to them. In one of *Boyz*'s first scenes the gentrified mother of Tre, who has moved out of the ghetto, brings the boy back to his father Furious Style (Lawrence Fishburne) because she feels incompetent to educate him.

Conforming to a 'sacred' version of 'blackness' that sees 'the separation from other cultures' as inevitable, black culture seems isolated in the ghetto, and to exist in a sort of vacuum. The interaction with members of other communities is almost non-existent and, at any rate, insignificant. Whites occupy the center, from which blacks are excluded. Whites are teachers (*Menace*), social workers (*Straight*), and cops (*Menace*). Yet there cannot be any dialogue and no meaningful interaction occurs, or seems possible between 'blacks' and other ethnicities (in *Menace* the main character O'Dog kills a couple of Korean grocers).

What is also of interest in these films is that the dialogue that is negated within the film is instead posited at the level of the language employed by these directors to tell their stories. While these films espouse a 'sacred' notion of authentic black culture, and as Tre's father in *Boyz*, refer to the necessity of a separate black public sphere, their cinematic style denounces a contamination of languages and of cultures. *Boyz*, *Menace* and *Straight* all construct their cinematic language in a conversation with the history of American movies. *Menace* obviously refers to Howard Hawks' *Scarface*, *Juice* mentions *White Heat* by Raoul Walsh. All these directors generally confess their admiration for Martin Scorsese, and the development of these movies' plots does not differ from Hollywood classical narrative (the *New York Post* called *Straight*, 'a 1950s melodrama'). In a sense, then, these films envision the language of American narrative film as the only place where meeting is now possible. In other words while, as Gates argues, these features portray a parochial and 'sacred' notion of black identity, at the level of cinematic language, of the means of communication, they hardly position themselves as 'exclusively' black films, pertaining therefore to a larger life-world than that possibly contained in an autarchic black public sphere.[17]

The construction of African American identity is made more 'profane' in the latest development of Spike Lee's *oeuvre*. Central in his recent work is a critique of any monolithic interpretation of 'blackness'. What varies, rather than what is homogeneous, is in the focus of his viewfinder. In *She's Gotta Have It*, African American identity was embodied in the three lovers of Nola Darling, each embodying a different 'type' of black maleness. In *School Daze*, the very shrine of black identity, the black college, appeared riveted by the divisions between Jigaboo and Wannabees, while out of the college race intersected with class to create new divisions.

It is interesting to compare the image of a working-class black neighborhood as depicted in *Do the Right Thing*, with its portrayal in the homeboys' films that has been legitimated by predominantly white critics as the true image of the inhabitants of inner city ghettoes. In Lee's film almost everybody works, though drugs and violence constitute a present, yet invisible, subcontext. 'In this script, I want to show the black working class. Contrary to popular belief, we work. No welfare rolls here, pal, just hardworking people trying to make a decent living.'[18]

More importantly, *Do* is a film about differences. Within a single street, people fight and argue about everything, from the content of American society to the relationship between genders and to the correct music to play. The ever-present *homeboy* is here dissected and removed, dissolved in a chorus in which individual voices are audible.

Interestingly, it is only at the end that the community finds its own unity when confronted with police brutality. Then it unites and performs politically by reacting to the cops and destroying Sal's pizzeria. The unity that can hardly be based on a sacred notion of 'blackness' is to be 'invented' when blacks act within the political sphere. Here, it seems, the film recalls what Patricia Williams has hinted at in her book, *The Alchemy of Race and Rights*:

> Being black is only one of a number of governing narratives or presiding fictions by which I am constantly reconfiguring myself in the world. Gender is another along with ecology, pacifism, my peculiar brand of colloquial English, and Roxbury Massachusetts.[19]

Yet discrimination, because of 'racial' difference, is also 'the most powerful social attribution' in her life, something that has to be counteracted in the public realm, for instance by energetic affirmative action policies.[20]

Spike Lee continued the problematization of any essentialist interpretation of blackness in his two next films, *Mo' Better Blues* and *Jungle Fever*, where he focused on black middle-class characters. In *Mo' Better Blues*, the story of a black musician in contemporary New York, the critical reflection on African American identity is left to the music. From the opening of the film when the young musician is forced to give up playing in the streets for the tedium of practice, Spike makes clear that musical prowess, the essentialist symbol of blackness, has more to do with *nurture* than with *nature*. If he is to succeed Bleek Gilliam, the black musician of *Mo'*, has to give up hanging out with the neighborhood youngsters and practice.

In *Jungle Fever* blackness is geographically dislocated. The film deals with an inter-racial affair between the Harlem architect Flipper Purifier (Wesley Snipes), and his secretary, Angie (Annabella Sciorra), a native of the Italian American district of Bensonhurst.[21] *Jungle* points to the similarities rather than to the differences between the two communities. Both communities shun the two lovers, and exercise pressures on them to break off their relationship. Both communities create 'niggers' out of the other, and even out of unequal gender relations since, as Gates has noted in his review of the film, 'Angie's exploitation by the men in her own family, also argues strongly that society creates "niggers" even in white enclaves such as Bensonhurst'. The sense of 'racial' difference seems to emerge only at the intersection, at the boundaries, when Flipper meets Angie.

It is, however, in *Malcolm X*, that Spike has constructed the most complicated meditation on African American identity. The premise of the movie is, as I take it, already conveyed in the first scene, with the American flag slowly consumed by flames until it is reduced to the X of the title. Consumed by the flames, the flag eventually reveals the scene of the brutal beating of Rodney King at the hands of a bunch of white policemen. By connecting Malcolm X and his refusal to identify himself with a name given to him by whites together with Rodney King, the American flag, and the political tradition of flag burning, Spike has visually woven a political narrative that connects Malcolm's message to the present day struggle against racism, both emphasizing the contemporary value of Malcolm's legacy within American reality and relocating this legacy within American political, oppositional, tradition (the flag burning). The racism denounced by Malcolm is still destroying African Americans' lives. Yet Malcolm's memory has to be relocated to the center of American public discourse. It is the United States, as a nation, represented by its national symbol, that has the task of coping with Malcolm's legacy.

Against any static interpretation of Malcolm, Lee's film has stressed the fluidity of the leader's personality at any stage of the production of *X*. As many have noted, the script for the film, originally by James Baldwin and Arnold Perl, and finally retouched by the director himself, is not based on historical research but almost entirely on Alex Haley's *The Autobiography of Malcolm X*. Haley's work, whose historical accuracy has been questioned by many, is geared to the various conversions of Malcolm, and assumes what Manthia Diawara, building on Werner Sollors's work, has called a 'conversionist' value.[22] Basing *X* on such a text, Lee has realized a film that emphasizes Malcolm as an ever-changing personality, exhalting the itinerary along which Malcolm Little transformed himself from 'homeboy', to black Muslim, to a refined American politician possibly able to supply the cornerstone for an alliance of American progressive forces.

The ability to change, and the fluidity of Malcolm's personality, is cinematically expressed in *X* by Ernest Dickerson, the phenomenal cinematographer of all Lee's movies. According to Dickerson, Lee requested different colors for each stage of the leader's life in order to mark Malcolm's intellectual transformations.[23] Accordingly the cinematographer emphasized dark colors in shooting the gestures of Malcolm/Red; later in the film, the prison scenes were shot with a bluish light to exhalt an element of 'deadness'; the apparition of Elija Muhammad was marked by a golden light, and Malcolm's activity within the Nation of Islam had a very sharp light that gave precision to the objects' contour so as to emphasize Malcolm's determination: 'I used no diffusion at all to soften the image, like I had before. It's no non-sense. Like the Muslims themselves. Very sharp, very clear in their purpose.' Finally, colors and lighting are softened up again, when Dickerson shoots Malcolm after the pilgrimage to Mecca.[24]

X allowed Spike to focalize his political and cinematic project. This tale of continuous conversions has allowed Lee a critique of any 'static', 'essentialist', or, 'sacred' conception of blackness. Other than Lee's emphasis on Malcolm's capacity to interact with a changing world and with his changing self there is, in the film, a reticence in defining once and for all who Malcolm is, and implicitly what a model black man should be. In what I perceive as a symbolic act, from the credits of the film to the collateral merchandise that Spike has designed, the director identifies Malcolm with an X, the symbol of Malcolm Little's refusal to identify himself according to white America's power structure.

The final scene, in which several South African school children stand up and claim 'to be Malcolm X', stresses the 'performative', anti-essentialist value both of Malcolm's legacy and, implicitly, of blackness. Its meaning, as I take it, is certainly about the unity of black people all over the world, yet it also rests on its spelling a sophisticated slogan of 'postmodern' politics, where blackness, as well as Malcolm's memory, far from being denied, becomes part of what Professor Diawara calls 'a cultural performance inside the oppression'.[25] In a situation where racism has tended to dehumanize blacks, the affirmation of a radical notion of 'blackness' becomes a political strategy. To claim 'blackness', as much as to claim to 'be Malcolm X', has more to do with positioning in the political discourse than with any essentialist notion of identity.

At the same time the way Lee marketed the film is important to understanding his project. Lee's successful efforts to capture the covers of the mainstream press in the weeks before and immediately after the release of the film, his reticence to have it premiered solely at the historic Harlem Apollo theater (and instead his insistence in requesting the Ziegfield in the very center of Manhattan where the film in fact premiered), and the very cost of the movie ($33 million) all made an appeal to a crossover audience crucial for the movie's profitability that underscores his attempt to relocate Malcolm's legacy at the center of American public discourse.[26]

In sum I would argue that the way Lee has used Malcolm is an exemplar of what Benjamin has called the 'double edgedness' of the phenomena of consumer culture. In a sense, Malcolm has been commodified and turned into a hat or a T-shirt, yet he has also been relocated at the center of public debate. Haley's *Autobiography* was close to the top of the *New York Times* best-seller list between November 1992 and March 1993, while *Bowker's 1993–4 Subject Guide to Books in Print* has 56 titles under the rubric Malcolm X, a 115 per cent increase compared with the 1991–2 edition which had 26.

After the first two or three years of the new wave, it seems clear that these filmmakers' experiences simultaneously reveal both the potential and the limits of a public discourse fashioned by the new media.

The notion of 'authentic blackness' embodied in the blaxploitation wave of the 1970s was also predominantly 'male', and heterosexual, and its partial decentering has occurred also because new subjects have been able to claim a space within black cinema. The dissemination of media know-how outside

Hollywood, new forms of credit, and video technologies have made movies cheaper to make, and they can be now largely financed through credit cards and the help of a few wealthy friends, as Matty Rich, Leslie Harris (*Just Another Girl on the IRT*, 1993), and Robert Townshend (*Hollywood Shuffle*, 1987) have shown.

The new wave of black films also counts among its protagonists black women that have made movies from a 'gendered' black perspective, like Irena Zeinabu Davis (*A Powerful Thang*, 1991), Julia Dash, and Leslie Harris. Harris was able to make *Just Another Girl on the IRT*, her powerful film concerning the coming of age of a Brooklyn black female teenager, relying almost entirely on her resources, and even editing her film in her Brooklyn apartment. The fine film by Julia Dash, *Daughters of the Dust* (1991), centering on a day-long family meeting of African American women at Ibo Landing on South Carolina's Sea Islands, was made for less than $1 million thanks to Dash's personal resources and a few grants. This film embraced a consciously Afro-centric point of view, and ran counter to Hollywood's narrative tradition by fashioning its narrative style after an African *Griot*'s tale. At the same time, however, Dash destabilized a sacred notion of 'blackness' by consciously trying to explore its gendered dimension across racial lines. Her film, she says, was constructed around the point of view of black women, with men 'just on the periphery', and was meant for 'black women first, the black community second, and white women third'.[27]

For one million dollars collected from friends, credit cards, and a few grants, Wendell Harris was able to make *Chameleon Street* (1990), a radical attack on any essentialist notion of identity. This film, fraught with references to Ellison's *Invisible Man*, Rostand's *Cyrano*, and Cocteau's *The Beauty and the Beast*, uses the gestures of William Douglass Street, a con-man from Flint, Michigan, who successfully passed for a *Times* reporter, a medical doctor, a Yale co-ed, and a lawyer, to probe the way 'blackness' is a social construction. When he interacts with others in society there is no 'real' Douglass Street. He only conforms to what the others want him to be. White stereotypes of blacks is certainly the major determining factor. But any collective definition of 'blackness', even the one given by the community itself, becomes a cage in which Street is imprisoned. In a telling scene he listens with a friend to African music, yet the off-screen voice tells us that he prefers 'the classics', from Debussy to Vivaldi to Jimi Hendrix.

The limits of this process are also evident: many more movies have been made, yet only a particular kind of movie has been able to capture the center of American public discourse. Only homeboy films, in fact, have succeeded in pleasing a composite audience of white suburbanites and inner city blacks, while hardly positing any concrete challenges to American society. Anybody who has been connected with these movies has been able to survive and prosper. Thus John Singleton signed with Columbia,

Dickerson with New Line, and the Hughes brothers and Matty Rich signed with Caravan.[28] Wesley Snipes, the hero of the neo-blaxploitation *New Jack City*, recently surfaced again in another film on the dark side of Harlem, *Sugar Hill*. A notion of black identity as male, 'sacred', and separatist seems to be quite consistent with box office success, especially if it does not radically challenge Hollywood's narrative conventions. Two fine movies by director/actor Bill Duke, *A Rage in Harlem* (1991) and *Deep Cover* (1992), espousing a clearly separatist and essentialist notion of blackness, have not had any problem in finding sponsors and distributors. The same can be said for Mario Van Peeble's neo-exploitation adventures, *New Jack City* (1991) and *Posse* (1993), and for black-focused comedies like *Livin' Large* (Michael Schultz, 1990) and *Strictly Business* (Kevin Hooks, 1991) that espouse an essentialist notion of blackness.[29]

Lee has been able to stay afloat while directing quite ambitious movies that refused to give simplistic answers to the question of black identity. This has a lot to do with his exceptional skill in marketing his works, and can only cautiously be seen as evidence of a major transformation of the public discourse. A master market strategist, Lee has become an expert of what he calls 'guerrilla filmmaking'.[30] This method, based on moderate production costs, self-promotion, and the marketing of an entire line of products collateral to his movies, has allowed him to make his film in relative independence from the studios, at least until the making of *Malcolm X*.[31] His first film, *She's Gotta Have It*, cost only $175,000 and was shot on location in Brooklyn in twelve days. *Schools Daze* cost $4.5 million and earned $13.9 million. *Do the Right Thing* cost $6.5 million. Until *X* his films cost much less than the average Hollywood cost of $25 million. 'When people give you six and a half million dollars [the cost of *Do the Right Thing*], they're going to let you do what you want to do, if they have any confidence in you.'[32] This marketing skill has afforded him an economic independence that others, coming later, or unable to obtain the same publicity as Lee, have not been able to achieve.

Filmmakers who have problematized the notion of black identity, but lacked Lee's ability to locate himself at the center of public discourse, did not do so well. Charles Burnet's *To Sleep with Anger*, a sophisticated rendition of how a middle class family deals with black roots, has been mismarketed by Samuel Goldwyn and has grossed only $350,000, notwithstanding its featuring a major star like Danny Glover. *Chameleon Street*, after winning the Grand Jury Prize at the 1990 Sundance Festival, is still looking for a distributor. *Daughters of the Dust* has been seen only in the art house ghetto, while *Just Another Girl on the IRT* was not distributed as widely as other films centering on ghetto life, despite the protests of Harris 'the studios are putting money into films that tend to be of this [homeboy] genre. It's unfortunate that the predominant image we see is of young black males toting a gun'.[33]

African American women filmmakers' marginalization is even more striking when we consider that, with the partial exception of Spike Lee's pictures, very few significant roles for women are to be found in the other films of the wave. The homeboy films again stand out for the minor roles women play in them, and, as the feminist black critic Jacquie Jones has pointed out, the new ghetto aesthetics consistently reduce women to 'bitches and ho's'.[34]

In conclusion I would argue that African American filmmakers of the 'new wave' seem to be in almost the same position as characters in the action film, *Deep Cover* (Bill Duke, 1992): at the beginning of the film, a white police executive is selecting a police officer for a difficult and well paid mission. The candidates are all black, and to each of them the functionary asks the same question: 'what is the difference between a black man and a nigger?' Whoever gives the right answer gets the job.

Like these police officers African American filmmakers strive for the opportunity to make films in a racist society. Their particular 'burden of representation' also requires them to supply a counter-definition of 'blackness' in order to decenter the dominant racist discourse. Like the officers in the film some will not pass the test. It also becomes clear that certain identities are more welcome than others. Anything does not go. For this reason the homeboy genre, with its violent heroes pleasing a cross-over audience of disenfranchised blacks and suburban whites, works. Yet, whoever wants to give more complicated answers had better adopt the precautions taken by Spike Lee.

Deep Cover seems to represent well the problem facing these filmmakers: like its police officers in the racist police department, African American filmmakers have continuously to define themselves as black, since the other qualification, 'nigger', is always present and has to be disclaimed. They have to carry their 'burden of representation'. It is also their constituency, the black community, that asks them to do so. But is it the only community to which they belong? Will they ever be allowed to be also women, socialists, gays, intellectuals, and to have these communities also inscribed in their texts as historical spectators? At the end of *Deep Cover*, the main character (Russell Stevens Jr., played by Lawrence Fishburne), has found what he thinks is the right answer for him: 'A nigger would even care to answer this question.' In a way, he is tired of identifying himself; maybe he only wants to be what he is. A few seconds after he answered the question Fishburne has to resign from the police department.

Notes

† This paper benefited a great deal from conversations I had with several people at New York University. In particular, I would like to thank Professor Thomas Bender, Anne Sophie Cerisola, Valentijn Byvanck, John Baick, Richard Abate, and Melissa Moore. While its faults are only mine, I would suggest that, without their input, it would have been much worse.

1. K. G. Bates, 'They've gotta have us: Hollywood Black directors', *New York Times Magazine*, 14 July 1991, p. 14.
2. E. Guerrero, *Framing Blackness: The African American Image in Film* (Temple University Press, Philadelphia: 1993), pp. 113–55.
3. Ibid., p. 158. See also Bates, 'They've gotta have us', p. 14.
4. N. Easton, 'New black films, new insights', *Los Angeles Times*, 3 May 1991, p.1.
5. T. Alaniyan, 'African American critical discourse and the invention of cultural identities', *African American Review* 26 (1992), pp. 533–7.
6. J. Baldwin, 'Sydney Poitier', *Look*, 23 July 1968, p. 56.
7. H. L. Gates, Jr., 'Introduction', in idem (ed.), *Bearing Witness: Selections from African American Autobiographies in the Twentieth Century* (Pantheon Books, New York: 1991), p. 3.
8. M. Warner, 'The mass public and the mass subject', in B. Robbins (ed.), *The Phantom Public Sphere* (University of Minnesota Press, Minneapolis: 1993), pp. 234–57.
9. *Newsweek*, 19 July 1993, p. 52.
10. *New York Times*, 10 June 1993, p. C13.
11. *Newsday*, *Parade Magazine*, 1 August 1993, p. 7.
12. *New York Post*, 22 May 1991, pp. 27–8.
13. *Los Angeles Times*, *Calendar*, 7 July 1991, p. 23.
14. J. Gelmis, 'Eyes on the prize', *FanFare*, 12 January 1992, p. 13.
15. H. L. Gates, Jr. 'Must buppiehood cost homeboy his soul?', *New York Times*, 1 March 1992, sec. 2, p. 11.
16. *New York Times*, 28 May 1991, p. C11.
17. The debate has basically crystallized into two positions, one arguing for the existence or at least the desirability of a 'pluralist decentered postmodern world', in which black identity would locate itself within a separate black public sphere; the second on the idea that the public sphere should more or less be coterminous with the political entity of which one is citizen. On this, and other related issues, see N. Garnham, 'The mass media, cultural identity, and the public sphere in the modern world', *Public Culture* 5 (1993), pp. 251–66.
18. S. Lee and L. Jones, *Do the Right Thing: A Spike's Lee Joint* (Fireside, New York: 1989), p. 30.
19. P. Williams, *The Alchemy of Race and Rights* (Harvard University Press, Cambridge, Mass.: 1991), p. 256.
20. Ibid.
21. H. L. Gates, Jr. 'Film view: "Jungle Fever" charts Black middle-class Angst', *New York Times*, 23 June 1991, sec. 2, p.20.

22. M. Diawara, 'Presidential Lecture', New York University, 7 October 1993; W. Sollors, *Beyond Ethnicity: Consent and Descent in American Culture* (Oxford University Press, New York: 1986), pp. 11, 19.
23. Gelmis, 'Eyes on the prize', p. 13.
24. *New York Times*, 18 April 1993, sec. 2, p. 14.
25. M. Diawara, 'Cinema studies, the strong thought, and black film', *Wide Angle* 13 (1991), p. 10.
26. *New York Times Magazine*, 25 October 1992, pp. 36–9; *Village Voice*, 10 November 1992, pp. 38–40; The Larry King Live Show on CNN, 13 November 1992; *Newsweek*, 16 November 1992, pp. 66–8. On the premiere controversy, see *The New York Amsterdam News*, 19 November 1992, p. 24.
27. J. Dash, *The Making of an African American Woman's Film* (The New Press, New York: 1992), pp. 33–40.
28. On the Hughes brothers and Matty Rich, see *Newsweek*, 19 July 1993, p. 52. On Dickerson, see *Variety*, 16 August 1993, p. 5.
29. On the essentialist notion of blackness, see Gates, Jr., 'Must buppiehood cost homeboy his soul?'
30. S. Lee, *Spike Lee's Gotta Have It: Inside Guerrilla Filmmaking* (Simon & Schuster, New York: 1987). Though I have not sufficient space to develop this point, I would suggest that Lee's genius lies also in his attempt to control the reception of each of his movies through the release of a book on the making of each film. This release is almost contemporary to that of the film. Authored either by Spike Lee himself, or by some trustworthy collaborators, these books partly try to redirect the interpretation of each film in order to appease segments of the audience that may find the sense of the film too ambiguous.
31. The director has also proved very effective in playing the media trumpet, appearing on the cover of *American Film*, the *National Review*, and *Newsweek*, before the release of *Do the Right Thing*, and of innumerable magazines before that of *X*.
32. 'Final cut: Spike Lee and Henry Louis Gates, Jr., rap on race, politics, and black cinema', *Transition*, no. 52 (1991), p. 180.
33. Cited in L. Beale, 'Menace II black image?', *Daily News*, 30 May 1993, p. 3.
34. J. Jones, 'The new ghetto aesthetic', *Wide Angle*, special issue on black cinema edited by M. Diawara, 13 (1991), p. 32.

For a complete list of Ryburn and Keele University Press books please write to

*Keele University Press
Staffordshire ST5 5BG, England*